"We Ask for British Justice"

"We Ask for British Justice"

WORKERS AND RACIAL DIFFERENCE
IN LATE IMPERIAL BRITAIN

Laura Tabili

Cornell University Press

ITHACA AND LONDON

First published 1994 by Cornell University Press.

Printed in the United States of America

⊗ The paper in this book meets the minimum requirements
of the American National Standard for Information Sciences—
Permanence of Paper for Printed Library Materials, ANSI Z39.48-1984.

Library of Congress Cataloging-in-Publication Data

Tabili, Laura.
  "We ask for British justice" : workers and racial difference in late imperial Britain / Laura
Tabili.
      p.   cm. — (The Wilder House series in politics, history, and culture)
  Includes bibliographical references and index.
  ISBN 0-8014-2904-8
  1. Blacks—Employment—Great Britain—History—20th century.   2. Minorities—
Employment—Great Britain—History—20th century.   3. Seamen, Black—Great
Britain—Social conditions.   4. Blacks—Great Britain—Social conditions.
5. Minorities—Great Britain—Social conditions.   6. Great Britain—Race relations—
History—20th century.
I. Title.   II. Series.
HD8398.B55T33   1994   94-7305
331.6'396041-dc20

Contents

Acknowledgments

THE WELCOME OCCASION at last arises to thank the many people who contributed to this project both directly and indirectly, many of them over a long period of years and in multiple ways. First thanks go to James Cronin and Carole Shammas, formerly of the University of Wisconsin–Milwaukee, who have encouraged and inspired numerous students of history. Jim Cronin first encouraged me to pursue graduate work, and has continued to offer both practical support and astute counsel. Carole Shammas urged me to undertake the Ph.D. and inspired by her example an impeccable standard for feminist scholarship and teaching. For practical and political education I am also indebted to fellow members of U.W.–M.'s Progressive Student Forum and to the Milwaukee Alliance study groups, as well as to a broader community of progressive and feminist scholars now scattered across the United States and Britain. Their commitment to extending the lessons of history beyond the academy continues to delight and inspire.

At Rutgers University, John Gillis and Allen Howard responded to early drafts with unfailingly meticulous commentary and criticism. Generous with their time and attention, both also offered sound and patient guidance in practical as well as scholarly matters. Thanks are also due Karen Anderson, Bill Bartholomew, Alan Bernstein, Gail Bernstein, Kimn Carlton-Smith, Scott Cook, Richard Cosgrove, James Cronin, Bob Dean, Peter Fraser, Alison Futrell, John Charles Heiser, Nancy Rose Hunt, Richard Price, Hermann Rebel, John P. Rossi, Pat Thane, Douglas Weiner, and Winthrop Wright, all of whom read substantial portions of the work in progress and offered valued criticism. So did the readers for

Cornell University Press, editors Roger Haydon, David Laitin, and George Steinmetz, and members of the Wilder House seminar.

Alistair Tough, Richard Story, and Christine Woodland of the Modern Records Centre, Tim Thomas of the India Office Library, Jagdish Gundara and Diane Nair of the Institute of Education Centre for Multicultural Education, Ken MacMillan, Dougie Harrison of the Scottish T.U.C., Arthur Marsh, and the staff and archivists at Friends House Library, London, the Institute of Historical Research, the Institute of Race Relations, the Public Record Office, Rhodes House Library, the National Maritime Museum at Greenwich, the Merseyside Maritime Museum, and the U.S. Department of Labor Library in Washington, D.C., not only provided access to relevant materials and other facilities but in many cases smoothed the researcher's path in other ways. Quotations from Crown copyright records in Oriental and India Office Collections of the British Library and from Crown copyright materials in the Public Record Office appear by permission of the Controller of Her Majesty's Stationery Office. Quotations from records of the National Union of Seamen appear by permission of Mr. Jimmy Knapp, President of the National Union of Rail, Maritime, and Transport Workers.

Critical financial support for the early stages of the project came from a Rutgers University Graduate College fellowship, while the Social and Behavioral Sciences Research Institute of the University of Arizona supported the later stages, both through a mini-grant in summer 1989 and a Research Professorship providing a semester's release from teaching in spring 1991. The Office of the Vice President for Research at Arizona provided a research grant for summer 1989 and a grant from the Provost's Author Support Fund.

For their generous hospitality to an itinerant researcher, I am indebted to Anna Clark, Victoria Berman, Deborah Mabbett, Bob and Pippa Little, Angel Chiu and "the Boys," Peter Coombes, Judy Coombes and Russell Thomas, Helen Jones and John Mattson, and Judith Rowbotham and Maria Dowling. Rudy Bell, Kelly Boyd, Steve Rappoport, John P. Rossi, Susanna Treesh, and Kimn Carlton-Smith initiated me into the mysteries of microcomputing. Mr. and Mrs. John A. Rossi stored my belongings during two extended research trips. John P. Rossi and my mother, Carol Tabili, provided advice, emotional support, and timely cash subventions in various crises.

For comradeship, moral support, and welcome distraction, many thanks to friends, family, and colleagues in New Jersey, Wisconsin, England, Maryland, and Tucson, especially Anne Apynys, Bert Barickman, Bill Bartholomew, Polly Beals, Jack Bernhardt, Lynn Berrettoni, Kelly Boyd, Fran Buss, John Campbell, Kimn Carlton-Smith, Anna Clark, Lis Clemens, Phyllis Conn, Linda Darling, Roy Domenico, Maureen Fitzgerald, Todd Garth, Kim Grant, Paul Greenough, Gay Gullickson, Colette Hyman, John Kelly, Michelle King, Gary McCann, Laura McCloskey, Melissa Mac-Kinnon, Susan Morgan, Suzanne Morris, Kathy Morrissey, Spike Peterson, Leigh Pruneau, the Rossi family, Lael Sorenson, Gracie Southall, Carolyn Strange, the Tabili family, Susanna Treesh, and Vicki Weinberg. Without the support of Karen Anderson and Doug Weiner I would not have survived in Tucson.

Finally, thanks are due to my parents, Thomas and Carol Tabili, and my "adopted" parents, Kenneth and Elizabeth Mosley. With our migrant forebears, Elisabetta and Filippo Tabili, Ottilie, Karl, and Edward Krause, they first taught the lesson that people make their own history in the struggle for bread but also for roses. This work is dedicated to them with gratitude and love.

LAURA TABILI

Tucson, Arizona

"We Ask for British Justice"

Introduction

IN THE 1920S AND 1930S imperial racial categories and racial subordination were reconstituted on British soil. The episode was critical to the ongoing dialogue between colonies and metropole that continues to shape Black people's lives in Britain. Recontextualizing race within the global dynamics of Britain's imperial system challenges explanations for conflict that rest on ahistorical assumptions about the universality and naturalness of xenophobia and racism. Evidence of widespread structural and institutional support for racial subordination, when coupled with a record of popular action and Black resistance, demands reconsideration of racism's origins and persistence.

Consider a scuffle in a union hall in Salford, the port of Manchester. On 19 May 1930, J. H. Borlase, an official of the National Union of Seamen, (N.U.S.) Britain's major maritime union, was manhandled and slightly injured by a crowd of seamen assembled in the union's offices in Gladys Street. The men, whose ranks included "200 Empire-born Negroes," objected to the rumored union-sanctioned hiring of an Arab crew from another port by the steamship *Paris City*. One of Borlase's assailants, James William Andrews, a West African resident of Manchester, "appeared to be acting as spokesman for both the white and coloured men present." After the police arrived, two white and two Black seamen came forward to inspect the discharge books—work credentials—of the six Arab seamen. They returned the books when satisfied that the six Arabs were "local men," who subsequently sailed on the *Paris City*.[1]

The details of this incident defy the assumptions that have informed much scholarship on British racial conflict. An incident in which West African, Arab and white seamen all defined themselves and one another

as "local men" confounds prevalent understandings of Black men as "archetypal strangers" and of racial difference as an ineluctable impediment
to social harmony.[2] We must ask how James William Andrews and the
six Arab firemen who sailed on the *Paris City* came to be defined as
"insiders" by white rank-and-file seamen, when so many scholars assume
African and Arab seamen alike remained forever "strangers." Such seeming
anomalies perhaps explain why British historians have been reluctant to
integrate Black people and racial analysis into the "mainstream." Evidence
of interracial solidarity makes no sense when we have reified racial difference as an inevitable source of conflict.

Within British social history, devoted until recently to questions of class
and latterly gender, Black people and racial dynamics indeed remain marginalized and underanalyzed. Many historians treat racial difference as a
natural attribute, both impervious to historical analysis and inherently
disruptive, while Britain's numerically small Black population is dismissed
as insignificant. What the Salford incident suggests, conversely, is that
Black men's status as "local" or "stranger" was conditioned and contingent,
subject to negotiation—well within the purview of historical investigation.

The purpose of this work, then, is to reconstruct the historical context
in which racial conflict or interracial cooperation occurred, and to show
how that context, and with it the meaning of racial difference itself, altered
over time. Beyond restoring Black people to the landscape of British history
and their voices to the historical narrative, it illuminates the material as
well as the ideological underpinnings of racial stratification, locates the
meaning of racial difference and the sources of racial conflict in their global
and imperial context, and provides a historicized approach to current
debates. The Salford incident challenges a "consensus" view of Britain as
a monolithically racist society, demanding that we specify who had the
means to promote racial exclusion and inequality, who benefited from it
and how, and under what conditions other members of British society
were persuaded to participate or resisted participation. The purpose is not
to deny the racism prevalent in British society but to hold historical actors
responsible for their choice to engage in racist practices. Disaggregating
British society reveals there was no racist consensus in the early twentieth
century but, rather, conflict and struggle among historical actors with unequal means to realize their goals.

The intensity of this struggle is incomprehensible until viewed in the
broader context of British imperialism. For the few thousand Black seamen
living in Britain were only the most visible of a global and multiracial
colonized population whose labor sustained Britain's imperial power.

Their position in the labor force of the mercantile marine, a single but crucial industry that drew workers from all parts of the empire, shaped their status as insiders or outsiders.

Although Black people have lived in Britain for centuries, the men in question probably began settling in British ports in the late nineteenth century, as the industry responded to international competition by recruiting cheaper labor in the colonies. Yet the same dynamics of imperial expansion and industrial decline that brought Black men to Britain increasingly rendered their presence problematic. In the 1920s and 1930s, a period of imperial and domestic instability, employers, the state, and organized labor expended substantial resources to police, subordinate, and exclude this small population, well before the much-publicized conflicts after the Second World War. These efforts formed an episode in a continuing dialectic among colonial and metropolitan societies and structures.[3]

While racial conflict in Britain is frequently attributed to the intellectual and cultural legacy of imperialism, the economic and political processes through which imperial racial inequalities were reconstituted in Britain have remained largely unexplored. Yet this work shows that the political economy of Britain's declining maritime empire created structural conditions conducive to conflict. The dispossession of colonized people was part of the structure of political and economic inequality fundamental to British society and politics, economic might, and specifically imperialism.[4] Britain's global dominance had been supported by the world's most powerful merchant navy, and shipowners continued to wield extraordinary political, economic, and cultural influence. The conflicts of the interwar years grew out of maritime employers' efforts to extend colonial levels of control and exploitation to workers in the metropole. Struggle ensued among elites with competing agendas, including employers and government ministries and Black and white elites in various colonies, and between elites and nonelites that included Black and white seamen and their advocates.

Continual resistance by Black seamen and others with less wealth and power demonstrates the incompleteness of elites' power to determine outcomes, or—as the Salford incident suggests—to predict or control seamen's response. Yet while agendas were contradictory and ill conceived, while results were often partial or unforeseen, outcomes largely benefited employers, reinforced racial subordination, and disadvantaged Black seamen and other workers. Interwar practices in effect recolonized Black seamen in Britain, giving maritime employers privileged access to their labor with reduced responsibility for their social reproduction.[5] This was the outcome of a political process that effectively deprived Black working men of the freedoms and choices available to white men. Thus, racial difference was neither an inherent source of conflict nor a personal quality independent of larger historical processes. Instead, the same struggles over wealth and power that shaped other aspects of interwar politics and society also constructed racial difference.

Understanding race as "a relationship, and not a thing," shaped by an ongoing and contested process of racial formation, owes much to Marxian understandings of class and class formation. In early twentieth-century Britain, the reconstitution of racial difference as a political and economic disability took shape in the context of struggles that destabilized and redefined citizenship in relation to nationality, race, and gender. From the 1890s the definition of British nationality assumed new urgency as the massive displacement of population spurred by global industrialization brought large numbers of migrants to Britain. Immigration restriction in 1905, 1914, and 1919 involved recodification of British nationality, the franchise was broadened in 1918 and 1928 to include women and dependent men, efforts to enforce a race-blind "imperial standard" of citizenship in the Dominions failed, and mounting demands for colonial political autonomy compelled the reconsideration of racial inequality and with it the imperial project itself.[6] These events were only the most immediate of centuries of struggles to establish political rights, a process that continues in current debates about full citizenship and rights for women, racial and cultural minorities, and former colonial subjects. Legal definitions of British nationality functioned to perpetuate inequalities by confining rights to certain groups. Arguably, racial "affinities" were as much a product of these state-sponsored constraints as an inspiration for them.

Yet contrary to understandings of British national identity as a monolithic or static category of inclusion or exclusion, evidence suggests that the relationship between race and empire, and in turn the definition of Britishness—like the material goods racial subordination was designed to preserve for whites only—were actually contested. Since the distinction between subject and citizen was not formally codified until late in the twentieth century, the conflicts of the interwar years that were a prelude to this codification involved Black British subjects' efforts to assert and exercise the rights of political and social citizenship on the basis of their British nationality.[7]

While Britain's liberal "tradition of tolerance" had been much compromised by the First World War, overt mechanisms of racial subordination like those in the colonies were largely absent from the metropole. But in the 1920s and 1930s colonial mechanisms and the racial categories they supported were reconstructed in Britain. Racial subordination in Britain, both in the labor market and by the state, was a legacy of colonial and imperial racial processes—but not simply a cultural or sentimental one. Understanding the imperial impact requires an analysis of the political economy—the material processes—of racial subordination as well as of the historical construction of myths of racial inferiority and exoticism—two discrete although interdependent processes. This work offers an analysis of employers' promotion of racialized inequalities within the maritime workforce, and of union and state capitulation. It also describes how these extrinsic material factors—economic benefits, political process—interacted with or mobilized an already existing and evolving ideology of racial difference also shaped by the imperial experience.[8]

As the incident in Salford suggests, Black workers challenged and destabilized this system of racial subordination at both the material and the ideological level. They initially defied imperial inequalities by migrating to Britain and later by evading the controls established to deter their migration. In addition, they appropriated and refashioned imperialist arguments in defense of their rights as they defined them. The ideology of empire and nationality was more than simply a tool of oppression: Black British subjects as well as white racists struggled to define its meanings and uses, albeit with radically unequal power at their disposal.

This prehistory of officially sanctioned racial subordination demands rethinking of postwar British race politics. State-sponsored exclusion of Black migrants in the 1950s, 1960s, 1970s, and 1980s has been interpreted as a response to public pressure or popular racism. In much of the postwar debate, Black people have been portrayed as strangers and intruders, bearers of an alien and polluting culture. Black people's poverty and powerlessness has been attributed to cultural impediments to the "assimilation" process common to "immigrants."[9] White hostility has been depicted as a natural, justifiable response to cultural exoticism.[10] Images of "Other"-ness, deviancy, and white revulsion have prompted institutional efforts to minimize racial conflict through minimizing the Black population in Britain. These have included the manipulation of immigration and nationality law in the 1960s, 1970s, and 1980s to restrict Black Commonwealth subjects' access to Britain, and ultimately to disenfranchise them of citizenship. These images have also legitimated official interference with Black families and communities in the effort to eradicate imputedly "deviant" or "pathological" cultural practices that supposedly perpetuate Black people's marginalization while inviting white people's hostility.[11]

In view of Black people's cultural diversity, holding their "cultures" responsible for their subordination is unconvincing. Attributing their problems to unfamiliarity ignores their centuries of life and work in Britain, and mystifies the imperial hierarchies that render their presence anomalous. Criticizing the focus on culture to the exclusion of questions of power and class struggle, scholars have begun to incorporate both the material and the cultural aspects of racial domination, and to locate British race relations within the global history of imperialism and postimperialism.[12] The most successful efforts to do this have come from Birmingham's Centre for Contemporary Cultural Studies (C.C.C.S.), whose adherents adopt a Gramscian analysis of hegemony, and from the Institute of Race Relations in London, which relies on more conventional class analysis. Although their approaches differ, their analyses of working-class and Black cultures within structural and materialist frameworks that include political and social context offer much to labor and social historians. The most provocative recent work posits race and racism as irreducible to class, but, like class and gender, historically contextual and contingent.[13]

Informed by these approaches, this work builds on the already substantial literature on Black people in Britain, while avoiding the conceptual limitations that have kept this history unrecognized. In the immediate postwar years, two pioneering works of social science sketched in the broad chronology of Black people's history in Britain. Studies of Cardiff in the 1940s and Stepney in the 1950s traced the Black presence in Britain back to the time of Elizabeth I, and offered a *précis* of significant events from which subsequent authors have borrowed heavily.[14] In the ambitious surveys of the 1970s and 1980s, historians painstakingly reconstructed more of Black people's centuries of experience in Britain, pushing the chronology back to the time of the Roman occupation, providing substantial detail on Black political and labor activism, and restoring Asians and women to the record.[15] Case studies have supplied additional detail on individual settlements, putting particular emphasis on racial conflicts.[16]

Other British historians may be justly criticized for their continuing neglect of this history, yet its marginalization stems in part from the way racial questions have been conceptualized. Even though most historians of Black people in Britain have avoided entering into the "race relations" debates, they have tacitly incorporated some of its assumptions. They tend to present Black workers as obvious scapegoats in an otherwise homogeneous population, and to view conflict as the inevitable if deplorable response to economic or sexual competition between two mutually exclusive and naturally antagonistic groups of working men.[17] Some accept the view of Black people as "immigrants" and "minorities," virtually conceding their marginality in British society, and their irrelevance to larger historical processes.[18] Such interpretations leave unchallenged the idea that racial hostility is latent in social relations, resurfacing in any crisis. In addition, they take for granted the objective or fixed quality of racial difference itself, and its inexorably divisive effects. But events such as the Salford incident problematize such assumptions.

Because of the failure to engage "culturalist" or essentialist assumptions, the history of Black people and racial conflict has not been well integrated into British historiography, nor has this history been articulated with the imperial processes that formed it. Treating racism as epiphenomenal has absolved the shapers as well as the scholars of broader historical processes of responsibility for racial questions. Focusing on "attitudes" and behaviors detached from an analysis of underlying structures neglects the ways that Black and white working people were positioned in relation to each other within a system also fissured by class, gender, skill, and other dynamics.[19] Apparently inconsistent practices and behaviors were actually products of differences of power and interest among the central and local government, the press, union leaders and ordinary working people, white as well as Black.

To view racist policies as the state's response to popular demand or a reflection of union influence promotes unwarranted "consensus" view of a social formation riven by structural inequalities and consequent conflict. The motives of the white rank and file are extrapolated from those of union leadership; local police are held responsible for nationally promul- gated policy; and working people are assumed to share and act on the racist and imperialist propaganda promoted by elites. Yet if we investigate the most notorious examples of racial subordination in interwar Britain, such as the Coloured Alien Seamen Order of 1925, we find that actions commonly attributed to popular racism demonstrably had other sources. These conflicts stemmed neither from essential racial or cultural differences, nor from the inherent xenophobia of ordinary people, but from material constraints negotiated among specific historical actors with explicit goals.

After the Salford incident, for example, the *Morning Advertiser*, under the headline "Arab Seamen Sent Back: Union Offices Stoned by Coloured Sailors," portrayed the incident as a racial conflict between African and Arab seamen. Shipowners' representative Captain Dill reinforced this with the explanation that it was "not advisable to mix Arabs and West Africans" on shipboard. The verdict of the Home Office and local police, however, was that conflict had been introduced into the situation by the employers and Borlase, and was exaggerated by the local press. Days before the incident, Borlase had made unsubstantiated statements to the press alleging the arrival of Arab seamen "from other districts" in an area of high unemployment: "If the position with regard to the s.s. Paris City had been made clear at the outset," wrote a local constable, "there would not have been occasion to call upon the police for assistance."[20]

As the discrepancies between accounts of the Salford incident suggest, uncritical reliance on press reports and other popular literature can result in an incomplete and insufficiently nuanced understanding.[21] A focus on such evidence neglects the institutional origins of race policy in interwar Britain and their influence on the actions of ordinary people. Comparison of such evidence with letters, memoranda, minutes, correspondence, and other materials left by the actual participants in state policymaking—the Home Office, the India Office, the Board of Trade, the Colonial Office, the International Transport Workers' Federation (I.T.F.), and the National Union of Seamen (N.U.S./N.S.F.U.), and petitions, letters, and other testimony from Black and white seamen themselves—was tedious work. Yet it has yielded a more complicated and richer story—of conflict and negotiation rather than consensus; of resistance, evasion, and protest rather than simple oppression; and of a surprising variety of responses by different historical actors, sailors and civil servants, shipowners and union leaders, and Black and white men and women.

This more complicated story requires that we consider not only what people did, but the meanings they and others ascribed to what they did. In this task we can be aided by insights derived from emerging analyses of gender, race, and ethnicity. Scholars in many disciplines are rejecting the view of race and gender as natural attributes, instead viewing them as dynamic power structures given shape by particular historical contexts. Definitions of racial difference, like masculinity and femininity, have been sensitive to economic and political change, mediated by class and gender, and manipulated by elites in the pursuit of power.[22] Literary scholars have been the most emphatic in arguing for the social and historical construction of racial as well as gender differences.[23] Yet their current focus on imperialist and racist discourses was presaged in anthropological and historical literature that presented race or ethnicity not as a static condition so much as a "positional" relationship made and unmade in historical contexts.[24]

Rejecting the view of ethnicity as a *völkisch* quality gradually destroyed by industrial capitalism, these scholars have explored the ways identity has been shaped by the dynamics of imperial domination and indigenous resistance or in the process of global economic integration.[25] Racial and cultural groups are thus not objective entities but are both made by external factors, and remake themselves through choice and action. The notion of racial groups as static and homogeneous is further undermined by endemic "boundary problems" and by internal stratification and conflict on lines of gender, class, and other social divisions. In light of such understandings, to reify racial or cultural differences as sources of conflict appears naive. The question for historians is the process through which originally value-neutral physical attributes or cultural practices acquired value-laden positive and negative constructions or interpretations in particular historical contexts.

Scholarly as well as popular discourse, moreover, betrays significant slippage among notions of race, culture, and ethnicity.[26] I use the term "Black" because it is used by scholars in the discipline; because it is preferred by contemporary Black Britons, who comprise an equally diverse population; and because the term "coloured" is anachronistic and sometimes offends. That struggle continues about the terminology describing racial categories as well as their composition betrays their inherent instability.[27]

Early twentieth-century Britain, indeed, offers compelling evidence of how racial differences were constructed and assigned meaning, and of how these meanings changed. In Britain as in the colonies, the epithet "black," or the more polite "coloured," described Africans and West Indians, South Asians and Arabs. "The problem" of "the Negro," according to one official, involved "Adenese, Arabs, Berberans, Somalis and Egyptians," while the terms "Arab" and "Somali" were applied with similar imprecision to Sudanese, Adenese, Somalis, Yemenis, Zanzibaris, and Egyptians.[28] This diverse population shared neither physiognomy nor culture; they were united by a political and historical relationship of colonial subordination. Thus "Black" was a political label rather than a physical description: the boundary between Black and white was not drawn on the basis of physical appearance, but on relations of power, changing over time and continually contested. As the history of the Coloured Alien Seamen Order found in chapter 6 will show, in the course of several decades this flexible category shifted and broadened to encompass new groups, conditioned by economic imperatives, gender relations, and domestic, labor, and imperial politics.

British racial processes were shaped not only by the material demands of industry and the state, but also by an ideology of racial difference. This racial ideology was not epiphenomenal, but historically contingent, derived from colonial labor and political relations, and influenced by domestic social relations. From the late nineteenth century, Britain's political and eco-

nomic subordination of non-European people was buttressed by an ideology of European and specifically British racial and cultural superiority.
Supporters of European empire building argued that British and European
success in dominating non-European peoples was proof of their entitlement and fitness to do so.[29]

British imperial identity was increasingly constructed around class-
specific and gendered images of a predatory masculinity that was also race-
specific—"imperial manhood." Like race, masculinity was a political category as well as a personal and social identity. Manhood was defined by
privileged access to social resources and the concomitant capacity and duty
to exercise control over the self and an array of inferior Others: women,
children, colonized people, animals, foreigners, the natural world. For this
process of self-definition involved the construction of a Manichean "Other"
embodying those characteristics excluded from the masculine ideal: colonized men were depicted as less than men—effeminate, childlike, and
brutal, rightly subject to white ruling-class control. The view of Indians
as "feeble even to effeminacy," "sedentary . . . delicate . . . languid," "ener-
vated" was echoed in Carlyle's view of the "West Indian negro," and in
Richard Burton's ascription to Africans of the "worst characteristics of the
lower Oriental types."[30]

While scholars debate the relative impact of political factors and autonomous intellectual and cultural trends in the making of racial ideology,
maritime employers, as chapters 3, 4, and 8 will show, drew on them
pragmatically to justify their labor practices to the union, the state, and
the public, and, perhaps most important, to themselves. The power of
racial ideology, indeed, even within a particular historical context such as
imperial Britain, resided less in its cogency or plausibility, which was
minimal, than in its flexibility and opportunism. For the analogue with
gender is imperfect. Whereas gender is constructed around relatively consistent physiological differences between men and women, definitions of
race have been constructed around no discrete and coherent set of differences. Skin tone, often posited as a universal signifier of racial difference,
was hardly a factor in defining Jews as racially different from other Europeans, for example. Likewise, the political economy that constructed
Jews as racially Other in Europe differed from the political economy that
constructed colonized people as racially Other in the British empire, or
that constructing racial differences in, to take another case, Latin America.
Neither scientists nor laypeople have ever achieved consensus on the set
of differences—physiological or subjective—that consistently define race.[31]
That individuals have been able to "pass" from one category into another,
transgressing their permeable and indeterminate boundaries, confirms this.

Racial constructions or representations instead proved adaptable. This was reflected, for example, in Captain Dill's assertion that Arabs and West Indians were inherently incompatible. As his remark suggested, maritime employers manipulated notions of race and culture in an effort to control both Black and white workers by controlling racial discourse. Lumping all colonized workers together as racially inferior justified subordination, while emphasizing, accentuating, or inventing cultural differences among them obscured their common experience, keeping them divided.[32] For just as there was more than one Black "culture," British culture was far from monolithic, but conditioned by variables such as gender, class, region, skill, and age. That the racial Other was feminized, infantilized, and bestialized should alert us to this.

As the conflicting accounts from Salford reveal, white as well as Black people's understandings of the meanings of racial difference were mediated by class, gender, and skill.[33] As the discussion of war service and of interracial settlements shows, Black Britons' cultural identities and loyalties could be plural or overlapping, and could change over time and in response to discrimination and conflict. The relationships among race, culture, nationality, and entitlement—how people defined themselves and one another—have all changed as relations among people have changed, and have varied over time and in space. The Salford incident, for example, tells us that what was at issue was less "colour" than economic and political relationships of which "racial" difference was one signifier among several.

Indeed, preoccupation with the structures of white oppression and Black sailors' accurate depiction as a "reserve army of labor" for the British shipping industry risks portraying Black workers solely as victims.[34] Yet scholars are increasingly rejecting the image of the migrant as an unsophisticated bumpkin borne along by forces beyond his or her understanding. Migration, they argue, was a pragmatic response to an expanding global system. Individuals migrated for a complex of personal motives including maintenance of institutions such as the family, already threatened by industrial expansion in the "Old World."[35] As the actions in Salford suggest, Black workers in interwar Britain were far from the naive and easily bullied "coolies" scorned by their adversaries and pitied by their advocates. Those who came to Britain before, during, and after the First World War aimed to enhance their individual welfare, to aid their kin, and to claim their "rights" as they defined them. Their migration to Britain was itself a blow against colonial domination and exploitation.

Evidence about their migration, organization, and activism found in chapters 4, 6, and 7 shows that Black workers themselves profoundly influenced interwar British race policy. Through resistance and protest,

Black workers challenged racial subordination and blunted its force. Exploiting inconsistencies in the imperialist position, they appropriated the rhetoric of fair play, of entitlement derived from service in the world wars, and of the British promise of eventual reward, to place claims on the state and to demand power and control over their lives and work. Their evasion and subversion of the mechanisms of exclusion, their tenacious claims to rights earned through military service, and their stubborn maintenance and defense of family and institutional life forced the state to refine and intensify policing measures and ultimately to redefine the relationship between race and nationality itself.

The two world wars that flanked this period were critical in forming ideology and practice. Commonly understood as occasions for Black migration to Britain, the wars also exposed the stresses and contradictions in imperial racial policy. The Black experience examined in the first and last chapters is consistent with scholars' view that "total war" offered shortlived episodes of apparent opportunity for women, workers, and colonized people, accompanied by state expansion and enhanced surveillance and control. Colonized workers generally, not only seamen, were used as a "reserve army of labor" to be drawn into the industrial or military workforce in times of expansion and then excluded from the system as demand for labor contracted. Interwar struggles were in part about efforts to "expel" colonized people who had collectively and symbolically if not always personally entered the metropolitan workforce during the war.

The second chapter demonstrates how the challenges facing British elites in the postwar world shaped Black workers' structural position. These challenges included Britain's precarious global economic and political status, and the related drive for political and economic democratization manifested in heightened colonial and working-class militancy. This chapter also describes the specific predicament facing maritime employers after 1870, to which cheap labor appeared to be a solution.

As the third chapter explains, although small in number and so confined to the ports that many white Britons remained oblivious of their presence, Black seamen who migrated to Britain prompted a disproportionate response from employers, the state, and the union. The maritime industry that brought them to the metropole rested, paradoxically, on an empire-wide system of racial stratification and subordination that rendered their presence in Britain anomalous and even alarming. While many scholars have blamed union racism for Black seamen's disadvantaged position in the workforce, this investigation reveals that contract labor and other employer-initiated practices created structural inequalities that chronologically antedated the union's formation and shaped its response to Black seamen.

In Britain Black seafarers and other workers confronted institutions such as the Home Office, the Colonial Office, the India Office, and the seamen's unions, whose efforts to reconcile the conflicting imperatives of imperial profits and imperial unity ultimately refashioned colonial racial divisions in the metropole. The fourth chapter suggests how the effort to maintain vast numbers of contract laborers in a somewhat hermetic system conflicted with employers' desire for a smaller pool of Black sailors who could be more flexibly deployed, even at the cost of somewhat higher wages. Given all parties' internally contradictory agendas, it is not surprising that it was difficult to design state policy to meet them. State efforts to impose accountability for the social costs of these practices were subverted to further subordinate Black seamen.

Many scholars have held the union almost solely responsible for interwar racial subordination and exclusion.[36] Yet chapter 5 shows that union race policy was ambivalent, discontinuous, and inconsistent, and that the union resisted the principle of unequal pay until after the First World War. This investigation also illustrates the pressures that eventually moved the union to capitulate to employers' racial practices, and union efforts to benefit from racial divisiveness. The chapter also discusses Black seamen's anomalous position within the union.

The state itself lacked a consistent approach to Black workers. Chapter 6 shows that such racist policies as the Coloured Alien Seamen Order were the outcome of conflict and negotiation among different groups within and outside the state. That Black seamen continued to call on the state as a protector, demanding "British justice," suggests they were well aware of these conflicts. All the same, the outcome of these struggles was that state power was deployed in particular ways, in ways that disadvantaged Black seamen and other colonized people on the basis of race. However ineffectual in accomplishing particular goals, measures such as the Coloured Alien Seamen Order created and reified racial boundaries and hierarchies within the workforce and the community, not only in Britain but in the empire.

Chapter 7 returns to interracial port settlements to explore the local impact of these broader processes. Local race relations were volatile and unpredictable, but racial difference, however constructed in policy and practice, did not unavoidably cause conflict. The 1920s and 1930s also witnessed a process of racial formation analogous to class formation: a "racial" identity and a culture of resistance took shape, expressing Black

Britons' sense of commonality and claims for participation in political, economic, and social life. Further, displays of solidarity between Black and white workers repudiate contemporary and current expectations about racial incompatibility.

The British case challenges essentialist explanations for racial conflict, illustrating how race, class, gender, and other social divisions have been created and re-created in struggle and negotiation among historical actors with conflicting and often contradictory agendas. In exposing the critical links between British labor struggles and the race, labor and political relations in the empire, this history situates Black colonized workers inside rather than outside of British class formation. Racial divisions and animosities, far from atavistic and innate human qualities, were reproduced in the course of interwar struggles, structured by relations of power and interest integral to the historical process—not independent of it, and by the dynamic and volatile interaction between domestic and imperial politics. Responses to postwar migrants to the United Kingdom from the Caribbean, Africa, and India, far from an inevitable or natural reaction to "strangers," were in large measure conditioned by the imperial mechanisms and categories reconstituted in Britain between the wars.

CHAPTER ONE

"I Can Get No Justice":
Black Men and Colonial Race
Relations on the Western Front

We have been caught just as fish are caught in a net. Now what I hope is that since I have eaten the Sirkar's salt for so many years and have cheerfully fought so many fights and have come over here to conquer land for the Sirkar, I shall not be beaten. The government will be victorious and I shall gain reputation and my parents too will become famous, and if I am killed my name will go down to posterity.
—Gurkha soldier, October 1915

The coloured men have mostly served in the Forces, Navy and transport. They are largely British subjects, and are proud to have been able to have done what they have done for the Empire.... The majority of negroes at present are discharged soldiers and sailors without employment; in fact, some of them are practically starving, work having been refused them on account of their colour.... Some of us have been wounded, and lost limbs and eyes fighting for the Empire to which we have the honour to belong...We ask for British justice, to be treated as true and loyal sons of Great Britain.
—Statement by a delegation headed by Mr. D. T. Aleifasakure Toummanah of the Ethiopian Hall, Liverpool, June 1919

IN THE STRUGGLES of the 1920s and 1930s, Black seamen and other workers frequently invoked colonial support in the Great War. Their argument, that colonial subjects' war service had encumbered the British state with implicit and explicit obligations, proved difficult for the authorities to resist. The wartime experiences of Black troops and laborers in Britain and France help to illuminate the making of that bargain and its continuing ambiguities.

Although Black people have lived in Britain for centuries, the First

First epigraph: L/MIL/5/825/1162/67. Second: HO45/11017/377969/f16.

World War is commonly viewed as a moment when large numbers of Black working men first arrived in Britain and Western Europe to fill wartime manpower shortages. For colonial troops and working men, as for women and other workers, participation represented an opportunity that proved hollow even before the peace. Fearing that Black military assistance in a "white man's war" would undermine imperial racial strat-ification, British military and colonizing elites strove to preserve colonial racial practices and power relations in the metropole.[1] In the context of total war, colonial mechanisms of racial subordination were deployed in service of new actors and imperatives in Europe.

Scholars agree that colonized people who served Britain in the Great War anticipated postwar rewards such as political autonomy or self-rule, but were disappointed instead by "broken promises and reaction."[2] Yet in spite of official efforts to limit and control Black men's wartime expe-riences, colonial racial practices and hierarchies were not simply trans-planted but were also transformed in the European setting. Interwar protests show that the war experience proved a usable past, empowering Black working men to place claims on British resources and the state, and compelling the state to respond. It was this new sense of entitlement, not simply their larger numbers, that lent urgency and credibility to postwar demands.

Indian and other Black British subjects served in the First World War as soldiers; as noncombatant laborers, medical and other personnel; and as merchant seamen. The West African Frontier Force, the King's African Rifles, Black West Indian combat regiments, and "experimental" combat units of "coloured" South Africans served in West and East Africa, the Middle East, and Jamaica. In addition, at least one "Coloured" unit was formed by men living in Britain. These Black combat units did not serve on the Western Front with white troops from Great Britain, Canada, New Zealand, Australia, Fiji, and South Africa. The authorities feared mutiny at worst and erosion of racial boundaries at best if Black soldiers should fight side by side with white ones in Europe. The only non-European combatants in the British forces on the Western Front were from the Indian Army.[3]

Over a million Indian soldiers served in the First World War, more than from any other British possession, including the white Dominions. Of them, 138,000 fought on the Western Front. In addition, hundreds of thousands of Black and Chinese noncombatant laborers and other per-sonnel, from British possessions in Asia, Africa, and the Caribbean, served in Western Europe. Although the number of Black seamen involved in the war is unknown, men on "Asiatic" labor contracts alone constituted well over a fifth of the 15,000 merchant seamen killed.[4] Merchant seamen's contribution is particularly noteworthy because it was they who largely built Britain's interracial seaport settlements, and first confronted systematic racial barriers in Britain.

The decision to use non-European personnel on the Western Front was a practical one, but shaped by imperial race and labor relations. British troop strength eroded within weeks of the declaration of war, and manpower shortages intensified as the war continued. Consistent with colonial labor practices, the military treated Black and Chinese manpower as a resource to be exploited and manipulated for the benefit of the empire and its white rulers.[5] "Coloured" laborers and troops could be treated with less care: in military transports they "would be packed much closer than white troops."[6] The object was to save money: explained Lord Derby, Secretary of State for War, non-European "labour is not only the best but in the long run the cheapest."[7] Still, this pragmatic decision had political consequences, for Black war service carried implications for ongoing struggles over racial capacity, political rights, and material and ideological rewards in Britain and the empire.

As Black troops and laborers arrived on the Western Front, the dilemmas of imperial power arrived with them. In the colonies, Black people's economic and political subordination was justified by a contradictory rhetoric that assumed colonized people's racial and cultural inferiority while it implied that cultural assimilation, accompanied by an unspecified amount of biological or racial "evolution," would be rewarded by equal treatment eventually. The ambiguity of this rhetoric permitted multiple interpretations: how much assimilation, how long an evolution, the meaning of terms such as "equality," the content of the "reward," were vigorously contested among colonial and metropolitan elites.[8]

Before, during, and after the Great War, ongoing debates in Britain and the colonies equated military service with citizenship, nationality, and manhood, forming a pretext, for example, for withholding the suffrage from British women. Similarly, imperialists premised their argument for continued British rule on India's inability to defend itself. Accordingly, many Indian elites and their British sympathizers, and to some extent imperialist elites, saw the war as the occasion for colonized people to "prove themselves" or decisively fail to do so. The adequacy of Indians' military performance would be a test of their fitness for greater political autonomy and responsibility. In the words of the Indian press: "The prerogative of British citizenship involves . . . the right and the duty to bear arms in defence of one's country and King."[9] Elites also linked military service to imputed racial capacity: in view of the threat to imperial unity posed by the white Dominions' contemporaneous efforts to exclude Black British subjects, many hoped the war would promote interracial "under-standing," as the "gallant troops" of the Dominions "fought side by side and shoulder to shoulder with the equally gallant troops from India."[10]

Yet within the broad equation, war service carried different implications for British authorities, colonized elites, and the Black soldiers, laborers, or sailors. Hailing India's "demand to share the responsibilities as well as the privileges" of empire, Indian elites welcomed the war as an opportunity to renegotiate India's political status, and to challenge racial hierarchies in India and the empire. In their view the imperial government incurred implicit obligations by accepting India's outpouring of arms and patri-otism. *The Hindu* typified the Indian press in anticipating "a concession . . . which will raise us in our own estimation, as well as in the eyes of the world at large." Many African elites also supported the war in terms that explicitly linked wartime patriotism and postwar opportunity; service and "citizenship."[11]

Colonized people were encouraged to expect postwar rewards because of wartime promises and concessions by British administrators, politicians, and civilians. Indian recruits were promised pensions, grants of land, and more king's commissions. To woo the Indian public, Indians were ad-mitted to the upper civil service, the cotton export excise was removed, and the notorious Indian indenture system was abolished—the latter to facilitate recruiting for wartime labor companies. In many critical matters the British War Cabinet was hamstrung, however. For example, liberals such as India Secretary Edwin Montagu favored immediate postwar self-rule for India, while imperialists such as Lord Curzon favored a lengthy period of tutelage lasting as long as several centuries. Official pronounce-ments at once encouraged extravagant expectations, while inconsistent official actions fostered disillusionment and suspicion.[12]

The war's meaning for Black soldiers, laborers, and sailors remains a matter of contention. Some scholars argue that the war stimulated support for colonial independence movements, producing "new-found pride in race," showing that Europeans were "vulnerable" and "couldn't be trusted," and speeding "changes already underway." Since white coloniz-ers' fears of armed revolution by Black war veterans proved groundless, another scholar disputes the thesis that the war was modernizing or pol-iticizing for ordinary soldiers, arguing instead that it reinforced a "con-servative" impulse among "loyal subjects."[13] Evidence suggests that the war simultaneously strengthened troops' reciprocal bond with the monarch and conferred a sense of entitlement that was ultimately subversive of the imperial order.

Like elites, ordinary footsoldiers entered the war with explicit hopes. Perusing their testimony reveals much about the sources of political disaffection, and ultimately of mobilization and resistance among ordinary people in the colonies and in Britain. Rank-and-file soldiers, like Indian elites, perceived the call to arms as an implicit bargain, but their interpretation of the bargain differed. Their professed goal of distinction in combat meshed with personal and family honor, loyalty and obligation to the state. This not only reflected the colonizers' success in assimilating Indians' religious, kin, and military traditions to British purposes, but also rank-and-file agency in constructing the meaning of their military service and of British paternalism in culturally and politically usable ways.

One could argue that many of these men came from an isolated and unrepresentative segment of the Indian peasantry. The British rulers of India had historically cultivated a relationship of clientage and protection with the groups they styled "martial races"—cultural and kin groups that they considered racially suited for warfare. The British military in India built on indigenous solidarities of "blood, region, speech, religion and caste" through the device of "class companies." Companies and sometimes whole regiments might consist of men of a particular village, family, occupational group, religion, or caste. Religious and intergenerational kinship bonds reinforced political allegiance, and kin relations were conflated with relations of authority: the Subedar-major was often an older man who acted as a sort of confidant or "village elder," while the British officer was treated as the "father" of the unit and referred to the soldiers as his "jawans"—"youths." "Class" companies possessed collective identity and *esprit*. They fought not only for pay, but out of "a sturdy love of serving and fighting in defence of their country and in the service of their King-Emperor."[14] The patriotism of the "martial races" was at once an expression of personal pride and discipline, "a prestigious career," "a moral obligation," and "a path for religious fulfillment." The "martial races" were the foundation of British military power in India and in turn they were protected.[15]

The extraordinary wastage of human life in the First World War, however, rapidly exhausted the supply of "martial races" and over the years men from outside those groups entered the Indian military. Although most new units were rapidly disbanded after the war, their successful performance helped discredit notions of the "martial races'" unique capacities. It also seems to have imbued non-"martial" groups with similar expectations of postwar rewards.[16] Indeed, testimony during and after the war shows how soldiers, laborers, and sailors all placed claims on the state in the name of colonial war service.

Indian soldiers served for a combination of personal interest and political allegiance. They interpreted their sacrifice and its reward in terms of honor, rights, and "justice." During the war, official bungling and colonial racial practices undermined Indian soldiers' confidence in British honor and fair play, eroding their commitment to the war and anticipating the unraveling of imperial loyalty. In addition, fraternization with Europeans changed their view of themselves and of their colonial rulers. Even before the war's end, voices from the battlefield began to articulate the sense of a compact betrayed. Evidence of this process appeared in the reports compiled in 1914 and 1915 by the Censor of Indian Mails for the Indian Expeditionary Force, and was corroborated in the experiences of the Indian, African, and Chinese Labour Corps.

Intended to detect disaffection, mutiny, or subversion in France or India, the censor's monthly reports and dozens of appended fragments of trans-lated material afford a glimpse into the perceptions of Indian troops at the Front in France and in military hospitals in Britain.[17] The sample is highly selective, but no less valuable for it. The letters were self-censored, as the men were aware they would be read en route. In addition, men who could not write depended on scribes, and those who could not read on someone to read letters to them. In some units incoming letters were read aloud to the group. In view of this lack of privacy, a remarkable number of intimate observations survive. Conversely, as a somewhat public and social product, these letters may be viewed as a barometer of sentiments widespread among Indian troops—even as a counter in a heavily hege-monized negotiating process with the wartime state.[18] That is one reason why the censor read them.

Like the thousands of Englishmen who flooded recruiting offices in the first months of the Great War, Indian soldiers, their testimony suggests, shared patriotism and a sense of obligation to the empire, entwined with personal and group interest, kin and religious loyalty. In spite of the war's disorganizing impact, men's words and actions were reinforced and me-diated by their battlefield community and their religious convictions and guided by their families in India. Enthusiastic professions of political loy-alty, allusions to family honor, and to the maintenance of religious practices even in battle, and intense of personal commitment were soon eclipsed by deteriorating morale as these interests appeared to conflict with the British military and political agenda.

"You ask me when I am coming home." wrote Dogra Bali Ran from Brighton to a correspondent in India, "The answer is, when the enemy is completely defeated and our King is victorious. We have eaten the King's salt all our lives, and now is the time that we are wanted." Bali Ran boasted of his newly acquired "fame" as a casualty of battle, without which "I should have remained wholly unknown."[19] Wrote a Punjabi to a kinsman in France: "The people of India who are now fighting in France will return in due course, carrying the banner of victory," not only to be "welcomed by their kindred and people" but "the Govt will reward them suitably for their services." In turn, "The man who . . . does his duty by the government with absolute loyalty need have no fear for the future."[20]

Many initially reconciled the potential conflict between their Islamic faith and service of a Christian monarch. Men frequently requested pocket-sized copies of the Qur'an suitable for use in the trenches, and discussed modifications of prayer ritual in battlefield conditions: "I think you ought to say prayers with your boots on and not to omit the prayers. The ablutions can be performed with earth, if the water is cold."[21] Efforts to maintain religious practice in combat bespoke continuity between prewar and wartime experiences and values, and Indians' confidence that imperial loyalty could be reconciled with their own cultural practices.

Letters from home enjoining men to valor on the battlefield for the sake of God and family reflected the identification of personal and family honor and integrity with military service. A correspondent commended a soldier in France for "repeating the deeds of your ancestors. . . . in the time to come the new generation of India will be able to recall your acts of heroism."[22] Another urged the claims of posterity: "Remember always God and his prophet . . . do good work, so that the name of your tribe be exalted. He is a (brave) man, who renders illustrious his own name and the name of his tribe, not he who disgraces himself and his tribe."[23] At times such admonitions provoked irritation. A member of the 40th Pathans cautioned, "As for what you wrote to me telling me not to blacken our name—if you write like that again you and I will quarrel."[24] Another warned that such letters, when read aloud before the assembled company, provoked laughter.[25] Such sentiments suggest that wartime experience was unraveling the mesh of personal, kin, religious, and political loyalty. At the same time, as British authorities feared, Western Europeans' unfamiliar race, class, and gender relations challenged Indians' views of themselves and of their colonizers. Colonial power was sustained by race, class and gender hierarchies in which white colonizing men exercised authority and power over colonized men and all women, children, animals, and the natural world, and manipulated the boundaries among them. In the colonies a labor system in which class and racial difference unambiguously corresponded was reinforced by social and sexual boundaries drawn along lines of race, class and gender, obscuring the disunity and ambiguity within both racial groups.[26]

Observing and sharing Western Europeans' relatively relaxed social relations disrupted Indian sojourners' prior understanding of social hierarchies. Fraternization and comradeship with white civilians helped destroy "the mystique of invincibility"—the idea of European infallibility reinforcing imperial power.[27] In addition, Black men gained a new sense of confidence and entitlement, as military service was detached from the hierarchical, paternalistic, and racist ethic of the "martial races," and linked instead to more egalitarian treatment they had apparently earned.

At first, the authorities attempted to preserve the mystique among non-European war personnel. Aboard troop ships the absence of European officers too ill to appear before the men was explained through lies about "other duties," for "an officer off-colour is an anomaly." Canadian troops and Chinese laborers on the same ship were forbidden to fraternize, although they did so covertly. The labor companies' noncombatant status was depicted as proof of their racial inferiority: a British officer assured a Chinese laborer that "he hadn't the beans to become a Tommy in one hundred years." Daryl Klein, an English officer who "went home" with the Chinese Labour Corps, described with amusement their first encounter with a European manual worker, the ship's carpenter on the transport carrying them to France. Because of his shabby dress and his dexterity with his tools, Klein reported, they refused to believe he was a European at all, concluding he was "a Chinaman in disguise."[28] This possibly exaggerated anecdote suggests how Black workers' and troops' exposure to class, race, and gender relations in wartime Europe undermined the imperial mystique and the naturalized hierarchies that sustained it. This was particularly marked in Indian soldiers' interactions with Europeans and especially European women.

"The white people make great pets of us Indians," reported a young man after a visit to London.[29] In keeping with the suspension of peacetime norms entailed by total war, many French and English troops and civilians lavished unaccustomed approval on the Indians who were fighting their enemies in Europe. "In this place natives of Hindustan obtain great attention, but only those who wear turbans," wrote Mithan Lal from Milford. "Often when the English ladies and gentlemen meet me they salaam graciously and speak kind words to me." The opportunity this presented was not lost: "Out of devilry I assume a slight limp, from which they conclude that I have been wounded."[30] Another man drew a political lesson: "The Englishmen at home are also very good people. It is only the ruling class that thinks so much of itself and stands in the way of any Indian reform."[31]

European women too proved more receptive in Europe than in the overseas empire. In the colonies strict taboos inhibited sexual or romantic relationships between white women and Black men, while white men's exploitation of Black women was routine.[32] Consistent with this unsavory legacy, peer pressure among Indian soldiers as well as protests from their families in India discouraged fraternization with European women.[33] Colonial authorities, conversely, feared such socializing would jeopardize the race, class, and gender barriers necessary to maintain colonial domination.[34] Yet in spite of official, group, and family disapproval, Indian soldiers like other Black men mixed relatively freely with English and French women in wartime Europe, eroding the mystique of European difference and superiority.

Salvation Army Adjutant Mary Booth, granddaughter of the organization's founder, wrote of "the Indian Camp" with undisguised fascination: "The various castes and types of Gurkhas, Sikhs, Pathans, Hindus, etc. are here. Magnificent physique, intelligent faces, fiery eyes." Booth's encounters with Indian men were a model of propriety: "One of them followed us the other evening from one Camp to the other," she reported, "one of his best friends was in the Salvation Army. He took tea with us." While Booth's primary concern was the state of the men's souls, many interactions were not so innocent. Commented one man, "The apples have come into excellent flavour. We wander in the orchards all day"; and another wrote, less circumspectly, "The ladies are very nice and bestow their favours upon us freely. But contrary to the custom in our country they do not put their legs over the shoulders when they go with a man." Indeed, with increased contact, gender relations assumed a familiar form: "The girls of this place are notorious and are very fond of accosting Indians and fooling them," wrote N. D. Sircar from Brighton, "They are ever ready for any purpose, and in truth they are no better than the girls of the Ada Bazar of Indore."[35]

Military authorities historically have viewed sexual access to nonelite women as a problematic but necessary outlet for fighting men, an implicit reward for their sacrifices to the state. Evidence suggests that the authorities tacitly eased access to local women in implicit exchange for Black men's participation in the war. For instance, British authorities defied the commander in chief of the Indian Army, permitting English nursing sisters and female visitors in Indian convalescent hospitals—but not without trepidation. As some white elites feared and others apparently hoped, this temporary suspension of colonial sexual and racial taboos may have held broader lessons for Black fighting men. In the context of imperial interdependence and the negotiation implied in total war, men previously inhibited by colonial proscriptions may have interpreted unrestricted access to the mother country, and social interaction with their white fellow subjects, especially white women, as part of the reward for war service.[36] Encounters with working-class white people and white women "no better than" prostitutes at home also challenged the race, class, and sexual hierarchies learned in the colonies, undermining British authority and credibility.

By late 1915 morale in the Indian Army was deteriorating. Men may have been demoralized in the first instance by their inability to discharge their duties in what they were satisfied was an honorable manner, due to the unfamiliar conditions of "the first industrialized war."[37] A Sikh soldier expressed his dilemma:

> What you say in your letter about not being disloyal to the Emperor, and it being the religion of the Sikhs to die facing the foe—all that you say is true. But if you yourself could be here and see for yourself! Any shrivelled charas-sodden fellow can fire a gun and kill a score of us at our food in the kitchen. Ships sail the sky like kites. Wherever you look, machine guns and cannon begin to shoot, and bombs fly out which kill every man they hit. The earth is mined and filled up with powder; when men walk upon it the powder is lit and up go the men. There is no fighting face to face. Guns massacre regiments sitting 10 miles off. Put pikes and staves in our hands and the enemy over us with like arms, then indeed we should show you how to fight face to face! But if no one faces us what can we do? . . . You tell us to fight face to the foe. Die we must— but alas! not facing the foe![38]

Similar sentiments were not uncommon among European troops, but Indian troops' disillusionment was heightened by the widening disparity between political and personal commitments. Long absences also wrought havoc in men's private lives. Many attempted to conduct their affairs from

a distance, but their absence exacerbated family tensions. Personal griev-
ances could become political disaffection: confessed one man, "I have made
myself unfit, because I have been passed over three or four times for
promotion."[39] Low morale also spread from India.[40]

Although the censor dismissed "the enemy's brand of pan-Islamic propaganda" as a threat to Indian morale, political and religious considerations
did produce disillusionment. Islamic British subjects, for example, had
reason to mistrust Britain's ambiguous war aims toward the Ottoman
empire. The British viceroy had early dismissed religion as a factor in the
war, yet statements by politicians such as Asquith and Lloyd George, as
well as the caricatured rhetoric of the press, suggested otherwise. In addition, press censorship and political repression in India taxed Indian
civilians' loyalty. By late 1915 the apparent link between religion and war
service began to weaken as home-front disaffection filtered to Muslim
troops on the Western Front. In the wake of the sultan of Turkey's alliance
with Germany, the rhetoric of God, King, and Country dominating earlier
letters waned, as some families urged desertion on their loved ones in
France. Yet in spite of both personal and political grievances, desertion
was widely discouraged as a dishonor to family and country.[41]

Low morale was aggravated in military hospitals in Britain, where colonial paternalism and control were transplanted to the metropole. On
active duty Indian soldiers had access to French civilian life, but once
wounded many Indian convalescents were segregated from British civilians. Self-styled "victims of love"—an ironic comment on the suffocating
paternalism of hospital authorities—men complained they were treated as
"prisoners," denied "freedom," "liberty," and "justice." Men complained
that the wounded were treated as "malingerers" and returned to combat:
"I am ordered to the front . . . I cannot walk, and I can get no justice."
Warrant Officer J. H. Godbole, describing conditions in the "Kitchener
Hospital Jail," invoked a sense of the wartime compact betrayed: "These
men have left their country and come here to die for the sake of the
Kingdom. This may well be called ungratefulness."[42] Thus the resumption
of colonial racial practices in wartime Britain also figured into the implicit
"bargain."

By late 1915, the British military, disturbed by low morale among Indian
troops, removed them from the Western Front. Many argued that Indians
had failed to "prove themselves" on the battlefield, confirming prejudices
about Indians' racial and moral inferiority, and reinforcing British reluctance to yield political power in India. Scholars have argued that this

"failure" was "self-inflicted" by the British, who deliberately ill equipped colonial troops to minimize the threat of mutiny, and sent "illiterate peasant[s]" to do battle in an "industrialized war."[43]

Evidence from the censors' reports suggests that the "failure" of the Indian Army may have actually been a symptom of Indian politicization. Indian troops' fusion of personal, political, religious, kin, and corporate loyalties was undermined not only by the shock and stress of war but also by the challenges Western European experiences presented to colonial race, class, and gender relations, unleashing the potential for radicalization and militancy. While Black troops' experience produced neither the armed rebellion white elites feared nor the support for nationalistic political autonomy colonized elites promoted, it did shape the outlook of the Black rank and file, an outlook reflected in their appeals to British justice in the 1920s and 1930s.

Even after the Indian Army was withdrawn to Mesopotamia, the British military continued to rely heavily on "coloured" manpower in Europe. Throughout the war, they employed thousands of white and "coloured" noncombatant laborers and skilled medical personnel from East and South Africa, Nigeria, Fiji, China, and India.[44] The composition and motivation of the labor companies differed from that of the Indian army and of Indian and African elites. Whereas the "martial races" were largely of "the peasant proprietary class," many labor corps volunteers were skilled craftsmen, scholars, or merchants who left secure and lucrative situations in India or South Africa to labor on the Western Front for minimal pay. Typical, according to Kasri Nath, a recruiting officer with the Third Indian Labour Company, was "an expert goldsmith, Jugal Kishore, who earned RS 50/– to RS 60/ per month, [who] joined as a labourer on RS 20/." The social composition of the Chinese labor companies and the British West Indies combat regiment was similar. Yet the bulk of the labor companies consisted of peasants or workers with less idealistic motives. Some were already part of the global labor force, like the Chinese veterans of South African contract service, the skilled men recruited from the Witwatersrand mines to do blasting in French quarries, or men lent to the Namibian forces by the South African Chamber of Mines. To such men recruiters explicitly promised political and personal rewards to no avail; African governments ultimately resorted to "press-ganging" to meet the demands of the imperial government.[45]

The labor companies did not enjoy the same symbiotic relationship with the imperial government that motivated the army. Those of artisanal and proletarian origins were perhaps more sensitive to imperial race politics than to the issues concerning colonized elites. As Indian migrants to the rest of the empire came from precisely these groups, racial exclusion by the Dominions may have concerned them particularly.[46] As men from such diverse backgrounds increasingly were drawn into the task of imperial defense later in the war, it is not surprising that a wider cross-section of colonized people became directly invested in the war effort, and expected to partake of postwar rewards, variously defined.

Imperial race relations were built into the labor companies. The deployment of Black manpower in Europe pitted the expedient interest of the imperial government and the military, faced with a labor shortage, against colonial governments' and white elites' determination to preserve race stratification. Colonial governments insisted that African labor companies be ill equipped and segregated from white units and civilians for fear that Black veterans might "demand the vote" or aspire to be "the equal of your wives and children." White South African officers, race-segregated barracks, inferior equipment, shabby uniforms, and disproportionate mortality attributed to "disease, overwork, and undernourishment" provoked mutinies among these units in France.[47]

Colonial patterns also pervaded the administration of the Indian Labour Companies. Indian workers received inferior food, clothing, shelter, and medical supplies, resulting in unnecessary illness and injury. Black noncombatants were used in combat zones to which white units were not assigned, yet they were denied military "sepoy" status, thus eligibility for pensions and other veterans' benefits granted to their white counterparts. Indian and Anglo-Indian officers were replaced by the dregs of the British officer corps because the authorities "regard an Indian as a 'black man' and not to be trusted"; and military commissions were withheld from Black and Anglo-Indian Labour Corps supervisors while white supervisors were commissioned. The last occurred through direct Government of India intervention, showing how racial subordination in Western Europe was enacted in explicit response to pressure from the colonial administration. A final offense was the refusal to honor promises made in India to commission Labour Company commanders, and manipulation to keep the men in Europe beyond their contractual obligations.[48]

Both the experience of Indian troops as expressed through the censors' reports, and that reflected in the record of the labor companies, reveal patterns of imperial domination and racial subordination that were reconstructed from the colonies to Western Europe during the First World War. This importation consisted not merely of cultural "norms" or "attitudes" but of material constraints, bureaucratic mechanisms consciously operated by human actors. Debates about colonial power relations, informed by estimates of colonized peoples' innate capacities, spilled over into daily practice during and after the war.

The apparent betrayal of Indian and colonized people did not arise simply from cynical calculation by the military and the British Government of India. Colonial racial subordination broke down in Europe because of disunity and tension among white elites, British and colonial, military and civilian, and between these elites and the white rank and file and white civilians. Many white Europeans were less committed to racial subordination than were colonizing elites, or perhaps they found their assumptions about colonized people challenged by experience. Even the military, whose demand for cheap and expendable manpower coincided with colonial governments' interest in preserving racial subordination, found flexible deployment of that labor and the maintenance of morale conflicted with colonial racial barriers.

As colonizing elites feared, and in spite of their negative experiences, Indian troops and other Black personnel emerged from the First World War with a heightened sense of collective confidence and entitlement. Their experiences helped dispel the colonial mystique of infallibility, while their service in the war and the concessions granted by an anxious imperial government gave them an enhanced sense of power. Black veterans' definition of the reward for war service was modified, "modernized," and perhaps democratized. Even though war experience was negative and disillusioning in many ways, it became part of the collective legacy of British colonized people, marshaled to support interwar demands. Appropriating the language of imperial unity, British justice, and fair play, and the reciprocal obligations of military service and patriotism, colonial subjects pressed the central government to reconcile their demands with the rhetoric of empire.

Indeed, the tension between retaining colonized peoples' confidence and maintaining colonial subordination only intensified with the Armistice. The war's economic and political results heightened the state's capacity for intervention in Black workers' lives in Britain and in their freedom of movement. The colonial legacy of paternalism and subordination and of Black men's claims to rights earned in the war was echoed in interwar struggles, and it remains in Britain's late twentieth-century race policy and in contemporary Black protest. The rhetoric, however hollow, of a harmonious multiracial empire based on British justice, in which colonized people had only to "prove themselves," was useful. In the decades of imperial instability, repression, and retrenchment that followed World War I, Black soldiers, laborers, seamen, and other workers repeatedly renegotiated the bargain struck over colonized people's service in the Great War. In resisting measures such as the Coloured Alien Seamen Order, 1925, they appropriated the rhetoric of imperial reciprocity and equality to legitimate their presence in Britain and to extract state support.

Thus the war experience was at once conservative in strengthening Black working men's claims on the British state, and radicalizing, in provoking a sense of betrayal—expressed not through the separatist impulse of nationalist elites, but through a militant demand to redeem their rights as imperial subjects.[49] The outrage Black men expressed in the course of interwar conflicts originated in the sense of a duty unreciprocated and a compact dishonored, a compact made on the battlefields of France.

CHAPTER TWO

"A Shame on Britain's Part":
Problems of Empire in the Postwar Order

We have never regarded our selves as *aliens* to Britain in peace or in war. . . . So long as the Union Jack flies . . . so long will we regard the word alien as a totally unsuitable word. . . . all these years all the British Black people have such love for the Mother Country England but since the great war things is turn look what happens to us in England in 1919 dont it is a shame on Britain part.
> —Excerpt from a letter from West Indian seamen in
> Barry Dock to the Colonial Office, 5 May 1925

With these solemn declarations before them and with their splendid record of sacrifice during the War, the seamen of India expected that a new order would be created for them by improving their miserable conditions of life and work. But to their great disillusionment no such order came into existence. . . . No doubt the British Empire was saved and made safer for British shipowners to exploit India's cheap labour.
This was how Indian seamen were rewarded for their splendid war services!
> —Dinkar Dattatraya Desai, Joint General Secretary
> of the Seamen's Union, Bombay

BLACK PEOPLE had lived and worked in Britain for centuries, yet in the years after the First World War their presence assumed a new and problematic prominence. Intensified control and policing were the outcome of efforts to preserve imperial power by reinforcing the global inequalities on which it rested. The war accelerated three interrelated processes contributing to postwar racial conflict: one was Britain's deteriorating global economic position; another was the tenuous condition of imperial unity; the third was the continuing struggle over the redistribution of wealth and power at home. Two specific developments provided the impetus and the means for enhanced racial subordination: one was the decline of the

First epigraph: HO45/12314/476761/17. Second: *Maritime Labour in India* (Bombay: Servants of India Society, 1940), 11.

shipping industry; the other was a redefinition of British nationality and its concomitant prerogatives.[1] These in turn were shaped by ongoing historical processes and exacerbated by the First World War.

The years preceding the Great War were anything but the golden autumn of popular nostalgia. Late Victorian and Edwardian Britain was racked by the stresses of domestic social conflict and global economic and political competition. After the war, colonized peoples' rising demands for political autonomy and economic "justice" threatened structural racial inequalities—economic, political, social, and cultural—intrinsic to the colonial system but superficially—at least until the 1920s—not found in Britain itself. At the same time elites were preoccupied by ongoing labor agitation within Britain: working-class activism manifested first in the New Unionism of the 1880s and later in the formation of the Labour party continued during and after the war.[2] These challenges prompted elite efforts to maintain and strengthen race, class, and gender structures supporting the existing distribution of wealth and power.[3] Specifically, the industrial crisis manifested in the decline of British merchant shipping stimulated efforts to reinforce the racial, geographic, and economic barriers between Black workers in the colonies and white working people in Britain.

In their late nineteenth-century drive to preserve global economic supremacy, British elites had pursued formal colonization to protect international markets, prompting a cycle of resistance intensified by World War I. The idea that colonial political autonomy could only follow a lengthy period of European tutelage lost credibility by the early twentieth century as British-educated colonized elites began to demand political power. By the eve of the First World War, the contradictory imperatives of a gradualist colonial policy—promising eventual power and equality to colonized people—and a domestic social policy based on the colonies' maintenance in political and economic vulnerability, were increasingly evident and odious.[4]

The war seemed to resolve these problems but actually intensified them. While jingoism, nationalism, militarism, and "Home Front" propaganda seemingly forestalled the dissolution of domestic order, total war in many ways accelerated the challenges to the distribution of power and wealth in Britain and the empire. At the war's end a new and more democratic definition of citizenship was embodied in the Representation of the People Act of 1918. Wartime intervention in the economy and social life made the state, not the workplace, the focus of working-class demands in the 1920s and 1930s. The interwar years saw sometimes bitter extraparliamentary conflict and negotiation among newly emergent "governing institutions" and ordinary working people in Britain and the empire. At issue was the use to which the state's enhanced power would be put.[5]

For colonized people, the war represented, in the words of one scholar, a "Pandora's box of misplaced optimism." Misled by wartime promises, Indian, African, and other colonized elites expected to share the white dominions' enhanced role in the future councils of empire and looked for an end to racial subordination in the colonies. They sought less to break ties with the metropole than to attain political and economic equity within the empire, through appealing to the British public's supposed sense of fair play and legality. Instead of the extension of political responsibility and civil and economic rights implied and even promised in prewar and wartime rhetoric, colonial subjects saw these possibilities receding with state retrenchment in the postwar years. Initially encouraged to regard their support for the war as the fulfillment of an explicit compact, they found their commitment unreciprocated as Britain adjusted to a diminished status in the world economy and politics. In 1919, after British troops massacred unarmed demonstrators in Amritsar, Punjab, agitation began in India, sensitizing the India Office to Indian public opinion.[6]

Colonized people's war service lent critical weight to their demands for political rights, because British citizenship itself was redefined in 1918 as a reward for participation in total war. "Home Front" support for the war effort had blurred the lines between military service and other types of war service, expanding the pool of legitimate claimants on state power and resources at the very moment when the state's responsibility to its citizenry also grew. The correspondence between war service and citizenship was affirmed when the suffrage was extended in 1918 to returning war veterans and women, presumed war workers. It was also implied in the extension of what scholars call "social citizenship" embodied in promised "Homes Fit for Heroes" and other postwar state provision.[7] Still, gendered and class hierarchies continued to structure British society and racial barriers continued to disadvantage Black working men in postwar Britain and the empire. Yet like "race" itself, the meanings of "equality," "citizenship," "rights," and "justice" were mutable and contested, depending on whether the person promoting them was a civil servant, a union leader or a sailor, a man or a woman, white or Black. In their struggles over power and wealth historical actors used these terms to articulate relationships and demands in particular situations.

The British state, in particular the India Office, the Colonial Office, and the Foreign Office, recognized the war's politicization of colonial subjects, especially the radicalizing effects of racial inequities among British, U.S., and French troops on the Western Front.[8] After the war, official efforts to preserve the empire from political and economic disaggregation included fastidious refusal publicly to countenance race discrimination.[9] Yet elites within and outside the state were themselves disunited in their understandings of the rights of Black British subjects.

By 1919 two contradictory traditions were already enshrined in law and custom. The principle of equal rights for all British subjects regardless of race was clearly and repeatedly enunciated in the course of the nineteenth and twentieth centuries, yet it was repeatedly abridged in law and practice. Queen Victoria's proclamation upon assuming direct rule over India after the 1857 Rebellion against the East India Company was understood to imply a progression to full rights of citizenship for Black as well as white British subjects. Imperial citizenship was explicitly extended to all colonial subjects in 1910, and reaffirmed in 1914.[10] In the 1920s and 1930s the principle of "equality" was invoked by some British policymakers to resist demands for exclusion of Black British subjects, and by others to deny the racial distinctions they promoted covertly.

Interwar governments were actually deeply involved in constraining and subordinating Black British subjects, using a mechanism developed during total war, the aliens control bureaucracy. Early twentieth-century aliens restriction had been developed in the context of a more restrictive race, class, and gender-specific redefinition of Britishness itself. After decades of agitation, aimed principally at Russian Jewish refugees, and of bitter Liberal party opposition, central government control of immigration was introduced by the weak Aliens Act of 1905, but accelerated by wartime xenophobia. The much stronger Aliens Restriction Act of autumn 1914 passed easily in the first wave of anti-German suspicion. To its public and parliamentary foes, immigration restriction itself was un-British, representing a dangerous abridgment of laissez-faire and a callous betrayal of the British tradition of political asylum. But the demands of total war made excluding undesirables by manipulating nationality legitimate and even patriotic. Severe wartime measures against Germans and Britons of German descent reinforced the principle of aliens' exclusion and set precedents for discrimination among categories of British subjects. Measures intolerable in peacetime seemed justified in wartime, on the pretext that individuals' loyalty, thus their citizenship rights, were in question. Wartime xenophobia, strengthened by postwar isolationism and economic protectionism, sustained antialien fervor into the interwar years, muting opposition to the Aliens Restriction (Amendment) Act of 1919, and the stronger Aliens Order of 1920.[11]

After the war the institutional apparatus for policing aliens and migrants was refined and strengthened, reflecting growing bureaucratization. Although the broad powers granted by the Aliens Restriction Act of 1914 stipulated its use "in time of war or on occasion of imminent national danger or great emergency," Home Secretary Edward Shortt rejected a return to the *status quo ante bellum*. Restrictions unthinkable before the war had become indispensable in his view, and palatable to Parliament. He proposed an even stronger act, to exclude "alien agitators," criminals, paupers, and "undesirables" and to prevent "mutiny, sedition or disaffection," especially "the promotion by aliens of industrial unrest."[12]

Shortt's remarks notwithstanding, nationality and immigration policy reverted from a wartime antisubversion mechanism to one frankly designed to regulate the peacetime labor market. Provisions for screening out Germans and pro-Germans were eliminated in favor of those barring alien workers when "it was thought that British labour could be supplied for the performance of the services required by the employer."[13] The wartime precedent of discrimination among British subjects on the basis of birth was retained and eventually turned against Black British subjects. In the succession of economic and civil crises during the 1920s and 1930s, the state, employers, and union leaders eventually resorted to the same measures against colonized subjects that they had advocated against British subjects of German or "alien" descent a few years before. Cloaked in vaguely patriotic guise, aliens restriction served a number of purposes, including economic protectionism, covert foreign operations, and simple empire building within the bureaucracy.

The postwar British state was not a monolith: different branches had differing functions and agendas, and each was facing new challenges. The India Office and the Colonial Office worked to preserve imperial stability, the Board of Trade to maintain British economic power, and the Home Office to control resurgent civil conflict. The deliberations of the Joint Standing (Aliens and Nationality) Committee (J.S.A.N.C.), comprising members of all these bodies and others, reveals that from its wartime inception nationality policy contained an inexorable contradiction between exclusionary and racially based economic nationalism and the strategic impetus for empirewide rights. Hence the Home Office and the Board of Trade attacked Black workers, while the India Office and the Colonial Office defended them.[14]

Even accepting that any British subject was entitled to live and work untrammeled in the metropole, a principle much abridged by the close of the war, two factors made Black British subjects' rights especially tenuous:

one was their limited access to passports, documents virtually unheard of for ordinary people before the war and unavailable in many parts of the empire; the other was the ambiguous status of Protectorate and Mandate subjects.[15] The difficulty of determining whether an individual was a British subject was exacerbated by the ambiguity of the definition itself. Even the "experts" inside the bureaucracy had problems distinguishing subjects from other inhabitants of the empire. In 1928, Haldane Porter of the Home Office commented with unconscious irony, "It was difficult to explain even to the educated person the legal difference between a British subject and the British protected person, and quite impossible to make a coloured seaman himself understand."[16] Moreover, as we will see, for many purposes nonsubjects traveled with British credentials and were considered British nationals outside Britain. Who was a British subject and to what this entitled him were matters of interpretation, even to the law's administrators. The labor movement and rank-and-file workers, Black and white, had different understandings of Britishness and its prerogatives.[17] It would be difficult to argue that the popular definitions were any less valid than the official ones, which were, in any case, repeatedly renegotiated by interested state ministries in the course of the 1920s and 1930s, and redefined again by the Nationality Act of 1948.

Although nationality is often understood as a matter of birthright, immutable and unqualified, the definition of who was entitled to British citizenship and what citizenship entailed actually shifted and blurred. In the 1920s and 1930s it was determined not merely by culture or birthplace, but by relations within the empire and with foreign governments; the effort to regulate the domestic British labor market; and the impetus to conceal state functions from public oversight. Legal codification often complicated rather than clarified individuals' status.

In the interwar years nationality policy evolved gradually into a means of race and class subordination. The Home Office aliens bureaucracy became its mechanism largely by default. Yet as a relatively undeveloped arm of the state in 1919, the Aliens Department's initial reluctance to undertake policing Black seamen perhaps dissipated with the realization that such work could become a source of power. The history of early negotiations with the Treasury Department suggests that some of the excessive aspects of interwar aliens policing may have stemmed from the effort to justify the Aliens Department's existence and its continued financial support. It also suggests that the abusable "dragnet" approach, and the delegation of authority to local police and officials of unreliable scruples, may have resulted from inadequate resources for more systematic and possibly hu-

mane measures. In addition, antisubversion functions were retained covertly. In 1922 Major General Sir Wyndham Childs of Scotland Yard
successfully squelched Home Office plans to abolish the highly unpopular
visa system. Wyndham Childs explained that Foreign Passport Control
Offices facilitated surveillance of "revolutionaries" by the Secret Service,
a function he and the Home Office doubted that the Treasury could justify
publicly.[18]

The stated aim of this mechanism was to regulate immigration from
the continent of Europe. But the Aliens Department was increasingly
preoccupied with an unforeseen project for which its powers were ill
suited: the control of migration from British colonies and protectorates.
The bulk of such migrants were seamen, who routinely traveled internationally and required special concessions from local governments for their
brief periods ashore. The letter of the Merchant Shipping Act, 1906,
embodied a cluster of techniques designed to keep "colonial seamen" out
of Britain. But this proved impossible, for seamen were extraordinarily
mobile, and if they were British subjects they had a right to be in Britain.[19]
In the 1920s the state began to use the newly developed aliens bureaucracy
to treat Black British subjects as though they were aliens. The state was
pressed into this awkward role by the plight of British merchant shipping.

The mercantile marine was an industry deeply implicated in imperial as
well as industrial instability. Britain was an island nation whose nineteenth-
century preeminence rested on the twin pillars of industry and empire,
and merchant shipping was represented as indispensable to Britain's economic vitality as well as to its romantic and swashbuckling maritime legacy.
The industry thus carried emotional, historical, and nationalistic reso-
nances for many Britons.[20]

With interwar Britain's "ailing giants"—declining staple export industries including cotton textiles, shipbuilding, and coal—merchant shipping
claimed major economic and cultural significance while shipowners
wielded disproportionate political power both within the state and as a
pressure group outside it. Because this global industry drew much of its
multiracial workforce from the overseas colonies, maritime labor relations
had structural as well as cultural implications for twentieth-century British
race relations.

Merchant shipping had been critical to Britain's nineteenth-century
domination of the global economy. The British industry had historically
controlled a disproportion of world trade, and could only lose in the
interwar climate of economic protectionism and intensified competition.
British merchant tonnage quintupled between 1860 and 1914, constitut-

ing one-third of world tonnage by 1914. But since 1900 rival national industries had encroached. Only monopolistic conference arrangements with German, Dutch, Belgian, and U.S. companies had enabled the overcapitalized industry to limp toward 1914. The precarious equilibrium was disrupted by the First World War. Shipowners blamed the war and "the Hun" for the damage to their floating stock, and faulted the greedy U.S. industry for the postwar depression, but the industry's critics blamed owners themselves. The industry's decline relative to the United States and Germany was prefigured in the depression of 1901–11, and then exacerbated by the boom and bust of the immediate postwar years.[21]

Because business historians use success as the criterion of good management, they seem tacitly to agree with more radical critics that the industry's interwar problems stemmed from bad management. The Labour Research Department (L.R.D.) argued that "the direct effect of the war . . . has been a relatively unimportant factor in producing the depression in shipping." The L.R.D. argued instead that industrial instability was the "direct result of capitalist methods in shipping during and after the war." These included wartime profiteering; "hiding" of profits; inflation of the value of tonnage due to competitive bidding-up of vessels; overbuilding— also at inflated prices; and "watering" of stock. In short, the industry was overcapitalized immediately after the war, entailing high overhead costs and the inability to offer competitive freight rates. In addition, U.S., Japanese, Italian, and French industries had benefited from the war and continued their inroads into Britain's share of the market.[22]

The deluded effort to restore Britain's merchant tonnage to its already bloated prewar levels produced a brief boom followed by a dramatic bust in the early 1920s. Tramp shipping was particularly hard hit. Britain's overcapitalized fleet already faced competition before the war from the lower-waged Greek and Norwegian industries. After the war the market for heavy goods carriage moved from tramps to more reliable liners, house fleets, and specialized vessels such as oil tankers and refrigerator ships. Yet specialized fleets were never entirely adequate and tramps continued to provide the elasticity that interwar trade demanded. Unlike the large liner combines, tramp ships tended to be owned by small independent firms, especially vulnerable to the vagaries of the interwar economy.[23]

Historians differ as to whether these decisions were made out of stupidity, idealism, or greed, but they agree about the outcome. While world trade actually grew by 35 percent between 1913 and 1929, world tonnage grew faster, by 45 percent, and was 20 percent more efficient than prewar stock. The result was a permanent surfeit of overpriced and, in the case of tramps, obsolescent vessels chasing a constricted volume of goods. Throughout the 1920s and 1930s the industry remained unprofitable. The situation was aggravated by the decline of international migration resulting from aliens restriction in the United States, Britain, and elsewhere; by economic nationalism which hurt historically maritime nations; and especially by the Depression. State-assisted scrap-and-build programs brought temporary relief in the 1930s, but by that point shipowners had already begun moving capital out of shipping to more profitable investments. They also shifted ships to foreign flags of convenience to evade state and union oversight, a trend that continued throughout the century.[24]

The industry was also highly concentrated. By the 1920s the "Big Five," the Peninsular and Oriental, the Royal Mail, Cunard, Ellerman, and Furness Withy, controlled one-quarter of U.K. merchant tonnage. The Shipping Federation, Ltd., the Employers' Federation of the Port of Liverpool, and the Railway Staffs' Conferences comprised the bulk of employers in three highly centralized organizations. In spite of the industry's deterioration, maritime employers retained impressive economic and political power. Shipping interests were well represented in interwar governments. Even during the 1924 Labour administration, sixty-six members of the Commons and seventy in the Lords were "known to be directors of [Shipping Federation] affiliated companies." Sometime Board of Trade President Walter Runciman owned the Moor Line.[25]

In the 1920s and 1930s, shipowners used the industry's "parlous state" as a pretext to cut wages and to enlist National Sailors' and Firemen's Union's support for assaults on the state and on other nations' shipping industries. Nonetheless the uncompetitive industry was genuinely suffering. Owners and union representatives spoke frankly of wasted resources and overcapitalization: during 1921 wage negotiations Havelock Wilson of the seamen's union asserted, "There are some ships in England to-day which could not be made to pay even if the seamen went without any wages at all, and also had their food cut off." Shipowner Sir William Noble, to whom the remark was addressed, agreed. At the end of the war British seamen accepted a 15 percent wage cut.[26] Wages fell further in the 1920s and 1930s.

But as the Labour Research Department noted, the reasons for unemployment were different from the reasons for the drop in profits, and were largely attributable to reductions in the manning of individual ships. Even as the volume of trade improved in the early 1920s, unemployment continued high as a result of manpower reductions and resultant speedup. Some jobs were lost due to the switch from coal to oil power and the shift of capital from freight to passenger trade. Others were lost when skilled workers were replaced by apprentices, boys, and unskilled men.[27]

Technological innovation aggravated unemployment. Diesel or oil-powered ships replaced smaller, slower, and costlier coal-fired steamships. Between 1920 and 1925 diesel tonnage quadrupled and in 1927 diesel tonnage under construction surpassed that of steam. Since firemen were now employed to watch engines rather than stoke them, oil-burning ships permitted a drastic reduction in stokehold crews, dispensing with half the firemen and all the coal trimmers.[28] Thus it was a particular branch of the industry, tramp shipping, which was most affected by the constriction of international trade, and a particular section of the workforce, firemen or stokers, who shoveled coal into the boilers of steamships, who were most affected by technological unemployment. Black seamen were prominent in both workforces, constituting a labor reserve filling the least desirable and least steady jobs. In the mid-1930s the Tyne and the Bristol Channel ports, where tramp shipping dominated, were the principal sites of racial conflict.[29]

Seafarers' unemployment was aggravated by poor labor relations, for shipping employers were notorious wage cutters and union busters. Labor organization was fragmented and disunited well into the 1920s. Working conditions compared unfavorably with those of other maritime nations. The seafaring workforce was mobile and employers wanted it so. In prosperous times British sailors deserted seafaring for less unpleasant and more remunerative employment; even in slumps the need to seek work in the indefinite interims between voyages made the workforce extraordinarily fluid. The occupation was categorized as "casual."[30]

We will see that shipowners refused responsibility for their workforce between voyages, and the state was powerless or unwilling to constrain them. Its regulatory functions proved most effective against relatively defenseless individuals rather than powerful corporate entities. As later chapters will show, in an effort to contain the social impact of maritime labor relations, the government reluctantly began policing Black workers through aliens control mechanisms, redefining them as aliens in the process. Black workers' prominence in this faltering industry was thus unfortuitous, for the task of dealing with Black people in Britain devolved first upon those authorities concerned with the detection of crime and the prevention of civil disorder: the Home Office and local police. Yet the sensitive nature of imperial relations meant it was impolitic overtly to exclude British subjects based on race alone, and the Colonial Office, the India Office, and vocal sections of the public vehemently opposed racial distinctions.[31] For this reason the Home Office and its minions intervened only on the pretext that the men were aliens.

Wholesale exclusion was mediated not only by the manpower demands of the industry, but by India Office and Colonial Office concern to preserve the credibility of imperial promises. For instance, they squelched a 1921 proposal for an empirewide passport conditioned by racial criteria.[32] This pattern recurred in interwar race policing: the Home Office, fearing domestic disorganization and civil conflict, made repeated assaults on Black people's access to livelihood in Britain. Each such move was resisted by the India Office and often the Colonial Office and the Foreign Office, who argued it damaged British credibility, jeopardizing imperial unity.

Twentieth-century race relations thus developed in the context of threats to Britain's world dominance. The disproportionate official attention to Black workers is explicable when placed in its imperial context; conversely, close examination of their situation illuminates the racial dimension of imperial decline and dissolution. In the early twentieth century, nationality policy was used to keep colonial workers out of Britain and in the colonies. Official definitions of citizenship and entitlement were adjusted between 1914 and 1942 to meet the fluctuating demands of the labor market, to quell agitation in the colonies or at home, and to justify wartime conscription.

Thus the contradictory stresses of domestic conflict and imperial instability were played out in struggles over the use of state power among employers, state ministries, organized labor, and Black workers and their advocates. The recolonization of Black workers in twentieth-century Britain—accomplished through administrative manipulation of definitions of citizenship, nationality, and entitlement through the aliens control bureaucracy—can be seen as the outcome of global pressures converging on the multiracial workforce of one economically, politically, and historically significant industry.

CHAPTER THREE

Black Seamen in British Ships:
The Uses of Race for British Shipowners

I showed that one fireman in every six committed suicide . . . met by the charge
that these suicides were due to drink. Then, when I showed that the same
thing was prevalent among Lascar firemen, I was told that it was due to
religion.
>   —Joseph Havelock Wilson presenting merchant seamen's mortality
>   figures to the House of Commons, 21 April 1909

The employers, and their agents, the reactionary trade union leaders of America, England and France, are fostering race hatred among the white sailors
and dockers against their coloured class brothers. In this way the Negro
workers become the victims of the worst forms of discrimination; the bosses
give them the heaviest and dirtiest work, and pay them lower wages than the
white workers. The Negro sailors are put in the most dirtiest and overcrowded
parts of the ships. They are being given the worst food and they are forced
to work under the most terrible conditions.
>   —The Negro Worker

RACIAL CATEGORIES and racial subordination in early twentieth-century
Britain were materially influenced by labor relations in the mercantile marine. Shipboard labor relations in turn bore the imprint of the empire of
which the industry was so integral a part: a racial division of labor and a
racial hierarchy prevailed aboard British ships, structured by imperial economic imperatives and racial inequalities. It was Black seamen's efforts to
shift their position within this structure, not their numbers alone, that
rendered their presence disruptive. An appreciation of how racial dynamics
infused maritime labor relations should compel labor historians to confront
the use of race to divide and control British working people. It should
also prompt us to seek beyond national borders for a global view of labor
relations that corresponds to employers' global reach.[1]

First epigraph: quoted in *The Seaman* 2 (August 1912): 103. Second: 2 (April 1932):
21.

Within the empire, colonized people's labor was systematically under-valued and the surplus appropriated by metropolitan elites. The case of merchant shipping illustrates the material mechanisms whereby imperial political and economic inequalities and colonial racial mythologies were imported and refashioned in Britain. In the early 1900s, racial and ethnic divisiveness formed part of employers' repertoire of strike-breaking and union-busting techniques.[2] These practices and the rhetoric that supported them did not simply privilege white sailors over Black ones. They enabled employers to reproduce, preserve, and even intensify aboardship the hier-archies that kept British workers disunited ashore.

In the first half of the twentieth century, the British seafaring workforce, numbering about 200,000 men, was divided into three groups, each de-fined by levels of wages and working conditions, and by attributed ra-cialized characteristics. By far the largest group—roughly two-thirds of the workforce—were seamen of European origin, most of them British but many of them Scandinavians or other Europeans. From 1901 through the 1950s the other third of the British seafaring rank and file were "black" or "coloured" men—to use contemporary parlance—from East and West Africa, India, the Caribbean, and the Arabian peninsula. Most were British subjects from the colonial empire. Only a small fraction of them—a few thousand—worked under conditions and at rates of pay comparable to those of white seamen. Even these men were hardly competing with white men for the same jobs, for while they were legally indistinguishable from white seamen, informal segregation and discrimination kept them in the worst jobs at the worst pay.

In any case, by far the bulk of this one-third of the workforce were kept entirely separate from white seamen by anomalous labor contracts, chiefly those called "Asiatic" or "Lascar" articles of agreement. Hired in colonial ports at colonial wage levels and exempt from state or union-sanctioned protections, Lascars and other contract workers were paid one-third to one-fifth as much as white or Black seamen who operated in the nominally free European labor market. The appalling conditions of "Asiatic" labor contracts reflected employers' view of colonized people as super-exploitable and expendable labor: they provided low pay, squalid living and working conditions, and constraints on sailors' occupational mobility and freedom to bargain. Thus the racial division of labor and inequalities of well-being between Black and white people in the British empire were reproduced aboard British ships. In addition, employers reconstituted imperial social relations on shipboard, infusing domestic class and gender definitions with racial content imported from the colonies.

1. Masters and Men of the SS *Oolabaria*, ca. 1900. Reproduced by permission of the National Maritime Museum, Greenwich.

This racially segmented shipboard labor system took shape in the late 1800s, as the technology, the work process, and the structure of Britain's once unrivaled merchant marine responded to foreign competition. The imperatives of capitalist accumulation—indeed, of the industry's very survival—demanded wage cuts and technological innovation. Freed of the obligation to hire British seamen with the 1849 repeal of the Navigation Acts, employers began to hire men of any race or nationality who would accept lower wages than British seamen (see Table 1). In the words of shipowner Thomas Brassey, M.P., "foreign seamen keep wages down."[3] Joseph Havelock Wilson, President of the National Sailors' and Firemen's

TABLE I. Monthly pay for categories of seamen, 1928

Rating	European standard rates	Bombay Lascars	Calcutta Lascars
Quartermaster	£9 10/	£4 10/	£4 2/6
Sailor	£9	£2 5/–£2 8/	£1 17/6
Greaser	£10	£2 12/6–£3 6/	£1 19/
Fireman	£9 10/	£2 6/–£2 5/	£1 14/6
Assistant steward/ general servant	£8 5/	£2 11/–£3 15/	£2 11/

SOURCE: Figures taken from House of Commons debates for 15 June 1928, *Parl. Deb.*, 5th ser. vol. 218(1928):1331–32; figures in the center columns have been converted from shillings; also *Monthly Labor Review* 9 (October 1919): 157; Leslie Hughes Powell, *The Shipping Federation: A History of the First Sixty Years, 1890–1950* (London: 52 Leadenhall St., 1950), 46–47; Memorandum from the All-India Seamen's Federation: "Indian Seamen in the Merchant Navy" per S. Alley MT9/3657 M.14184.

Union (N.S.F.U.), Britain's major maritime union, complained that employers, seeking a "more docile" workforce, employed a succession of non-British seamen, including "Norwegians . . . Germans, Dutchmen, Greeks, Spaniards and Turks. It was after these had made demands that they turned to Asiatics."[4] For after the N.S.F.U. successfully organized European seamen, employers next sought cheap labor in the colonies.[5]

Employers ultimately resorted to colonized seamen, and in particular to Indian seamen, because a preexisting contract labor system limited their access to the British labor market and inhibited their organization by British unions. Lascars served on special two-year contracts first codified in 1834, although the institution was much older. Like the term "coolie," "Lascar" denoted both race and occupational status, and, in the mouths of the British, was somewhat pejorative.[6] Most were Indians, but Malays, East Africans, and other non-European seamen were found among them.

For their own protection, unionized seamen were required to sign new articles of agreement for each ship, but two-year "Asiatic" labor contracts precluded this. Employers could legally abridge this contract any time after the first three months, while crewmen had no legal grounds for quitting, nor any mechanism for recovery of wages due. In 1913–14, employers were required to provide 120 cubic feet of shipboard space for each European seaman, while Lascars were alotted 72 cubic feet per man. Even when requirements were upgraded, a differential remained. In 1959 the Elder Dempster Company reported that an incentive for the "Africanisation" of their crews was the need to upgrade facilities if white crews were retained. Asiatic articles also exempted employers from British social wage provisions such as unemployment insurance and pensions.[7] For all these reasons Black contract seamen were more cheaply and flexibly deployed.

Working conditions, notorious for seamen in general, were worse for contract workers. Defined in the British and Indian Merchant Shipping Acts, Asiatic articles were a caricature of protective legislation: Lascars were to be carried only in temperate latitudes because owners declined to provide sufficient clothing in cold climates, incidentally reinforcing racist notions of genetic suitability for tropical climates, and for heavy hot work like stoking boilers. Amounts and frequency of meat and fish, quantities of vegetables, and antiscorbutics were minutely specified, as they were for European seamen. Employers resisted buying European-quality food for their Lascar crews on the pretext of the religious dietary strictures of the "Eastern races," yet they covertly abridged them, in one case feeding a Muslim crew margarine containing lard from tins painted over and labeled "ghee."[8]

Fleet Surgeon W. E. Home attributed Lascars' suspiciously high death rate from pneumonia and tuberculosis to their inferior working conditions. While European seamen's "sickness rate" in the tropics was a common excuse for employing African and Asian seamen on grounds of genetic suitability, Asian seamen's higher death rate may, paradoxically, have reinforced beliefs that they were physically inferior. Black firemen's high mortality and frequent "disappearances," deaths from beri-beri, "heat apoplexy," heart failure, "dementia," and suicide, suggest that many men, particularly firemen, may literally have been worked to death.[9]

A ship carrying Lascars might have two contracts: one for men on Asiatic articles and one for men on standard articles. This reinforced a hierarchy of status and living standards along with a division of labor, all defined by racial difference. Some conditions of work were governed by the Indian rather than the British Merchant Shipping Acts, impeding unified action on all seamen's behalf. In India, Asian seamen were subject to underemployment and corrupt recruitment practices in which employers colluded. Bribes to *ghat serangs*, labor brokers, generally amounted to about a month's wages. In the 1920s the two largest shipping companies in India, the Peninsular and Oriental (P.&O.) Company, and the British India Steam Navigation Company (B.I.S.N.), recruited labor through the Seamen's Union of Bombay, of which one of their agents, Ligori Periera, was president. Men of other colonized peoples such as Goans, Chinese,

West Africans, and Trinidadians also served in the British merchant marine on irregular contracts and at reduced wages. As shipowner Charles Ainsworth explained, "The food and wages required to maintain one British seaman equal the needs of six or more Chinese; moreover, native crews work longer hours and can eat and sleep anywhere."[10]

Employers' bargaining position with Lascars and other colonized workers was enhanced by British colonial governments' interest in keeping those populations unorganized and politically and economically subordinate. As late as 1938, only 5 percent of Indian seamen worked in ships registered in India. The bulk worked in British ships, enabling metropolitan employers to maintain control over them and their wages. While Lascars, like other Black seamen, had long manned British ships, employers extended Asiatic articles, traditional in South Asia, to new sections of the workforce in the twentieth century. With state sanction, special articles were imposed on Adenese in 1903, on Somalis and men from Port Said in 1918, on some "white natives of India" in 1923, Goans in 1925, men from the Red Sea ports in the late 1920s, and, with modifications, Chinese seamen and West Africans. From 1901 until the Second World War, relative numbers of men on Asiatic articles grew steadily at the expense of unionized white and Black British seamen—from less than a fifth (18.5 percent) in 1901 to more than a quarter (26 percent) in the late 1930s (see Table 2). As an increasing proportion of the workforce was forced from the "free" labor market into contract labor, "Lascar" like "Black"— became an expandable and mutable category. British civil servants themselves admitted the "difficulty of defining the term 'Lascar.'"[11] In practice British authorities often treated all Indian seamen as if they were Lascars, and all Indians and many other Black working men in Britain as if they were seamen, or, more precisely, deserters from labor contracts.

In addition to providing employers with a virtually captive pool of cheap labor, Asiatic and other irregular articles kept colonized seamen in a class apart from European seamen by hiring them in the colonies for round-trip voyages only. In spite of their global mobility, Lascar seamen's movements were tightly controlled. Men hired on Asiatic articles had to be discharged in British India, or carried to an Indian port after discharge, "securing the return of the Lascar or native to his own country." Re-engagement in the United Kingdom or another non-Indian port had to be approved by a Lascar Transfer Officer—commonly a Board of Trade Mercantile Marine supervisor—to ensure that contracts signed were not too far outside the bounds of legality. Shipmasters were technically bound to keep track of Lascars during their voyages or in the United Kingdom,

TABLE 2. Seamen employed in British Ships, 1901–1938

	British		Foreign		Lascars		Total
1901	136,010	(.675)	28,073	(.14)	37,392	(.185)	201,475
1910	179,422	(.716)	27,117	(.11)	43,934	(.175)	250,473
1920	175,239	(.729)	14,760	(.06)	50,227	(.21)	240,226
1925	164,117	(.71)	11,869	(.05)	54,969	(.238)	230,955
1930	160,410	(.68)	18,899	(.08)	56,416	(.24)	235,725
1933	125,599	(.676)	11,089	(.06)	49,080	(.265)	185,768
1936	130,830	(.70)	7,830	(.04)	47,310	(.25)	185,970
1937	133,110	(.698)	8,720	(.0457)	48,660	(.255)	190,690
1938	131,885	(.685)	9,790	(.05)	50,700	(.26)	192,375

NOTE: Figures through 1935 are from the Board of Trade papers, MT9/2737 M.4541; those for 1936–38 from Behrens, *Merchant Shipping*, 157. The category "Foreign" included alien seamen, white and Black, as well as many Black seamen who were British subjects but undocumented; the category "British" included some documented Black British subjects. Hence the difficulty of estimating the numbers of Black seamen on standard articles. Figures in parentheses represent percentages. Since approximately one-third of men listed as "British" were officers, who were usually white, the proportion of Lascars in the workforce is under-represented by these figures.

but this was rarely if ever enforced. Originally intended to protect men against abandonment in distant ports, these provisions made it difficult for a Black man to get from many British colonies to Britain legally.[12]

All of this no doubt encouraged a Black seaman to evade Asiatic articles and migrate to or jump ship in Britain where he could seek a job under standard contractual conditions, with improved wages and rations, shipboard quarters, and chances of surviving the voyage. In Britain he could also claim other prerogatives, such as union membership, denied him in the colonies. For in addition to tens of thousands of contract laborers, a few thousand Black seamen lived in Britain, joined the union, and worked in conditions roughly comparable to white seamen. Exempt from the protective provisions of either Asiatic or standard articles, these men saved shipowners money on wages and in other ways. In addition to accepting lower pay, Black seamen on standard articles were unprotected by state- and union-backed "social wage" provisions, such as the requirement to "repatriate" a man to his home port after a one-way voyage.[13] The changing structure of the industry created a demand for their labor.

As foreign competition intensified from 1870 onward, tramp ships, which plied from port to port in search of odd cargoes, formed an increasing proportion of the British merchant fleet. They were an unreliable source of employment and voyages could last months and even years.

Tramps were thus undesirable to a man with a family or other commitments in port. They also paid poorly due to the industry's chronic ill
health, and its domination by smaller, economically vulnerable firms. Unable to sign Lascars for voyages of indefinite duration or outside temperate
latitudes, tramps offered employment to Black seamen on terms resembling
union-mandated articles, but often paid them less than white seamen and
relegated them to the worst jobs, notably stoking. Liverpool investigator
David Caradog Jones reported in 1932, "Negro firemen and greasers are
very frequently employed in the West African trade, as their wages are
less than those of white men."[14]

In addition, Black seamen on both Asiatic and standard articles were
part of an intricate shipboard racial hierarchy and division of labor derived
from and justified by the racial hierarchy and division of labor in the
colonial empire, and linked to the industrialization of seafaring in the late
1800s. For in the same years as employers cut wages by hiring increasing
numbers of Black men, European competition was forcing technological
innovation on British shipowners, as on their fellow industrialists on land.
The late nineteenth-century transition from sailing to steamships involved
new shipboard tasks and a new working environment—intensified pro-
letarianization and de-skilling.[15]

The workforce of a steamship was divided into three distinct "crews":
sailors on deck, firemen below stoking the steam boilers that powered the
ships, and, in passenger liners, stewards in the catering and housekeeping
crews. Up to half of crewmen were now engaged in jobs not traditionally
found on sailing ships—stoking, engineering, and catering. Even deck
crews' work had changed: complained "an old-time sailor" in 1917, "the
sailor's tools of trade are paintbrushes, squeegees, and wads of cotton
waste. They know nothing of the seaman's art." Although shipowners
debated whether steamships attracted an improved "new race of seamen"
or "injured seamanship," many deprecated these new shipboard tasks as
less than proper seafaring.[16]

In the eyes of employers and perhaps of the men themselves, each of
these jobs carried a status based on its perception as manly or menial,
skilled or unskilled. Stewards' jobs were dismissed as "women's work" and
stoking "is not seafaring...it is arduous, dirty and hot...with no sea-
going traditions to support it." These jobs were also typecast on racial
lines, and Black seamen more often filled them while white men dominated
deck crews. Blue Funnel ships had put Chinese in catering and stokehold
crews and white men on deck; the Palm Line used Nigerian catering
departments, "Somali" firemen and white deck crews. Goans, although

Portuguese rather than British subjects, had a traditional monopoly of saloon crews. Cunard refused to hire Black men for the highly visible deck crews of their passenger liners until the 1950s, when Black seamen "fought for" and won access. "In Lamport's," reported Black seaman Hermon McKay to historian Tony Lane, "they'd only allow colour in the galley." Consistent with the definition of unmanliness, catering and housekeeping crews of certain lines were alleged havens for homosexuals and transvestites.[17]

Stoking a steam engine with coal was indeed heavy, hot, dirty work. Yet it was also extraordinarily demanding of both skill and endurance, and white stokers could sometimes command more pay than deck sailors— especially in the tropics. On large ships, the fireroom, "hotter than hell or Panama," might have twenty boilers with three or four fires apiece. At each boiler worked a fireman, responsible for "throwing" coal on the fires and for "slicing" them with a hundred-pound iron bar to keep them burning:[18] "If full pressure of steam is to be maintained, [he] will need both skill and experience to keep his fires burning with a nice, even intensity over the whole grate area. He will need good coal too and nothing will break his heart so effectively as a run of ill-burning, heavily clinkering stuff, which must be raked and sliced continuously if it is not to stifle its own combustion." For every three firemen, the "stokehold watch" carried two coal trimmers, to break up "the coal in the main bunkers so that a regular flow is maintained through the exits on the level of the stokehold floor, thus providing a constant supply within reach of the fireman's shovel."[19] In less efficient ships, coal passers supplied coal to the firemen by the wheelbarrowful: "You had to go as fast as you could to keep up with the firemen, because if the fireman needed to make a pitch and there was no coal you were fired." The pace of work, thus the speed of the ship, was maintained by the "leading hand" in the department: "The fireman would often pass out from exhaustion and the heat, and the leading hand would go over to him and give him a kick, to see whether he was . . . just faking it."[20]

By the early twentieth century the least desirable jobs—catering and housekeeping, stoking, and tramp crews—had fallen to Black seamen on standard articles. By the 1920s they most often found work on cargo ships, especially the "dirty little tramps," rather than on liners which had shorter, regularly scheduled runs and the highest wages. Black seamen stoked the furnaces of now old-fashioned coal-fired steamships, rather than staffing more visible deck crews. When cleaner oil-powered ships were introduced, "the fireman ceases to be a laborer and becomes little more than a watchman"; these jobs were given to white sailors. Even after the Second World War, seaman Hermon McKay reported, many of the most desirable jobs, such as the steady jobs on Shell's oil tankers, were closed to Black seamen: "On those it's mostly company's men and it's mostly white."[21] Apologists for the industry alleged that Black men only filled the jobs that white seamen refused, while critics charged employers with using Black seamen to undercut white seamen's wages and working conditions.[22] Both were correct.

Owners' explanations that white seamen refused work in the stokehold is insufficient, for seafaring had always been notoriously squalid, and by all accounts conditions had improved by the early twentieth century, largely due to unionization. In 1914 Adam Kirkaldy called the seafaring workforce "some of the most highly skilled and valuable labour employed in the United Kingdom." But since Black men on standard articles filled the worst jobs they did keep white seamen from bidding up the wages and terms of the worst jobs. It was precisely in the stokehold and in the tropics, where white men demanded extra pay due to the arduousness of the work or the "unhealthy" climate, that Black seamen had the firmest foothold.[23]

Yet the number of Black men actually competing with white men in the "free" labor market was small—a few thousand in a labor pool of over 200,000. Even these men were often consigned to jobs white men had abandoned. By the interwar years, Black seamen on standard articles had become a normalized part of the workforce. In 1935, after fifteen years of union and state-sponsored anti-Black campaigns, the Board of Trade continued to expect a certain number of Black seamen, for instance, firemen, to remain "part of the normal supply of labour" whether they were British subjects or not, because their services were needed.[24] In the early 1900s, tens of thousands of underremunerated contract laborers constituted a genuine and growing threat to both white and Black seamen on standard articles of agreement. Yet the small number of Black men on standard articles became the focus of employer, state, and union attention.

In spite of their considerable economic benefits, employers remained ambivalent about Black seamen on standard articles. Black sailors on both standard articles and labor contracts not only saved employers money but enabled them to better control and more flexibly deploy their workforce, white as well as Black. The underpaid pool of Black men served as a tacit threat to discourage white seamen from militancy. Yet the price of this flexibility was ambiguity and continual conflict regarding the relative status of Lascars, white seamen, and Black seamen on standard articles.

Because unequal wages and working conditions for contract laborers were justified by emphasizing racial differences, the miniscule proportion of men on standard articles jeopardized the subordination of the majority. These few thousand workers represented a metaphorical and actual "leakage" from the Lascar labor pool and from the larger colonized workforce into the "free" and better-remunerated metropolitan labor market. Though useful to employers and even indispensable to the operation of the industry, this "leakage" had to be controlled to safeguard the structural inequalities undergirding the industry, and indeed the imperial system.

Further, the vulnerability that made Black seamen on standard articles so attractive to employers derived in large part from the institution of contract labor and the imputation from the unions, the state, and employers themselves that Black men were illicitly on standard articles and should rightfully be on labor contracts. The employers and, as we shall see, the union, albeit for different reasons, blurred the distinctions between the growing number of Black contract laborers and the far smaller number of Black men on standard articles. As if to reinforce the all too permeable boundaries between contract labor and "free" labor of either race, their practice and their rhetoric reinforced racial differences between white and Black men. The same stigmas invoked to confine Black seamen on standard articles to the worst jobs justified inferior wages and conditions for Lascar seamen who worked in all ships' departments. To justify the subordination of Black sailors on both Asiatic and standard articles, employers imported and rehabilitated colonial racial ideology.

Shipboard racial divisions and hierarchies did not begin and end with Asiatic articles. While scientists and intellectuals inconclusively debated the nature and boundaries of race, maritime employers made the ambiguities and inconsistencies in racial ideology work in their favor, pragmatically deploying notions of hereditary capacity, racial inferiority, and cultural difference to extend colonial racial subordination to the metropole. As in the colonies, Black men were not only feminized and assigned women's work, but also depicted as bestial, infantile, dehumanized, and exotic to justify their relegation to unskilled work. At the same time employers stigmatized white sailors with class-, race-, and gender-specific characteristics to justify employing underpayable Black labor.

The composition of ships' crews was determined in the first instance by their ports of call. Passenger liners carried crews from Asia, Africa, and the Caribbean, while tramps tended to recruit in East Africa, the Red Sea ports and the Arabian Peninsula: the Sudan, Aden and the Yemen, Somalia and Zanzibar. The "Arabs" who proved so troublesome to the Home

Office in the 1920s were tramp firemen. The Peninsular and Oriental Lines and Ellerman's recruited in India and South Asia while Elder Dempster carried West African crews. Harrison's carried Barbadians and Blue Funnel recruited men in the Far East: Singapore, China, and Hong Kong.[25]

Still, certain nationalities or "races" were typecast into certain jobs. In the 1920s deck crews were commonly composed of Hindus from Bombay and other ports in Western India, and stokehold crews of Muslims of Bombay and Karkaris. By the 1940s, however, employers were recruiting cheaper labor from Eastern Indian ports, showing that rigid notions of appropriate work were flexible enough to allow for wage cutting. Similarly, the P.&O. hired Punjabis and Pathans precisely because of their unfamiliarity with the work and its traditions, in an effort to undercut other Indian seamen.[26] Shipboard divisions, hierarchies and rivalries were intensified through the use of ethnically or racially homogeneous departments and white officers, or supervisors recruited from different ethnic and racial groups than their subordinates.

On some ships, Black crewmen routinely received inferior or leftover food, watered beer, cheaper cigarettes, and accommodation inferior to that of white crew members. Thus the "lower standard of living" in the colonies, a product both of less monetized economies and of imperialist exploitation, was mystified and "naturalized" as a product and proof of cultural backwardness. Such practices, accompanied by frequent reference to Black men's "excitability" and "fatalism" and liner officers' habit of summoning crewmen by clapping their hands, suggest that Black seafarers were treated much as children or beasts. Black seamen recognized shipboard racial divisions as an extension of the class distinctions between officers and men: "To them you were even less than the ordinary crew members who were white." State- and union-sanctioned agreements, indeed, provided a larger number of Black men to do the same job as a smaller white crew, on the pretext that they were "less efficient" or physically inferior, tying lower wages to imputed differences in competence and skill. Pay scales by no means matched these differentials, for the real motive was of course to get more labor power at bargain prices: while twenty white seamen were judged as "efficient" as twenty-nine Lascars, the latter were paid barely a quarter of standard wages.[27]

National Maritime Board (N.M.B.) regulations, by exempting all-Black crews from equal pay, rewarded race segregation and discouraged mixing "coloured" and white seamen in the same department. But, then, these regulations themselves were formulated with employers' participation. Race segregation enjoyed the endorsement of self-styled experts. Adam

Kirkaldy deplored the "mixing in common quarters of men of very different habits and nationalities." Employers, conversely, asserted that racially segmented crews were "more amenable to discipline" and "easier for the masters and officers to . . . control"—an approach reminiscent of colonial "divide and rule" strategies.[28] Somewhat contradictorily, shipowners extolled Black seamen's tractability in comparison with the fractious freeborn—and unionized—Englishman:[29] "Stokehold staffs recruited from Malta, the Punjab, British Somaliland and other British possessions . . . are better firemen and do not get drunk. The British fireman has never been satisfactory and never will be."[30]

It would be an error to see in these arrangements a division of labor that simply benefited the white rank and file at Black seamen's expense. The skills and relative status of shipboard tasks themselves were subject to negotiation and redefinition. Stoking, for example, was scorned as unskilled, yet when white men did it they were paid more than white deckhands, and "skilled men acquainted with steam" were a valued and scarce resource.[31] Shipowners, moreover, apparently felt a need to justify the division of labor by denouncing white as well as Black seamen as unfit, incompetent, unmanly. These deficiencies justified white men's replacement with Black men, and employers' resistance to wage rises for both.

Shipowners justified hiring Black men by arguing that they possessed virtues white seamen lacked—diligence, obedience, and sobriety. Conversely, and contradictorily, employers argued they must underpay and minutely control these docile, industrious workers because they were deficient in masculinity: the very traits that made them tractable, thus superior to white seamen, also made them inferior—"in an emergency they are practically useless"—for it was in this hour of crisis that the Englishman excelled: "Not a winter passes but brings evidence of their ability to meet with an every-day, undramatic heroism the cold-blooded perils of the sea. Meanwhile, from the standpoint of domesticity, they are a somewhat casual and shiftless commmunity."[32]

White seamen were stigmatized with a different set of images that defined the boundaries between middle-class and working-class masculinity: rebelliousness, drunkenness, indiscipline, and lack of control. Thornton deprecated British seamen's willingness to live in shipboard "squalor," while an employer who replaced his Chinese crew with a British one complained that work his Chinese crews completed in two days took the British crew three and one half; moreover, "the British firemen do not seem to worry about steam as the Chinamen used to."[33] As these examples illustrate, employers' rationales, like the inequalities they explained and helped to perpetuate, were riddled with internal inconsistencies, frustratingly elusive if taken at face value. Yet their appearance in the historical record cannot be ignored, for employers used them to legitimize shipboard racial divisions.

Turn-of-the-century definitions of masculinity involved contradictory demands for independence and self-discipline, initiative, and emotional and sexual control. Class distinctions were also infused with racial and gendered connotations. The boundaries between these dichotomized categories were fluid rather than fixed, reflecting an imperial social formation in which race, gender, and class hierarchies were mutually and dialectially constructed. Thus it was not difficult for British maritime employers to measure their workers, Black and white, against an internally contradictory as well as a race- and class-specific ideal of British manhood and find them all wanting, particularly when power and profit were at stake. By "splitting" white seamen from Black and defining each as deficient in some essential characteristics, employers justified both replacing white sailors with Black contract workers and paying both groups less.[34]

Employers' dichotomous view of Black seamen was echoed in a similarly inconsistent view of white seamen—particularly British ones. Shipowners not only promoted colonial ideologies of racial inferiority, but also exploited a mythology of British race, "the Imperial Race, the Island Race, the Island Breed." During and after the First World War they celebrated merchant seaman's wartime heroism, invoking the "reckless courage and daring" of Drake, Frobisher, and Raleigh. By romanticizing seafaring as essential to Britain's posterity, shipowners exaggerated their industry's importance beyond its waning economic significance, attempting to identify the national interest with their political agenda: "Our losses on the sea must be made up, . . . We are a maritime race. The sea is in our being"[35]

Praise for seamen's wartime sacrifices coexisted uncomfortably with fierce complaints about the wages the maritime hero could now command, a threat both to profits and to class distinctions: wage increases, employers complained, had enabled "the industrial classes . . . to compete for commodities, and thus artificially add to the cost of living."[36] Employers sought state assistance with labor supply and control in terms that identified British race with maritime skills: "Thanks to the hereditary salt in the blood, we have an unlimited supply of embryo seamen." Comparing maritime Britain to ancient Athens and Carthage, they invoked prewar fears of imperial decline, calling for "a steady supply of respectable British lads to respond to the call which is in their blood." "Our home-bred seamen have first call for employment on British ships. . . . It is their birthright."[37]

Since employers before, during, and after the war continued to employ men of any race or nationality who would accept lower wages than unionized British seamen, one suspects that these boys with briny blood were summoned to displace skilled adult workmen and to flood the labor market to keep wages down. In the late 1930s, after the National Union of Seaman succeeded in restricting British shipowners' access to Black and alien labor, this was precisely the source to which many employers turned to find underpayable labor. Throughout the twentieth century, employers continued to cut costs by replacing unionized adult men with apprentices, boys, unskilled men, and contract workers. They continued to contrast the virtues and deficiencies of the maritime race with foreign and Black seamen, who "know as much about keeping steam or launching a boat as they do of the differential calculus or the fourth dimension."[38] Lower pay for Black seamen was justified because white British seamen alone had "salt in the blood." Thus, like much of employers' race-, gender-, and class-specific rhetoric, the nationalistic campaign for an enhanced supply of British sailors with "salt in the blood" suggests an attempt to dilute the pool of well-paid unionized labor while reinforcing the racial subordination and segmentation of the lower ranks, both under cover of racist and imperialist rhetoric.

Employers correctly stressed the intimate connections between British merchant seafaring and the fate of the empire. The racial divisions and hierarchies that took shape aboard British ships were a response to the nation's faltering imperial power in the face of foreign contenders. Black mens prevalence in British ships reflected employers' efforts to maintain their declining profits by splitting the labor force along racial lines and threatening each group with replacement by the other should their demands escalate. Shipboard hierarchies not only minimized wages but kept white and Black seamen mutually intimidated, suspicious, and vulnerable—under control. To the extent that we can determine employers' agendas, then, it seems that occupational race-typing was not "economically irrational"; racial ideology presented a "countervailing advantage" that employers could turn to their own purposes by creating a "caste" of racially distinct "victims."[39] Shipboard labor relations also reflected imperial and domestic social relations. Employers found a ready source of cheaper labor colonized seafarers, and an adaptable rationale in the colonial mythology of racial and cultural difference.

Arguments about racial proclivities were used not to drive Black sailors out of the industry—far from it—but to enforce shipboard race segmentation, itself an extension of imperial economic and power relations. Racial ideology legitimated a division of labor and racial wage hierarchy that not only saved employers money, prolonging the life of the deteriorating industry, but enabled them to better control and more flexibly deploy their workforce, white as well as Black. Contrasting images of British sailors as a "maritime race" with "salt in the blood" with those of feminized, child-like, and bestial "tropical races," shipowners refashioned colonialist and racial images to the purposes of twentieth-century power and profit.

In addition to justifying the economic benefits of shipboard racial in-equalities, racist propaganda enabled interwar shipowners to enshroud their political and economic goals in the draperies of Britannia, simultaneously borrowing from and reproducing a nation- building project of inclusion and exclusion. Spokesmen for shipping industrialists linked nationality with race, patriotism, and imperial glory, invoking a nostalgic maritime legacy to identify their interests with those of the nation. Emphasizing racial differences between Black and white seamen on standard articles obscured their common vulnerability to contract workers. Blurring the occupational distinctions between Black contract workers and Black men on standard articles displaced attention to the smaller group and impugned their legitimacy as part of the British workforce.

Black seamen, whether on labor contracts or standard articles, were not without resources to resist. In 1908, the crew of the *Nairn* appealed to the High Commissioner for India against a Norwegian captain. Presaging interwar seamen's claims on the British state, they wrote: "If we tell him anything about the Board of Trade to the captain . . . he says black men can't do nothing . . . but we must have somebody to look after us, shipping office or the Board in British subjection."[40] Other crews mutinied, refusing to work, or appealed to the India Office, the union, and other authorities for aid. But their chief method of resistance was to seek jobs in Britain with standard wages and contractual conditions.

Because many Black seafarers' migration to the United Kingdom was designed to evade contract labor and the colonized condition it perpetuated, Black settlements' formation and persistence in Britain was intimately related to the existence of nondomiciled "Lascars." Lurid rumors of how men got from ship to shore tinged their presence with illegitimacy and low status. More important, the Black presence in Britain constituted a *de facto* threat to and defiance of imperial inequalities.

It was also in the wake of the First World War that Black seamen on standard articles became controversial in Britain, as employers sought to preserve their industry by intensifying racial hierarchies within the labor force. In the 1920s and 1930s both the union and employers portrayed

Black men on standard articles as interlopers who took low status jobs scorned by white sailors, and as illicit escapees from Asiatic articles. Black men on standard articles had a specific and constricted role in the British mercantile marine, providing elasticity in the labor supply, and facilitating the control of both Black and white labor. Yet they threatened shipboard and imperial racial hierarchies. The effort to reconcile this contradiction drew the state, employers, and the union into tortured and protracted negotiation for decades, while it shaped the experiences of Black sailors and seaport settlements in Britain.

Shipowners sustained racial barriers and inequalities in their workforce only with the tacit consent or active collusion of both the seamen's union and the state. Thus we may not assume that Black sailors' mere presence in a crowded labor market was the catalyst that mobilized latent popular racism. We must recognize that conflicts over Black seamen on standard articles were part of a larger context that included the ongoing struggle between shipowners and the National Union of Seamen, and the state's ambivalent role. To these questions we turn in the following discussion.

Chapter Four

A "Blot on Our Hospitality": Recolonizing Black Seamen Ashore in Britain

> The more they mix with the Europeans, the more ambitious they become to obtain European wages and European conditions.
> —Michael Brett, Shipping Federation representative

SINCE BLACK MEN'S RESISTANCE to their subordinate position in the seafaring labor market involved migration and settlement in Britain, access to housing and life ashore became a site of class struggle between employers and Black seamen. At several critical moments in the 1920s and 1930s, different branches of the British state came to intervene in these struggles, attempting to exert control over seamen and employers alike. Specifically, the state sought to make employers accountable for the social costs of their racialized labor practices. Employers resisted or sabotaged state efforts to systematize racial barriers, however, for they threatened the very ambiguity that made Black seamen useful. Thus although different branches of central and local government brought their own agendas to these negotiations, the outcome was that state power was deployed in ways that disadvantaged Black seamen while failing to constrain employers. The process effectively recolonized Black seamen in Britain through withholding economic, political, and social rights other British subjects enjoyed.

These episodes illuminate how workplace racial practices could shape racial formation in the wider society, illustrating, in turn, a broader dialectic between workplace hierarchies and divisions, and social and political relations outside the workplace.[1] They also illuminate the much-debated role of the state, for in the cases at hand the state functioned neither as a simple appendage of capital nor as an autonomous actor with power to

Epigraph: India Office Records, L/E/7/1152.

coercively harmonize conflicting interests.[2] Instead, outcomes were unpredictable and partial, shaped by the relative power of workers, industrialists, and the state; by internal contradictions in their agendas; and by Black seamen's continuing resistance. Yet in the end, colonial racial subordination, imported from the colonies to shipboard, was further extended from shipboard to shore with the aid of the British state.

The first episode began in spring 1922, in the maritime districts of London's East End. In May, Dr. F. N. Kay Menzies of the London County Council (L.C.C.) Health Inspectorate complained to the High Commissioner for India, state-designated advocate for Indians in Britain, that employers routinely housed Indian seamen ashore on Asiatic contracts in common lodging houses "unlicensed for seamen" instead of in the officially approved Strangers' Home for Asiatic Seamen in West India Dock Road, Limehouse. Kay Menzies suspected that the shipping companies' agents, in this case agents of the Ellermann Line, chose common lodging houses instead of the Strangers' Home because they were cheaper. The L.C.C. objected to Indian seamen staying in common lodging houses because these houses were not equipped for seamen. Luggage was stored in the kitchen and "men have to be left all night to guard it, taking their rest on the boxes." Added District Inspector H. A. Jury, as "the men have to use the same common kitchen and conveniences as the white men there is very little privacy for them." During his recent visit to 106, 107 St. George Street, Stepney, Jury had observed "Lascars engaged in prayer, standing on their mats on the kitchen tables, in the presence of all the lodgers."[3] Jury urged the High Commissioner to press shipowners to house "these poor strangers" in the Asiatic Home, or, alternatively, the home for Scandinavian seamen.

Ignoring the fact that employers' agents and not individual seamen selected housing when Asiatic articles were in force, Sir Walter Lawrence, the High Commissioner, dismissed the problem by invoking racial ideology: "My experience of the Oriental is that he will go for the cheapest." As well as contempt for the people he was meant to protect, Lawrence's response reflected longstanding official reluctance to intervene. Shipboard conditions were governed by ill-enforced Merchant Shipping Acts favoring employers over seamen, but responsibility for seamen ashore was open to dispute and negotiation. Crews on Asiatic articles, engaged for round-trip voyages, were the legal responsibility of the employer while in British or other ports. Even Indian and other Black seamen who sailed on standard articles and resided permanently in Britain were treated in many ways like men on labor contracts. The High Commissioner and the India Office were legally and financially responsible for Indian subjects in Britain, but rarely became involved unless approached for relief.[4] The Home Office and other ministries assumed the men were temporary sojourners or deserters; their presence was illegitimate and of no concern to the state. Yet the episode at hand illustrates how and why the state became involved, in service of conflicting and contradictory agendas, both domestic and imperial.

Consistent with the role and history of the L.C.C., Jury seemed genuinely concerned about the men's welfare, but perhaps also feared racial conflict, while it was Indian seamen's identity as imperial subjects that compelled the India Office to act. For L.C.C. personnel understood and skillfully manipulated India Office fears of imperial discord in pursuit of their more local concerns. Fearing "a public scandal," and frustrated by Lawrence's inaction, Kay Menzies next contacted Sir Cyril Cobb, M.P., who warned Lord Peel, Secretary of State for India, of "trouble, if any enemy gets hold of what I fear is a real blot on our hospitality."[5]

The response to India Office inquiries illustrated the obstacles to official reform of Black seamen's living and working conditions. With contradictory charges, countercharges, and denials emanating from various parties and with no real power apart from moral suasion, state actors were often impotent to establish basic facts, much less to effect change. Strangers' Home officials Mr. Whatmore and Rev. N. A. Lash resisted taking action: to explain why Jury found the Asiatic Home half empty, they invoked employers' arguments about occupational and cultural incompatibility: "Firemen refusing to sleep in the same dormitory as the seamen and vice versa and it being impossible to put Hindus and Moslems together." Lash and Whatmore insisted that the praying men Jury had observed "kneeling on the table in the kitchen of the lodging house carrying out their religious exercises in the presence of a jeering crowd of Britishers" were Goanese stewards, Roman Catholics who "did not require special privacy for the purpose of their religious exercises."[6]

Kay Menzies responded that "intimate experience of the Institution over a long period of years" indicated "the average number of beds occuppied in this institution is far below its capacity." He dismissed cultural incompatibility as "the common excuse put forward by Mr. Whatmore of the Asiatic Home," for "no such provision is made in the other common lodging houses," nor facilities for food preparation nor segregation by occupation or religion. Kay Menzies challenged Peel to a spot inspection of "an old hulk" at the Royal Albert Dock, in which the Peninsular and

Oriental Steamship Company (P.&O.) the major passenger liner company trading to India, housed their workers, out of L.C.C. jurisdiction: "I am given to understand, . . . that this hulk is an 'abomination' and a byword in the neighborhood for filthiness and unsuitability."[7]

Cobb determined to tour the lodging houses in question with a medical officer in tow. He invited India Office participation, and they in turn invited a representative from the Port of London Sanitary Authority, who had jurisdiction over the P.&O. "hulk." After months of delays a "surprise visit" was organized for the morning of Wednesday, 29 November 1922. The tour began at the Strangers' Home and proceeded to the house of Choy Sing at 70 High Street in the Pennyfields district of Poplar. Jury alleged that Choy Sing routinely housed seamen, although Lash and What-more denied it. The tour continued to other unlicensed houses, concluding with the P.&O. shed in the Royal Albert Dock.[8]

What they found confirmed Kay Menzies's charges. All were impressed by the Strangers' Home, whose facilities included "seperate cooking ac-commodation for Hindoos and Mohammedans." They found St. George's Chambers in Stepney and Choy Sing's house in Poplar clean, but their facilities "did not compare in any way favourably with those of the Asiatic Home." The party was shaken by their visit to the P.&O. "go-down." The hulk was "unsatisfactory in every detail. . . . Bunks arranged in tiers" against the walls blocked out light and air; the hulk was "dirty . . . badly heated" with "no proper cooking arrangements" and cramped, with in-sufficient "cubic space" for the number of occupants. Lord Winterton, Parliamentary Secretary to the India Office, "considered it a disgrace to any shipping company." The group concluded that "certain shipping com-panies care nothing for the welfare of the men."[9]

The delegation proposed several remedies, including publicity among seamen about the "advantages" of the Strangers' Home; warning em-ployers that they disapproved of common lodging houses; cooperation between the Strangers' Home and the Reverend George Dempster's British and Foreign Sailors' Society (B.F.S.S.) to handle overflow; L.C.C. and India Office monitoring of common lodging houses and potential de-serters; and remonstrance with the P.&O. regarding their dockside "go-down." Yet they hesitated: on the one hand humanitarian outrage at what they had seen was reinforced by concern about publicity in the colonies and desertion by "stragglers" into shore employment such as factory work or hawking. Yet their disapproval was tempered with reluctance to disturb their shipowning peers. They toyed with but rejected the African and Australian policy of fining shipowners for failure to locate deserters.[10]

The committee stalled until J. D. Gilbert, M.P. of the L.C.C., decided to make the matter public in the House of Commons, whence it eventually reached India and the floor of the Legislative Assembly. A joint India Office and Board of Trade conference hastily convened to draft a reply to Gilbert; to frame an approach to the P.&O.; and to arrange a conference with shipowners to "establish . . . standards in accommodation, food, etc.," and implement the rest of the recommendations of 29 November. The India Office invited shipping companies employing men on Asiatic articles to a conference on 22 February 1923. They relied on persuasion and good faith negotiation with shipowners: Peel initiated a discreet correspondence with Alexander Shaw of the P.&O., designed to save the company embarrassment.[11]

Several remedies were on the India Office agenda, including use of Lascar transfer officers to place Indian seamen in approved housing; publicity about the Strangers' Home among Indian seamen; fining shipowners; censuses of lodging houses; and race segregation. From among them, policing and segregation were eventually selected, because they served employers and the state alike. India Office and L.C.C. goals were largely ameliorative, albeit for different reasons, whereas shipowners had a different agenda, and in India Office concern they apparently saw a means to achieve it with state aid.

In the meeting of 22 February the India Office essentially bargained away a number of their goals to ensure shipowners' minimal cooperation. Most elements of the India Office and L.C.C. agendas were stripped away, leaving only provisions for monitoring and control that suited shipowners. India Office representatives stressed and all agreed the Strangers' Home was the most appropriate facility. Contrary to L.C.C. reports, prices in most common lodging houses were higher than those in the Strangers' Home, often for far inferior facilities. But the principal objection to these houses from Captain Segrave and the India Office, even those that were "clean, well-kept and sanitary," was that their clientele was "mixed . . . they take all nationalities, Europeans, Asiatics, everyone. One of our points is it is not desirable to mix up Europeans and Asiatics."[12]

The India Office objected to Indian subjects' freedom of movement in Britain because they feared racial conflict that would provoke adverse publicity in India. Peel explained, "If any scandal should arise in regard to Indian seamen in this country, . . . public opinion in India . . . would not unnaturally say, 'what has the S/S [Secretary of State] for India been doing to look after the interests of these fellow countrymen of ours?' " It was "not good in the interests of the Empire that seamen coming to this country from India, perhaps for the first time, should be put in these poor surroundings."[13]

This assumption, that racial mingling must produce conflict, was likely derived from employers' own rhetoric. Yet on this occasion employers' fears were different. Captain Michael Brett spoke for the Shipping Federation: "The more they mix with the Europeans, the more ambitious they become to obtain European wages and European conditions."[14] Shipowners believed that Black seamen's function as cheap labor would be jeopardized by contact with European seamen; that familiarity between Black and white seamen would result not in conflict but in heightened militancy. Employers welcomed state-assisted race segregation to reinforce inequalities and mistrust between their Black and white employees.

India Office representatives appeared unfazed by Brett's statement, perhaps because they too wished to limit Indian subjects' aspirations. Unlike the L.C.C., they were concerned less with Indian subjects' welfare than with containing Indian political agitation. Such activity, as colonial subjects' response to the First World War implied, might as easily be stimulated by positive experiences ashore in Britain as by racial conflict. Indeed, while cultural differences such as food and religion were invoked selectively to support contradictory arguments about racial conflict or harmony, both employers and the India Office frankly articulated the political and economic agendas served by race segregation.

Employers and the India Office thus favored the Strangers' Home because it offered specialized amenities and was reserved for non-European seamen—racially segregated. The B.F.S.S. hostel, which was also racially segregated, met India Office criteria that accommodation should be "unmixed" and "at some place which is not run for business purposes," protecting Indian seamen from exploitation. Yet shipowners' representatives balked at mandating their use. Brett, W. T. Fox of the Anchor Line, R. W. Scarff of the Ellerman City and Hall Lines, and Captain W. H. Sweney of the P.&O. objected to the "monopoly" of the Strangers' Home, and to automatic referrals from there to the B.F.S.S. hostel: "It is for us to say where the men shall go, not Dempster's or Whatmore and Lash's." When Scarff objected that the India Office was "limiting the range of the shipowners" the chair appeared to lose patience: the India Office had neither the power nor the wish to exercise compulsion, he stressed; they were "only asking you to assent to what we believe the interests of the Asiatic seaman to be." Mobilizing domestic politics for imperial ends, he warned of "public opinion in this country, which is very critical on the subject of the employment of Asiatic seamen at all."[15]

Shipowners' agendas soon became clearer, and were buttressed by racial ideology. Sweney of the P.&O. invoked race- and class-based fears of moral and physical degeneracy, arguing that men in "these homes . . . become more or less demoralised. They get a lot of drink . . . and they get diseases." But the company's real object was once again economic: "They are very much better in the Docks," Sweney argued, "where we can control their life and their movements generally and furthermore we can get some use out of them." Seamen "in the Asiatic Home," he complained, "are on full pay and are entirely useless. We cannot work them; we cannot take them from the home to the ships." Worse yet, once men experienced the superior amenities offered by lodging houses, even those deprecated by the L.C.C., they were disinclined to return to the hulk in the Royal Albert Dock and the employ of the P.&O., preferring the risks of the open market. Sweney undercut such evidence of resistance by borrowing colonial images of Black men as childish, impressionable, and undisciplined: "In these East End Homes they get in touch with outside people, who undoubtedly decoy them away and they decoy others away." The "go-down," he explained, "was satisfactory, but with the various societies there are about it got out of date." Sweney's comments met little official sympathy. The India Office was not opposed to company housing as such, but would not approve another facility that the L.C.C. could not inspect. They withdrew the offer to keep track of deserters, in spite of Sweney's plaint: "They wander away and we go to the frequented places to find them."[16]

The body stood at impasse, employers unwilling to commit themselves to the India Office agenda. The Reverend George Dempster of the B.F.S.S., in an attempt to salvage the meeting, raised the subject of deserters, hitherto a recurrent but submerged concern: "Possibly these Lascars become recognized British seamen after a while. They are no longer Lascars in the ordinary sense of the word. They get an English book [the discharge book was a seaman's work credential] and then traffic as ordinary English seamen." Implicitly recognizing desertion as a form of resistance to Asiatic articles, Reverend Dempster suggested that once a man went "missing" he would not likely be willing "to come back to the ordinary Asiatic conditions of work. . . . If something can be done to prevent that initial step . . . it would be a very good thing." India Office representative Captain Segrave agreed, alleging that lodging house keepers induced Lascars to desert with the promise of standard wages.[17]

Shipowners, like the chair, greeted the proposal to police deserters with enthusiasm. George F. Dean of the Harrison Line suggested that the police "report these men [deserters] to the shipowners as well as the India Office."

The India Office and the High Commissioner agreed to cooperate in policing seamen on Asiatic articles to prevent them deserting to better jobs in U.K. ports. Thus the agenda that emerged from the February 1923 meeting largely reflected shipowners' agendas. Keepers of common lodging houses must report "seamen, natives of India" to the High Commissioner within twenty- four hours of their arrival; the High Commissioner would supply shipping companies with lists of these men to use in tracing "deserters": the India Office would publicize a list of approved homes among Indian seamen. In spite of balkiness by Dean and. A. R. Qarke of the Bibby and Brocklebank Lines, men would be housed in the Strangers' Home and Whatmore and Lash would refer the overflow—not employers or their agents.[18]

So what began as a nominal effort to ameliorate Indian seamen's living conditions ashore became a program to frustrate their efforts to escape these very conditions. The unstated objective of the India Office was to "fix the responsibility on the shipowner" for destitute men and deserters and with it the costs. They failed. Shipowners refused to tolerate official meddling. Potential conflict between employers and the state was resolved at the expense of the men the India Office had set out to protect. E. J. Turner of the India Office explained to the British Government of India that the purpose of segregated housing was to minimize "racial disturbances."[19] Yet in the conference itself it appeared that the opposite was the case, and that employers anticipated rapid assimilation of Europeans' expectations about working conditions and pay if Black men were housed with European seamen and other workers in "mixed" common lodging houses. It was this possibility, threatening to shipowners and the India Office alike, that they hoped to prevent.

The state implemented its share of the bargain: the Board of Trade set about tracing deserters, while the India Office continued to pursue "approved" houses in Liverpool, Cardiff, and Glasgow. Local authorities were persuaded to enact "bye-laws requiring lodging-house-keepers to report the arrival of Lascars," and the High Commissioner agreed to inspect Cardiff housing regularly. Shipowners had successfully involved the local and central state in labor control, while committing themselves to nothing. In subsequent months their apparent disregard for the India Office program demonstrated the futility of official attempts at cooperation without powers of compulsion. Whatmore and Lash continued to send men to common lodging houses while the Asiatic Home stood virtually empty.[20]

The Board of Trade, responsible for oversight of trade and industry, further undermined the scheme, objecting that reporting all undocumented Black seamen as "deserters" was "too sweeping." Many non-European seamen were documented differently from European seamen: "A West Indian, a Kroo Boy or an Arab, even if he is a seaman, does not necessarily possess a discharge book." The scheme must therefore be limited to "persons who are or appear to be natives of India." In July and August 1923 a proposal to print posters for seamen listing homes the India Office recommended was scuttled by local port officials and the Board of Trade.[21]

The India Office backed out of pressing bylaws on the reluctant L.C.C., fearing humiliation if the matter came to a showdown. They hoped instead that lodging house keepers would cooperate voluntarily. The board's defection undermined India Office confidence, and the High Commissioner's suspension of tallies reduced the plan to posted notices in India and voluntary reporting of lodging house censuses. The India Office had no mechanism to enforce either measure. Their weakness was illustrated by the attempt to bluff all parties into conformity. The cancellation of compulsory measures was not to be publicized, Turner wrote, as it might "encourage the companies and the G[overnment] of I[ndia] to raise objections to performing their parts of the scheme." The plan rapidly disintegrated. By the following winter the India Office Judicial and Public Department reported that "in practice no purpose is served by passing the lists [of deserters] through them," suggesting the device had failed to track down any deserters. By spring 1924, shipowners and common lodging houses were back to business as usual, if, indeed, they had ever departed from it. After this abortive effort to regulate Indian seamen's living conditions, the British state resisted further pressure for reform until the Second World War forced them to act.[22]

We may never know what led shipping companies and the wardens of the Asiatic Home to subvert India Office plans. Kay Menzies had implied that shipping companies paid their agents too little to use the Strangers' Home. Perhaps they were pocketing the difference between the cost of the common lodging house and their allowance from shipowners. But the November deputation had found many common lodging houses more expensive than the Asiatic Seamen's Home. India Office officials apparently never entertained the possibility that money might be changing hands.

There were other reasons why the status quo may have seemed preferable to the India Office scheme. J. G. Dendy, Chief Supervisor of the Port of London, explained the shipowners' reluctance to control absolutely the free flow of labor. Echoing the employers' argument that "not one Lascar seaman out of 100 can compete with European in the ordinary market,"

Dendy explained that their presence in U.K. ports met employers' demand for men they could hire for one-way out-bound voyages but were not required to repatriate. The odd Lascar-turned-regular seaman offered an employer flexibility in manning a ship with no responsibility for the man after discharge. Eliminate this practice, Dendy argued, and "wilful desertions would automatically cease."[23] If Dendy was correct, the benefits of racial stratification—Asiatic or other special contracts for the vast majority of Black seafarers—were complemented by the advantages of keeping a smaller pool of Black sailors who could be more flexibly deployed, even at the cost of slightly higher wages. Thus the India Office effort to fix the boundaries between contract labor and free labor, impeding the flow of men from Lascar articles to independence, with its potential political or social costs, threatened to diminish employers' options.

In addition, like the P.&O., some companies may have wished to work their crews while ashore, or engage in other practices of which the India Office, the L.C.C., or the B.F.S.S. might not have approved. Perhaps it was a matter of sheer control: allowing local or central government to interfere in shore housing may have appeared an ominous harbinger of state supervision that shipowners felt compelled to resist on ideological as well as practical grounds. The scheme may also have encountered opposition, resistance, or even sabotage from crew-masters or agents of individual companies or ships with personal and possibly corrupt business arrangements and networks ashore.[24]

What the episode can tell us is how and why the state became involved in policing Black seamen ashore, and the reasons why state power was ultimately used against individual seamen instead of against shipping industrialists. The episode suggests that interwar governments' efforts to harmonize the interests of capital and labor were naive. Racially repressive policy was a product of convergence and negotiation among historical actors with different agendas and different degrees of power. Only those measures emerged that served the shipping industry's and the state's shared desire to constrain Indian seamen's mobility and expectations.

The plan to reform Indian seamen's living conditions ashore failed because the state lacked power to compel employers' cooperation. India Office concern to "protect" Indian seamen from racial conflict was a response to the threat of political agitation in India. Employers merely interpreted state overtures as the opportunity to enlist government aid in controlling their labor force. They showed no willingness to alter routine practices that maximized their control of the men while minimizing the costs of maintaining them. Colonial racial ideology proved a *lingua franca* that employers could rehabilitate and manipulate to excuse Black men's exploitation and to discredit their resistance. Enhanced control appeared a remedy for threats to racial hierarchy that included both interracial conflict and interracial harmony. Ironically, state concern for Indian seamen's welfare ultimately gained them no more protection—merely more control.

If the Lascar accommodation episode was a perhaps naive effort to harmonize employers' and seamen's conflicting interests, state intervention on shipowners' behalf was overt in a series of extralegal arrangements in the 1920s and the 1930s between the Liverpool-based Elder Dempster Company and the Home Office and the Board of Trade. The Elder Dempster Agreements, as they were called, permitted the company to evade British wage and nationality legislation by exempting their West African crews from the aliens legislation of 1919 and 1920 and from the Coloured Alien Seamen Order of 1925.[25] Like the Lascar accommodation scheme, the episode exposed how Black workers' exploitation in the colonies shaped Black seamen's subordination in Britain through employers' efforts to preserve shipboard racial inequalities ashore. It again reveals how and why state officials came to support employers' agenda, while failing to extract a reciprocal commitment from employers.

Elder Dempster and Company, Ltd., was the major cargo liner firm trading between Liverpool and West Africa. Founded by "that Great Imperialist the late Sir Alfred Jones," benefactor of the Liverpool and London Schools of Tropical Medicine, Elder Dempster and its subsidiaries the British and African Steam Navigation Company and the African Steamship Company, dominated the West African trade in Gambian groundnuts and palm kernels and cocoa from Sierra Leone and the Gold Coast, and ran mail and passenger services between the Cape and Canada, Galveston and New Orleans, the Canary Islands and Teneriffe.[26] Elder Dempster employed West African crews for this trade and was apparently indirectly responsible for the formation of Liverpool's West African "colony". Like other shipowners they regularly discharged crews after one-way voyages and refused to rehire men they found unsatisfactory.

Elder Dempster had employed West Africans at least since the beginning of the twentieth century. West Africa was known as "the white man's grave," making European crews expensive and hard to get. African seamen were judged physically suited to the climate and could be underpaid. What was new after the war was the aliens legislation of 1919 and 1920 requiring alien seamen—and in practice undocumented British subjects—to register with local police if their stay ashore exceeded two months. Among the professed aims of this legislation was to prevent illegal aliens from underbidding British workers: once a man registered he must be paid "British rates" of wages.[27] These minimal protective provisions jeopardized Elder Dempster's privileged access to cheap African labor.

Agreements concluded with the Aliens Branch of the Home Office in October 1922 and April 1924 exempted Elder Dempster's West African employees from aliens regulations, relieving the company of the obligation to pay British wages. In return, the company agreed to police the men themselves, freeing the chronically overburdened Home Office Aliens Branch from the work involved, and "keeping the Natives on Articles [that is, under contract] and thereby under control while in this country." Elder Dempster also agreed to repatriate "undesirables," deserters, and absentees at their own expense. The company used its "register card" as a sort of private passport and found "a threat of withdrawal," leaving a man undocumented, useful in enforcing discipline.[28]

Men from Britain's West African colonies were manifestly British subjects, and should not have been subject to aliens regulation at all. Colonial subjects who could prove it were entitled to disembark, to remain in the United Kingdom indefinitely, and to work for another company at higher wages. The Elder Dempster agreements, then, were frankly designed to impede West Africans from claiming their rights as British subjects, including the right to bargain over the price of their labor in the British market.

In 1925 owners were spurred to pursue new arrangements by another state regulation. The Special Restriction (Coloured Alien Seamen) Order eliminated the sixty-day "grace period" for Black seamen only, requiring those without British passports to register as aliens immediately. Unjust though it was, registration effectively regularized Black working men's presence in Britain, again implying British wage levels. In June 1925, E. N. Cooper, Superintending Inspector of Immigration for the North of England, wrote to Elder Dempster and to John Holt and Co. and Henry Tyrer and Co., their competitors in the West African trade, explaining the probable effect of the 1925 order: "Alien seamen in possession of a Police Certificate of Registration will endeavour to obtain employment in ships paying the port rate of wages." The Coloured Alien Seaman Order threatened to restrict employers' access to underpayable labor in another way, "due to the fact," they frankly admitted, that "many of the men . . . were, as British subjects, outside the [1925] Order," and their efforts to register would establish this.[29]

Anticipating employers' objections, Cooper offered a remedy: recasting

West African seafarers' articles of agreement in similar terms to Asiatic articles. Men would be signed for round-trip voyages terminating in West Africa and would remain under contract while in Britain. In addition, "If crews were engaged and discharged in West Africa" wrote Cooper, "wages to be paid would be determined at the port of engagement abroad." Special articles would also inhibit Africans from leaving Elder Dempster's ships in Liverpool to seek work at British wages, for "not being in possession of Police certificates of registration they would be unable to sign on any other ship in this country." Cooper promised state assistance "to return any deserter to his ship."[30]

Employers welcomed Cooper's proposal. John Holt and Co. feared that the Coloured Alien Seaman Order would "affect the supply of available men." Yet their main concern was not quantity but price: "Unless there be sufficient supply," they wrote to Cooper, "those who have certificates will be able to demand standard wages given to Europeans. . . . We are in favour . . . of crews being engaged and discharged in West Africa, as we are confident that this is the only practical method of control, and at the same time determines the correct value of coloured men's services."[31] In addition to direct cash savings, enhanced "control" was a secondary means to minimize wages by restricting African seamen's freedom to bargain outside the colonial context. Contracts would terminate only in West Africa, keeping wages low and giving Elder Dempster and other West African shipping lines a virtual monopoly of employment for West African sailors. The scheme's advantage to shipowners was clear, but it is less obvious why the state supported it. The Home Office had just concluded protracted negotiations ostensibly designed to prevent shipowners from substituting underpaid Black labor for union seamen. One might well wonder what moved them to assist shipowners in evading their own Coloured Alien Seaman Order.

Clues may be found in the language of "control" common to employers and civil servants alike. As noted earlier, control over the self and others distinguished ruling-class "imperial manhood," as both a political category and a personal identity, from women, children, the working class, colonized people, and the natural world itself. Yet such control was growing more complicated in the early decades of the twentieth century, as women, organized labor, and colonized people increasingly demanded a greater share of autonomy, political power, and social resources. While the India Office and the Board of Trade had imperial as well as domestic agendas to attend to when approaching Black workers, the Immigration Service and its parent entity, the Home Office, were charged with the maintenance of domestic order. Concerned with regulating immigration and containing civil conflict, the Home Office in the 1920s and 1930s found itself increasingly occupied with policing labor agitation.[32] Elder Dempster's promise to "control" a portion of that labor force was consistent with the intent if not the letter of their larger task.

Another clue may lie in the figure of E. N. Cooper, a lone activist in a largely reactive state bureaucracy. Cooper routinely exceeded the law by refusing Black Liverpool residents leave to land. He advocated the imposition of "native articles" on all Black seafarers, and lamented magistrates' frequent refusal to convict Black seamen under aliens law because they were British subjects.[33] Supervising from his post in Old Harbourmaster's House, Liverpool, and sometimes traveling to London or the other West Coast ports, Cooper personally oversaw the registration scheme for Black seamen.

"Control" to Elder Dempster meant restricting their employees' freedom to bargain for better wages and working conditions. But to Cooper and to some extent the Home Office, "control" was far more complex, perhaps reflecting the enthusiasm for statist solutions engendered by the First World War. Civil servants' ambitions extended beyond labor control to social control and sexual control, and they apparently harbored deluded hopes of controlling industrialists as well as workers. Cooper invoked the specter of Black and working-class volatility, drawn from both domestic class relations and colonial race relations. He predicted that if the Coloured Alien Seamen Order were extended to West African seamen, implying equal wages and working conditions, "we should . . . be soon face to face with the 'clash of colour' in our seaport towns." Mixing colonial sexual taboos and class-based fears of the poor, he warned that West African seamen ashore in Liverpool were likely to set up housekeeping with white women and to go on relief.[34]

Cooper betrayed his sense of personal vulnerability in an emotional account of "a surging sea of 500 negroes pressing round us" in a Cardiff seamen's waiting room. Reinforcing this implicitly sexualized view of Black men as uncontrolled and uncontrollable, irrational and overwhelming, Cooper defined his task as "stem[ming] the tide of each new breach in the defence." Cooper also revealed an inflated estimation of the state's control over industry, boasting that "the Immigration Officers have got a pretty tight hold of the companies now." The Home Office were apparently swayed, for they adopted his arguments for use in pressuring the Colonial Office.[35]

But the interwar British state was not simply a handmaiden to capital.

As in the Lascar accommodation episode, different branches of the state struggled and negotiated with employers and among themselves. At the Board of Trade, reaction to Cooper's proposal was cool: the agreements, while technically legal, were "contrary to the spirit of the Merchant Shipping Acts," and since "Elder Dempster are quite frank in admitting that they want cheap labour . . . the less the Board had to do with the scheme the better." They correctly feared that Elder Dempster sought to replace unionized seamen with underpaid West Africans.[36] In the end the scheme failed because the Board of Trade refused to give Elder Dempster an entirely free hand, insisting on minimal protection for their African employees, and because West African seamen continued to resist restrictions on their mobility, their freedom to bargain, and their claims to other prerogatives of British manhood.

The board's opposition was initially prompted by the transfer clause keeping men under contract while in port. To effect their purpose of round-trip voyages terminating in West Africa, Elder Dempster included an automatic transfer clause in their articles of agreement, but this clause was technically illegal, thus unenforceable. The British Merchant Shipping Acts required that regular seamen, for their own protection, must read, understand, and sign new articles specifying pay, working, and living conditions for each vessel: The Board of Trade "always insisted that seamen, other than Lascars, cannot be transferred [even] with their Agreement from one foreign-going ship to another." An automatic transfer clause would permit the company to move a man from ship to ship without signing new articles of agreement.[37] This would prevent him leaving their employ in a European port at the end of a voyage, or refusing a ship he found unsatisfactory.

The Board of Trade reluctantly permitted Elder Dempster to "bluff" West African crews into signing these illegal agreements, but if a man decided to leave the first ship in a U.K. port instead of returning to Africa on a second he was legally entitled to do so: "If the men could . . . prove that they were British subjects they might refuse to sign on again and eventually become domiciled in the U.K." The board also pressed the company to be responsible for men who fell ill in the United Kingdom. Insisting that they already provided abundantly for illness, repatriation, transfer charges, and fit living and working conditions, Elder Dempster resisted codifying any of their practices.[38] Although happy to benefit from state-assisted "control," the company was wary of reciprocal demands: "Should a man be in possession of a British passport, . . . neither we nor the Aliens' Officers would have any control over him, and if he refused to be repatriated, we, . . . would still be liable for his medical treatment and maintenance."

In 1927 Elder Dempster further stretched the already illegal transfer clause to encompass voyages to the United States and Canada en route to West Africa, their regular triangular route, evading North American as well as British wages and protections.[39] The Board of Trade initially resisted this. Suggesting that a man on a two-year contract might be transferred from ship to ship "whether a suitable ship or not," G. E. Baker probed, "would not the Superintendent in Sierra Leone find it very difficult to explain this clause to a Kroo boy and ascertain that he understands it before he signs it?" Baker mused, "Does the Department know what Elder Dempster really intend to do with their Kroo boys?" Just as the Board of Trade was about to abandon it, the Home Office stepped in to preserve the illegal transfer. Immigration Officers would refuse Elder Dempster crewmen leave to land without documentary proof of British nationality.[40] Yet even within the Home Office there was dissent.

In September 1927, Home Office Undersecretary Carew Robinson expressed doubts about depriving West African subjects of passports, critical to the plan. He anticipated "little sympathy from the Colonial Office for any suggestion that West African British subjects should be refused passports." To win Colonial Office support, the Home Office resolved to "draw attention to cases where such passports have been obtained by misrepresentation, the holder probably not being a British subject." Although, as Carew Robinson cautioned, "We have barely sufficient material for this," the Home Office made their material do, delivering a strongly worded complaint over the signature of Home Secretary Sir William Joynson-Hicks concerning the five cases they managed to scrape up. Admonishing Colonial Secretary Leopold Amery to discipline his staff from "apparently indiscriminating issue of British passports," they requested that passports for travel within Africa be issued on a one-destination basis only. The Board of Trade became resigned to the illegal transfer clause: if employers could not be constrained, it was some consolation that the scheme "keeps the crew under control and prevents them from landing in the U.K. [and] remaining here and claiming British nationality." Eventually the board bargained its consent to the illegal clause in exchange for Elder Dempster's nominal commitment to take financial responsibility for men they abandoned ill in Britain.[41] Thus with state support West African seamen were coerced to accept wages and working conditions inferior to those of unionized seamen, and inhibited from bargaining for better ones in the United Kingdom or in North America.

Yet in the 1930s the Board of Trade concluded that shipowners had failed to act in good faith. In spite of extensive state support and concessions, Elder Dempster defaulted on its agreement to repatriate "undesirables" to Africa, continuing to abandon "troublemakers" in Liverpool. The plan to keep West African seamen under contract in port was never extended to Liverpool, Elder Dempster's most important British port of call and the most substantial site of West African settlement in Britain, because the company was "alarmed" at the cost of keeping men "on articles" between voyages, and especially by the cost of repatriation. As late as summer 1927 the proposed European ports of operation remained Hull, London, Cardiff, and Hamburg.[42] By 1930, even Liverpool authorities conceded that "Messers Elder Dempster & Co. Ltd. wish to be relieved from any obligation . . . to extend the system of Sierra Leone articles to their whole fleet, and they have found the operation of the system . . . irksome . . . while the benefits at this end have fallen short of expectations."[43]

Cooper himself reported in May 1932 that Elder Dempster was violating the agreement by dumping "blacklisted" men in Liverpool. Of the hundreds of men so disposed of, most had found other jobs, but Cooper was concerned because 92 remained on relief.[44] By summer 1933, of the 371 initially registered, 168 were still on Elder Dempster's register, while 213 were no longer registered, having, in the words of an official, "escaped." In 1934 the Home Office surveyed 1,000 West African seamen currently in the United Kingdom. Only 224 of these were registered under the Elder Dempster Agreement, and 434 under the Coloured Alien Seamen Order. Of a total of 1,613 men employed since the beginning of the scheme, 1,000 were currently in Freetown, Sierra Leone, 320 on the "live" register in the United Kingdom, and the balance had been blacklisted by the company and remained in Liverpool.[45]

As a result, Elder Dempster cut their wages bill by hiring men at lower wages in West Africa, but continued to abandon those they found least satisfactory in Liverpool rather than returning them to the colonies as promised. Although the company declined to specify what sorts of activities or men they defined as "trouble, it is perhaps worth speculating whether men who rebelled by attempting to organize, or by challenging racial inequalities or labor discipline, might have enhanced the developing institutional and political structure of Liverpool's Black settlements.

The plan also failed because Elder Dempster's West African employees resisted it, developing strategies to remain in Britain and to seek better paid work. Many of these strategies of resistance were less collective and confrontational than individual and evasive. Since access to better wages and working conditions was contingent on individual men's status as British subjects, some 60 to 80 percent of West African seamen eventually armed themselves with passports, establishing their right to live and work anywhere in the British empire, including Britain itself.[46] Others married or set up housekeeping with local women, through which they officially established domicile in the United Kingdom, entitling them to relief and other social services. In addition, the authorities hesitated to deport married men, less out of respect for the conjugal bond than the fear of adverse publicity and the likelihood that their families, deprived of the breadwinner, would require relief.

A particularly embarrassing case was that of John Zarlia, whom the Home Office deported to Africa from Liverpool in 1928, stranding his wife and children, who then sought public assistance. Zarlia had lived and worked in Liverpool since before the war, both at sea and for the Liverpool Gas Company, but had lately fallen victim to Elder Dempster's "blacklist." In the House of Commons the Home Secretary, W. Joynson-Hicks, was asked why John Zarlia, deported as an alien, was "repatriated" to Sierra Leone, a British dependency. Joynson-Hicks, better known for his role in breaking the General Strike in 1926, supported the action, explaining that the man had no proof he was a British subject, and after his last voyage Elder Dempster had simply "decided to dispense with his services."[47] Subsequently the fear of bad publicity discouraged deportation of married men, and the West African settlement in Liverpool continued to grow, establishing an institutional and cultural nucleus for wartime and postwar Black settlement in Britain.

To the Home Office, this was simply evidence of failure. As early as November 1925, Haldane Porter, Chief Inspector and architect of the Home Office Aliens Branch had informed his staff that the scheme "is petering out." In late 1925 and again in 1935 the Home Office was prepared to scrap the plan, as it was apparently "breaking down" and absorbing excessive staff time. But Cooper resisted, arguing that "we are on firmer ground and have a better control of . . . coloured crews today than at any time." Without the agreements, "our control would immediately vanish."[48]

The company too rebuffed several proposals to abolish the scheme. Elder Dempster depended on bluff and intimidation to contain their employees' militancy both on shipboard and ashore, and the company's credibility was enhanced by apparent state support: "It would create a very bad impression on the negro colony in Liverpool if we [the Home Office] were to denounce the Agreement and throw the whole of the responsibility for controlling these men on the company." In December 1934 the Home Office again sought to scrap the special agreements and register undocumented West African seamen, including the bulk of Elder Dempster's workforce, under the Coloured Alien Seamen Order. This would force Elder Dempster to draw its labor force from the ranks of "men who have British passports" and pay them accordingly. Elder Dempster countered with a threat to provide their mostly British employees with passports, claiming that "the Company's green card was itself sufficient for entry to the U.K. for service with the company and guaranteed a man's employment so long as he behaved himself."[49] It is more than ironic that in 1920 it was the state that threatened Elder Dempster by issuing African seamen passports, while in 1932 Elder Dempster threatened the state with the same. In the interval the state had become deeply implicated in the industry's racial practices.

In September 1935 Elder Dempster was still recruiting new men in Africa rather than reemploying those already in Liverpool. Although Elder Dempster's business and shipping in general were reviving, numbers of West Africans on the dole in Liverpool, although modest, continued to mount, from 85 men in January 1932 to 110 in August 1934 to 149 in August 1935.[50] Yet neither the Home Office nor the Board of Trade had the power to compel Elder Dempster to honor their agreements.

Elder Dempster eventually solved the problem of controlling their West African employees by confining them to racially segregated company housing in Liverpool. In 1939 Ministry of Labour investigators reported with approval that the company had "provided a large hostel and insist[ed] that all unmarried negroes in their employ shall stay there between voyages." The hostel was located in Upper Stanhope Street, in the heart of Liverpool's historically Black settlement. Struck by its spartan atmosphere, the official visitors were assured that West African seamen expected a lower standard of living than English people—even in Britain: "The dormitories and rooms in which meals are eaten are rather sparsely furnished but it was stated that this was in keeping with the normal standard of living of West African seamen, who do not appreciate . . . many of the amenities enjoyed by the white races."[51]

By "naturalizing," thus "racializing" Black seamen's deficient living and working conditions as products of West African culture or nature, employers and their allies effectively suppressed the economic and political relationships between colonizer and colonized that kept African seafarers poor. As recently as 1959, Elder Dempster continued to employ the bulk of Nigerian seamen, to abandon those they found troublesome on "fictitious" medical discharges, and to discipline and control their employees with British authorities' aid.[52]

Like the abortive effort to control Lascar seamen ashore, the Elder Dempster Agreements were an example of state-industrial cooperation in which the state did the cooperating, employers got the benefits, and Black seamen paid the costs. Shipowners successfully enlisted state assistance to control their Black employees, sharing not only the material resources of the imperial government, but also its prestige. In the process, the state created legal and administrative distinctions and inequalities among British subjects, based on race.

The Elder Dempster Agreements were designed to enable the company to continue what they had long practiced, the undercompensation of their West African crews. Explicitly seeking to evade the minimal protective capacity of aliens legislation and to perpetuate imperial inequalities, employers and their allies mobilized pretexts of racial and cultural inferiority such as Africans' imputed moral degeneracy, physical inferiority, libidinousness, and lower standard of living. To the extent the arrangements worked, they undocumented British subjects were deprived of their legal rights and intimidated or bluffed into accepting technically illegal working conditions that undercut those of union seamen. Yet efficient exploitation of Black labor proved internally contradictory, as employers sought both to hire and fire men at will but also to keep their expectations about wages and working conditions distinct from white seamen's. Black seamen continued to resist imperialist "control," however: the large numbers of "troublemakers" blacklisted and abandoned in Liverpool were themselves a sign of West African seamen's ongoing refusal to acquiesce, while those who evaded Elder Dempster by providing themselves with documents or marrying, claiming their rights as British subjects and as householders, were refusing to tolerate continued exploitation in the Mother Country.

Two final episodes in the late 1930s demonstrated the British state's ineffectiveness in protecting non-European seamen. In the first, a state agent—this time the British Government of India—unilaterally granted a concession of value and benefit to employers while *ex post facto* attempts to extract reciprocal concessions failed. In 1938 a Government of India initiative to equalize conditions of work between Indian Lascars and regular seamen foundered. In belated response to 1936 International Labour Office recommendations the Government of India proposed to relax the "protective" latitude restrictions on Asiatic articles. In implicit exchange the Board of Trade sought employers' cooperation to limit hours and to institute overtime pay.

Latitude limits had already been subject to inconclusive negotiation in the 1930s. Public opinion in India favored their abolition because "lascars were being displaced by Chinese and Malays who were not subject to the restriction." But union opposition to any measure making Lascar crews competitive with Europeans, coupled with Board of Trade concern about Indian seamen in cold climates, squelched changes in 1934. By 1938, high unemployment and persistent public criticism in India prompted the Government of India to abolish unilaterally the restrictions on North Atlantic voyages for an "experimental period" of three years. Yet Government of India and Board of Trade efforts to obtain a commensurate wage increase for Lascar seamen, whose conditions of service were now no less arduous than those of men on standard articles, faltered in negotiation with shipowners and were opposed by the National Union of Seamen.[53]

Shipowners, while anxious to employ Lascar crews in the North Atlantic, refused to negotiate either with the British union or "irresponsible" unions in India. Their counterproposal fell far short of Government of India hopes, National Maritime Board conditions, and even the Board of Trade and the India Office's modest expectations. Although failing to obtain safeguards, the Government of India did relax latitude restrictions in June 1939.[54] Consequently, Indian seamen served extensively in the North Atlantic during the Second World War.

If this episode demonstrated the state's inability to protect Black seamen, events of the following year showed that racial ideology remained a *lingua franca* for owners and the state, obscuring and mystifying efforts to aid Black seamen. This was illustrated by negotiations in 1939 preceding the renewal of the 1935 British Shipping Assistance subsidy, a subsidy limited to vessels carrying British crews, but exempting contract laborers from National Maritime Board rates. Critics at the Board of Trade objected to paying the same subsidy for ships carrying contract laborers as those manned by men on regular articles, since Lascar wages had not risen at all since 1935, much less kept pace with N.M.B. increases. The Shipping Federation objected to a lower subsidy, indignant at the suggestion that employers of Lascars were "undercutting." Again, these arrangements were justified with racial arguments: "Climactic conditions, especially when the voyage is prolonged in the tropics, almost compels the employment of Asiatics or Africans, at any rate as firemen," while underpaying Black seamen was justified by "heavier manning and repatriation costs [which] counterbalance lower rates of pay."[55]

But the link with colonialism went beyond mere ideas or stereotypes. The Board of Trade candidly acknowledged the relationship between low wages for Black seamen and those for the far more numerous Black workers in the colonies, and their reluctance to jeopardize the deficient "colonial standard of living" critical to metropolitan prosperity. Lascar wages must be kept low, they argued, to keep colonial wages low: "It is not simply a case of exploiting coloured men, but the rates of pay of the seafaring population in any country are governed by the internal economy of that country, and there is no doubt that the [British colonial] Governments concerned are not generally anxious to see the seafaring rates increased to too high a level compared with those ashore." Low shipboard wages and poor working conditions not only benefited shipowners, but they indirectly supported the larger imperial project in which merchant shipping was enmeshed. Shipowners employing Lascars continued to receive full subsidy.[56]

These episodes help to explain how racialized shipboard labor practices, reconstructed from the colonial context, influenced racializing processes outside the workplace in Britain. This evidence tends to support those scholars who have proposed a dialectic between labor processes in the workplace and social and political relations outside the workplace. Shipowners frankly feared the breakdown of shipboard racial divisions in unsegregated boardinghouses and settlements ashore. To forestall this they sought to extend shipboard racial barriers to British soil, and in the process they involved the government.

The state supported the shipowners because it shared an interest in keeping colonized labor vulnerable and unorganized, and it had the means to do this. But beyond that their agendas diverged. The India Office sought to preserve imperial credibility by preventing "the clash of colour" ashore in Britain. Shipowners feared the opposite: contract laborers' eventual incorporation into the better paid workforce of the metropole, blurring the racial boundaries that disadvantaged white as well as Black seamen. Yet employers subverted state efforts too firmly to fix on racial lines the boundaries between contract and free labor. However contradictory, inconsistent, and incomplete these agendas, the outcome was that racist practices took shape in Britain through material as well as ideological projections of racial subordination and exploitation in the colonies, fostered by historical actors seeking to influence and manipulate race, class, gender and labor relations for economic and political ends.

The state's approach to Black seamen in Britain was shaped in negotiation and struggle among employers, various branches of local and central government, and Black seamen's resistance, and informed both by domestic and imperial agendas. Black men's subordination through this process was not the product of a consensual "tradition of intolerance": many inside and outside government saw racial conflict and disadvantage as "a blot on our hospitality." Yet state efforts to impose accountability proved a largely empty threat—in negotiation, protective impulses were subverted into repressive ones, while employers offered little themselves on issues that concerned the state. The case tends to corroborate arguments that the interwar British state practiced "indirect corporatism," providing services for capital but exercising no coercive power and failing to elicit cooperation.[57]

The outcome for Black seamen was abandonment by the government to which they looked for protection and support. Yet they continued to pursue the rights they claimed as British subjects, by acquiring passports in Britain or the colonies, by "making trouble" aboardship, by "wandering away" in search of better jobs and better lives, and by establishing and defending their families and settlements in Britain. Such actions were less dramatic forms of resistance, perhaps, than mutinies or strikes. Yet through these individual strategies of evasion Black seamen undermined the "control" of both employers and the state, and with it the larger imperial project. In addition, such strategies constituted a form of class struggle that also disrupted racial hierarchies through implicit assertions of manhood and Britishness.

Since the Board of Trade and other state ministries failed to extract shipowners' cooperation in containing the disorder produced by the maritime labor system, struggle between employers and Black seamen continued ashore. The apparent if illusory threat to social order involved the Home Office. The Home Office lacked even the minimal powers of compulsion on shipowners that the Board of Trade enjoyed. Consequently, in their hands state policy toward Black working people assumed the form it takes to this day. State power was invoked to constrain individual workers through the manipulation of labor and immigration regulation. In addition to the state, the National Union of Seamen was also persuaded to ally with employers in racist practices on shipboard and ashore.

CHAPTER FIVE

"We Shall Soon Be Having 'Rule Britannia' Sung in Pidgin English": The National Union of Seamen and the Uses of Race

The Chinaman ate rice with a knitting needle, while a Britisher wanted meat and a knife and fork, he clothed himself with a loin cloth while the Britisher wanted a suit of clothes; and he lived in a nest, while a Britisher wanted a house. The Chinese and Lascars were not to be brought up to our standard, but an effort was being made to bring our standard down to theirs.
—Mr. Tom King, M.P. for Lowestoft (a fishing port), addressing a mass meeting at Yarmouth, 1914

I have always believed that British seamen have done more to discover and establish the British Empire, and to develop it. It will be the task of the same men of the sea to keep it.
—Joseph Havelock Wilson, President of the National Sailors' and Firemen's Union

IN SUMMER 1929, Chris Braithewaite, a Black organizer for the National Union of Seamen (N.U.S.), Britain's major maritime union, reported a heated exchange with "Jimmie" Henson. Henson was a prominent N.U.S. official temporarily estranged from the union and organizing the Trades Union Congress (T.U.C.) Seamen's Section, a rival union. Henson rebuked Braithewaite for working for the N.U.S. and represented himself, Henson, as a better advocate for Black seamen: "Henson said he was the first man to have men of colour attend a conference here in London... so he has nothing against any man for his colour." Henson chided Braithewaite that "the boys in Cardiff will tell me a thing or two when they hear that I helped break up his meetings here in London." This remark stung, apparently, for Braithewaite reported, "I told Henson if he wished me to,

First epigraph: reported in *The Seaman*, 1 May 1914, 6–7. Second: Wilson, *My Stormy Voyage Through Life* (London: Cooperative Press, 1925), 44.

I will go to Cardiff tonight, or go to Hell with him or anyone who can discredit me in the eyes of my colour, as I have done nothing to be ashamed of."[1]

Although "Jimmie" Henson represented himself as an advocate for Black seamen, in the 1920s he lobbied actively, both in and outside the N.U.S., for state and union policies to bar Black seamen from the British labor market.[2] The intensity of Braithewaite's retort, conversely, perhaps reflected the painful choice he and other Black seamen faced, to join and support a union that subordinated and marginalized them or to remain even more vulnerable outside it.

As this episode suggests, Black seamen's efforts to protect themselves through trade unionism were impaired by the ambivalence and often antagonism of seamen's union leaders in Britain. Indeed, the story of the N.U.S. and Black seamen is one of tragically missed opportunity. In the early decades of the twentieth century, leaders of the National Sailors' and Firemen's Union (N.S.F.U./N.U.S.), initially resisted but eventually capitulated to the racialized inequalities dividing the maritime workforce. The union fruitlessly pursued exclusion of the few thousand Black seamen in standard conditions of work, while colluding in the displacement of white and Black unionized seamen by growing numbers of super-exploited contract laborers.[3] They rebuffed Black sailors' calls for union support and rejected overtures from colonial unions that might have forged an empirewide, thus global, labor movement to challenge continuing stratification.

Scholars have misinterpreted the role the seamen's union took in interwar racial struggles. The union has commonly received the dubious credit for exacerbating popular xenophobia, encouraging violent attacks on Cardiff's Chinese community during the 1911 transport workers' strike, and demanding state measures of racial exclusion such as the Coloured Alien Seamen Order of 1925 or the British Shipping Assistance Act of 1935, which effectively excluded undocumented Black British subjects from state-subsidized ships. These scholars also depict the union as opposed to Black seamen, rather than complicit in racial stratification. Such approaches slight the structural context described earlier, shaped primarily by employers and to a lesser extent the state, that conditioned union racial practices.[4]

Most Black seamen entered the seafaring workforce principally as contract laborers, inaccessible to union organization. Even those in the "free" market were systematically undercompensated relative to white seamen with the explicit aim of evading and undermining union-mandated conditions of labor. Both groups, like scabs in most contexts, were employed not only to cut wages but to intimidate unionized men. Union hostility to Black seamen, then, arose not simply from racial or cultural differences, but from their structural positioning as a threat to the union and its members. Black seamen on standard articles were the only small section of this vast pool of potential scabs accessible either to union organization or union-sponsored exclusion.

Yet union leaders did make choices, and failure to examine and learn from them is a continuing disservice to the constituencies the labor movement purports to represent. In the 1920s and 1930s, the union failed decisively to reject the racialized distinctions between contract and "free" labor that kept Black seamen cheap and exploitable, a threat to white and Black unionized seamen. In ostensible defense of white or British seamen's jobs—a point of ambivalence in itself—union leaders, like employers, blurred the distinctions between Black contract laborers and Black seamen on standard articles, focusing on the latter to obscure their retreat from militancy. In accepting employers' racial explanations for inequalities in the maritime workforce, union leaders neglected to confront the stratification that made Black workers attractive to employers and a threat to unionized seamen.

Yet, union leaders' stance toward Black seamen was not as uniformly hostile as many scholars have supposed. Instead, racial rhetoric and practice were inconsistent, ambiguous, and discontinuous in the years 1900 through 1950. Like Chris Braithewaite, Black men, perhaps as many as several thousand, did join the union, and pressed from within for support. Union leaders defended Black members, albeit inconsistently, while repeatedly denying that they practiced the "colour bar." Racist practice was not taken for granted, but was debated within the union and between the union and its critics.

This more complicated evidence demands consideration of broader questions in the history of British and indeed global labor movements. These are the related questions of the relationship between British labor leaders and the rank and file, and between the predominantly white and male trade unions and Black and other marginalized workers such as women, service workers, and the unemployed. British labor leaders have been charged with aggrandizing their power at the expense of the rank and file, and of neglecting to organize or represent non-"traditional" workers.[5]

Although the seamen's union could be dismissed as atypical in its estrangement from the mainstream labor movement and as the first union to encounter significant numbers of Black workers, its use of racial divisiveness resembled practices in many nineteenth- and twentieth-century

British unions. Union leaders have been accused of acting as brokers between employers and workers, deriving power and prestige from their capacity to discipline their members in exchange for concessions from management. Leaders of the National Union of Seamen fit this pattern in the 1920s and 1930s.[6] Leaders of the N.U.S. recognized that racial divisions disadvantaged white as well as Black sailors, resisting the principle of unequal pay, for example, until after the First World War. But through their eventual capitulation they established a privileged relationship with employers, consolidating their institutional power at the expense of more militant unions and of rank and file seamen, Black and white, British, colonial, alien and Lascar.

Union leaders benefited from and encouraged racial animosity instrumentally and for specific ends. Chinese and Black seamen formed the currency of compromise between shipowners and the seamen's union in the rapprochement that accompanied World War I. After the war the threat of Black seamen taking their jobs discouraged disaffected white sailors from militant actions that might imperil shipowners' confidence in union leaders. The campaign against Arab seamen in 1930 coincided with reconciliation between the renegade union and the rest of the labor movement in the aftermath of the General Strike. Union leaders also benefited materially from the contract labor system because money collected for nonbeneficiary Lascars supported the union's pension fund.

Formed in 1877, during the wave of New Unionism at the end of the nineteenth century, the National Amalgamated Sailors' and Fireman's Union of Great Britain and Ireland was reincorporated in 1894 as the National Sailors' and Firemen's Union of Great Britain and Ireland. Devastated in the 1890s by the Shipping Federation counteroffensive, the N.S.F.U. revived in 1910 with an infusion of energy from syndicalist Tom Mann among others. By 1913, the N.S.F.U. had seventy branches throughout Great Britain and abroad, and claimed 82,851 paid-up members, 90 percent of the organized seafarers in Britain. In 1911 the union gained its first twentieth-century victory in alliance with the dockers' union, and in the years immediately before the Great War it formed part of the powerful National Transport Workers' Federation (N.T.W.F.). In August 1925, after a period of turmoil and dissension in the early 1920s, the union incorporated Joseph Cotter's National Union of Ships' Stewards, Cooks, Butchers and Bakers (N.U.S.S.C.B.B.) to become the National Union of Seamen (N.U.S.). Today the union represents an atrophied but still multiracial workforce.[7]

The notion that Black seamen were a necessary sacrifice for the preservation of white seamen's jobs does not fit the evidence.[8] Instead, the
union's collusive race politics were consistent with its notorious lack of
militancy under Joseph Havelock Wilson, its "Founder and President for
Life," who dominated the union until his death in 1929. Wilson's personal
politics were a blend of trade unionism, pragmatic internationalism, and
naive corporatism. Wilson welcomed the Shipping Federation, an employers' combination created in 1890 in explicit response to the successful
London dock strike of 1889 and the burgeoning N.S.F.U.: "By having a
strong combination on each side we would have more respect for each
other." Rejecting socialism, "Class War," and "State control or Government control in the affairs of the workers," Wilson insisted that "seamen
had had more Government supervision than any other class of workmen,
. . . that the only way for them to obtain and maintain their freedom was
by combination."[9]

In view of the union's use of xenophobia, Wilson's personal views on
foreign labor were surprisingly pragmatic. At one point deriding foreign
seamen as "the sewer rats of Europe," he nonetheless insisted upon founding the union that "foreign as well as British seamen" be represented. "If
we excluded such men from membership," he explained, "the shipowners
would not be slow to avail themselves of the services of foreigners as
against the Britishers." Instead, foreigners with over four years of service,
7 to 10 percent of the 1901 workforce, were "admitted on the same terms
and conditions as Britishers." Thus the union accepted a customary definition of entitlement to work over currently developing notions based on
nationality. In the early years the N.S.F.U. organized all comers, regardless
of nationality, for "as long as foreign seamen accepted wages lower than
ours it would always be a menace to our trade." The N.S.F.U. sought to
organize "the enormous number of seamen who are engaged at Continental ports," providing German, Danish, and Scandinavian translators at
some meetings, and by opening branches in New York, Antwerp, Bre-
merhaven, Hamburg, and other foreign ports. In 1920 Wilson rejected a
demand from the Govan (a Glasgow suburb) branch that the union bar
"Aliens" from membership as "entirely contrary to the rules," and "asked
whether stopping the enrollment of Aliens would prevent them from
sailing on British vessels."[10] Throughout the interwar years the union had
a District Secretary for the Continent, Chris Damm, in charge of North
Sea ports.

Wilson's race politics, similarly, were neither overtly nor unreflectively
racist: in 1921 he rejected a proposal to openly exclude Black British

seamen in favor of white ones as "very foolish and very ignorant . . . it pits one race against the other, and it has entirely disrupted the seamen's movement in America." Throughout the 1920s his was a restraining influence on other union leaders' impulse to exclude Black seamen categorically from the union or from jobs at standard rates. Within the union, indeed, the relative status of Black and white British seamen was continually contested, as was the definition of who was rightfully "British." Henson, for example, reported that he failed to persuade the Colonial Office and the India Office that "the Arab seaman is not a British seaman [because] some of the coloured men . . . turned round and said that they had fought for the British flag." Thomas Chambers, another official, sought not to exclude all Arab seamen but simply "new men."[11]

Wilson's professed internationalism did not prevent the union from using racial and cultural slurs in the "Yellow Peril" campaign, or from covertly colluding in employers' subordination of Black sailors. But these remarks suggest the union's use of racial epithets and racial exclusion stemmed less from unthinking race prejudice than from pragmatic appreciation of their uses. Between the wars, the N.S.F.U. used racism consciously and tactically, and only after much debate. Consistent with the covert nature of much British racism, the N.S.F.U./N.U.S. repeatedly denied "race prejudice" or "colour bar" while deeply involved in racially divisive practices.[12]

From 1911 onward *The Seamen*, the union's biweekly "green sheet," was the mouthpiece of the union's contradictory and inconsistent racial program.[13] Race rhetoric in *The Seaman* went through three distinct stages: the teens were dominated by the language of Yellow Peril, abating during the war but reappearing afterward, ending only with the institutionalization of Chinese seamen's subordination through the National Maritime Board. The 1920s were a period of quiescence with no mention at all, for instance, of the Home Office's Coloured Alien Seamen Order of 1925. Racist rhetoric resumed in spring 1929 after Havelock Wilson's death, this time against a new menace, "alien Arabs." The Yellow Peril campaign of the teens foreshadowed those against "alien Arabs" and other Black workers in the 1930s.

In the teens and early 1920s, the union first departed from its policy of organizing in favor of a campaign to exclude Chinese seamen from British ships. The N.S.F.U. accused Chinese sailors of undercutting union men by unwittingly signing contracts with clauses authorizing illegal deductions from their wages. To combat this, the union initially sought equal conditions for Chinese seamen. As a member of Parliament, Havelock Wilson brought the abuse of Chinese seamen to the attention of that body, seeking to ensure that "Chinese and Lascars, if employed on British ships, should have the same conditions as Britishers." Employers blocked this legislative initiative in 1908, however, and the union failed to persuade the Board of Trade to mandate European ration scales for all, eroding Chinese seamen's advantage. After Workmen's Compensation provisions raised the social wage for British seamen, employers' efforts to replace British crews with underpaid Chinese intensified. By 1915 there were reportedly 14,224 Chinese seamen in British ships, or approximately 5 percent of the total workforce of some 250,000.[14] Still, as late as 1911 Wilson apparently harbored hopes of organizing rather than excluding them:

> At one time the European foreigner was sufficiently docile to play off against the Britisher. But now, seemingly, all European seafarers are a "drunken," "unsteady," "inefficient," lot, and the long-suffering shipowner turns reluctantly to the ASIATICS! But already history again begins to repeat itself. The Chinese are no longer all docility. They too are "becoming demoralized, insubordinate and defiant." Of course they are. Because . . . the conditions of employment aboardship are insufferable.[15]

Yet already the union's Yellow Peril campaign had begun to displace opposition from employers onto underpaid Chinese sailors themselves. For as their efforts to assist or incorporate Chinese seamen were frustrated, the union appealed directly to shipowners and the state to exclude them entirely.

Employers had already structured the debate about cheap labor on racial lines, contrasting white seamen's imputed laziness, drunkenness, and unruliness with Asian seamen's malleability and reliability. In the course of the decades the union adopted this racialized language to support their efforts to exclude Chinese seamen from British ships, and eventually to discipline the white rank and file. The N.S.F.U. was perhaps especially susceptible to arguments derived from the colonial experience. The industry's health depended on British domination of global merchant shipping, now threatened by overseas competition, and Wilson was an unabashed imperialist. During and immediately after the war the common language of racial difference eased the union's accommodation with shipowners. By the 1920s and 1930s underpaid and super-exploited Black and Chinese seamen had become the medium of compromise between the union and employers, while their continuing presence in the workforce effectively deterred unionized sailors from militancy. Thus it is useful to examine the anti-Chinese campaign as a foretaste of the union's stance toward Black workers.

The anti-Chinese campaign took several forms. A language test aimed at them was legislated in 1908. The N.S.F.U. leader, Captain Edward Tupper, manipulated anti-Chinese sentiment in Cardiff to garner violent support for the 1911 strike from town dwellers.[16] The union successfully gained the support of other trade unions, both in resolutions at the Trades Union Congress, and in wartime deputations to the Board of Trade. Before and during the war the union solicited rank-and-file support for Chinese exclusion through a letter campaign and a series of mass meetings in seaports. Finally, *The Seaman*, the union's tabloid, became the mouthpiece of anti-Chinese propaganda. Union leaders used the rhetoric of racial and cultural inferiority and the practice of racial subordination to elide their differences with shipowners and to appeal to the rank and file, the state, and other unions.

In 1908, after the 1905 Aliens Act made nationality a legitimate basis for exclusion, the union successfully promoted a language test for alien seamen. Men without adequate command of English constituted a hazard on British ships, they argued, yet the tests were aimed at aliens, specifically Chinese, suggesting that the motive was to restrict the labor market rather than to render British ships safer. The measure also cynically exploited the fact that few seamen, white, Black or Chinese, carried nationality documents: in Wilson's words, "I am sure that not one Chinaman out of twenty can prove that he is a Britisher." By 1913 the N.S.F.U. abandoned any pretense of interracial solidarity to campaign vociferously and at considerable expense for Chinese seamen's complete exclusion from British ships. In 1914 Wilson "fought the Parliamentary by-election solely on the Chinese issue."[17]

In this early campaign for racist exclusion, the labor movement appeared disunited and individuals, including Wilson, and *The Seaman*, seemed ambivalent on the question of Chinese and other non-European seamen. They denied racial animus and insisted instead that their objection to Chinese—and Indian—labor was economic, "Not a matter of nationality but of fair play," in the words of Harry Gosling, chairman of the N.T.W.F. *The Seaman*'s rhetoric was inconsistent and contradictory, reflecting the unsystematic and opportunistic character of racial ideology and perhaps also difficulty in reconciling racial exclusion with the union's previous inclusiveness. Nonetheless they muddled economic arguments with the

2. Pamphlet used in the National Sailors' and Firemen's Union's anti-Chinese campaign, 1912. Reproduced by permission of the International Transport Workers' Federation.

The Bosun's Mate (to new crew). "Now I'm goin' to read out some o' the things the Board o' Trade think you ought to know, an' if there's any of you don't understand English let 'im find out from the bloke next to 'im wot it's all about."

3. Cartoon impugning the effectiveness of the language test, from *Punch*, 22 June 1932, p. 692, reproduced in *The Seaman*, 8 March 1933. Reproduced by permission of *Punch*.

language of cultural and racial inferiority, displacing hostility from employers to underpaid sailors themselves. Illustrative was *The Seaman*'s vilification of a "group of greedy shipowners [exploiting] ... the half civilised Asiatic who can live on a handful of rice per day and who cherishes no disturbing notions about the rights of labour." Nationalism complemented and reinforced the language of race: "In China he might be a good citizen, but in this case he was introduced to undercut the Britisher."[18]

The Seaman, seeking to "repudiate" accusations of "race or colour prejudice," used cultural difference for the same purpose, asserting that the Chinese sailor, elsewhere denounced as the "economic man" who would work for less, heedless of labor solidarity, had "wholly different traditions and outlook upon life" preventing his successful assimilation of "true economic gospel." The writer concluded, "This is an economic and Trade Union question pure and simple." Invoking Orientalist imagery of the inscrutable East, *The Seaman* denounced "the gradual and stealthy advance of the Asiatic in his invasion of the British labour market." Wilson depicted the Chinese as a threat to "the Western standard of life" predicting, "we shall soon be having 'Rule Britannia' sung in pidgin English."[19]

In spring 1914 union leaders held a series of mass meetings in Hull, Cardiff, Yarmouth, and other ports. Spokesmen insisted that employers were their target. Gosling told a mass meeting in Hull on the first of May 1914, "They had got to see when a Chinaman entered a ship, factory, dock, mine or any other industry, that he demanded the same conditions and wages as Englishmen, otherwise they must regard him as a blackleg."[20] But in Cardiff Gosling urged his audience to "exterminate this Chinese evil," predicting that "cheap yellow labour ... will spread steadily like a cancerous growth until the whole industrial community is affected." The union's appeal reflected imperialist assumptions about racial and cultural superiority, depicting the "Heathen Chinee" as incompetent, insolent, and lazy, "dangerous and unsatisfactory," insubordinate, cowardly, mutinous, violent, excitable, murderous, docile, ignorant, cunning, dirty, and given to theft. Images of "semi-barbarians from the far East," prone to "opium and drink" and "savagery," and "physical and mental unfitness" for seafaring work clashed with others of "enterprising celestials" and "Chinese as German Spies," or "yellow heathens" who "laugh and jeer."[21]

Lascars and Chinese were paired in many discussions, obscuring the fact that unlike Chinese, Lascars were not competing with unionized men for jobs at standard rates. Although union leaders participated in reinforcing the structural barriers between regular seamen and contract laborers evermore rigidly in the first decades of the twentieth century, their rhetoric muddled these distinctions, exaggerating the "foreign" threat. Thus Wilson depicted Asian seamen, even Indian Lascars who were British subjects, as foreigners who were not entitled to work from British ports. "The Asiatic, the Lascar, the Chinaman," he asserted, "has a right to have a share of the work...on the coast of China." J. H. Borlase, an N.S.F.U. offical, told the *Evening Chronicle* that Chinese in British ships numbered 55,000, a figure he could only have reached by counting some 44,000 men on Asiatic articles.[22]

Although the campaign was avowedly against "cheap labor," racialized "othering" of the Chinese overwhelmed voices raised in favor of organizing them. In a 1914 meeting a motion in favor of equal pay for Chinese and British crews met resounding defeat. Mr. G. Williams, speaking for the majority, declared that "they had to recognise the fact that the Asiatic was not as good a man as the Britisher, and so not worth the same money. Therefore he thought it best to bar the Asiatic altogether."[23] In a front page editorial of 1 May 1914, the *Seaman* voiced the resolve to exclude even Chinese seamen who wished to join the union: "Hundreds of Chinamen would eagerly join tomorrow if they were allowed. But holding the views they do on the subject of Chinese Labour the Executive Council of the National Sailors' and Firemen's Union could not possibly tolerate any proposal for the admission of Chinamen to membership." Actually, some Chinese seamen did join the union, as lists of benefit claimants indicate. Reflecting "symbiotic intermingling of...racial and sexual themes," in one of his characteristic tirades, Wilson reinforced his basically economic argument with lurid references to "white girls [with] half-caste children...sufficient to make any Britisher's blood boil with indignation." Thus the economic threat of Chinese labor was transformed into a cultural, sexual, and political threat.[24]

The maritime unions sought the support of shore workers and fishermen by depicting the Chinese as a threat to them as well, and, indeed, the Yellow Peril campaign enjoyed the support and participation of Britain's major labor organizations. Delegates from the National Transport Workers' Federation, the Labour party, the General Federation of Trade Unions, and other bodies accompanied the N.S.F.U. to the Board of Trade. In 1917 the T.U.C. and the Triple Alliance of miners, railwaymen, and transport workers sent independent deputations.[25]

The union's turn from organizing to excluding Chinese seamen and other "outsiders" was not due simply to the persuasiveness of racial ideology but to the shifting balance of power among the union, employers, and the state. The anti-Chinese campaign straddled 1911, the year of the seamen's strike, the N.S.F.U.'s first twentieth-century victory, and 1917, the founding date of the National Maritime Board (N.M.B.), a wartime peak organization composed of employers and union representatives. At the beginning of the Yellow Peril campaign, the N.S.F.U. was still battling for recognition by employers and the state. Before 1917, successive Board of Trade presidents, David Lloyd George, Winston Churchill, even John Burns, rebuffed labor delegation after delegation. Although the Admiralty agreed in 1915 to give preference to "British or British Coloured" seamen, the resolution of the Chinese question was found not in direct state intervention but in a compromise between the N.S.F.U. and shipowners through the state-sanctioned N.M.B.[26]

The process of waging total war gave the N.S.F.U., like organized labor generally, *entrée* into the mechanism of the state. Seamen's bargaining power with employers was strengthened by the relative shortage of maritime labor. In 1917, to protect war transport from further work stoppages, the wartime state and shipowners consented to bargain with the largest and most conservative union in the industry, the N.S.F.U. While union leaders benefited from the accompanying accommodation, British seamen, Black and white, lost. Official recognition and a state-sponsored negotiating mechanism freed the union of the obligation to organize all sections of the workforce and gave it an advantage over rival seamen's unions—"what amounted to a closed shop." "Joint supply" boards composed of N.M.B. affiliated unions' and owners' representatives would now control the distribution of jobs; in practice sailors and firemen must join the N.S.F.U. to obtain employment. In 1922 the National Maritime Board instituted a document known as the PC5, or "work ticket," stating that a man was "in compliance with" the N.S.F.U., to qualify for a job. Withholding access to the PC5 was used to exclude members of rival unions and to discipline N.S.F.U. dissidents. Still, the Armistice terminated both state sanction and the wartime labor shortage, and the union was again bargaining from a position of relative weakness. Thus while the creation of the N.M.B. appeared a victory for the N.S.F.U. it also precipitated a critical shift to collaboration.[27] For through the N.M.B. the union participated in fixing unequal wage rates, perpetuating the threat cheap labor constituted to men paid standard wages.

The campaign to exclude Chinese seamen survived the war. In January and February 1918, navy chaplain and N.S.F.U. official Father Hopkins negotiated the clauses governing non-European seamen's wages through the 1950s. Chinese or "coloured" seamen would receive standard National Maritime Board rates—the same pay as their white shipmates—only when the specific department in which they worked contained white crew members. Even then, a grandfather clause exempted customary wage distinctions antedating the war. Another meeting fixed a lower wage for Chinese seamen on "European" articles and constrained owners from employing Chinese seamen until British white or Black seamen, or European (white) alien labor, were "absorbed." In April 1919 the National Maritime Board granted preference to British subjects over non-British Chinese and "Alien Coloured" seamen.[28] Thus subordination took the form both of lower wages and of a routine bias against hiring Chinese sailors.

Needless to say, Chinese and other excluded sailors suffered most, but this was altogether a bad bargain for the seamen's union. In refusing to organize Chinese and other non-European seamen, a course that could have eliminated their function as cheap labor, the N.S.F.U. bought into the shipowners' agenda. Lower wages gave employers an incentive to hire Chinese sailors while in practice the union was left with the task of enforcing their exclusion. Evidence of resultant confusion and conflict within the union suggests that some union officials themselves recognized this. In December 1919, a ship was blocked by industrial action in Newport harbor on the grounds that it paid Chinese seamen £8 10/, less than the standard rate of £11 10/. Edmund Cathery, N.S.F.U. secretary, when informed that Hopkins had recently negotiated this £8 10/ rate with the N.M.B., was outraged, instructing Hopkins to "terminate and cancel the Chinese Agreement." Hopkins assented but unequal wages survived through the 1940s.[29]

The lower wage for Chinese crews was only the most visible of a number of anomalous agreements between the N.S.F.U. and employers for the underpayment of non-European crews. In the 1920s and 1930s, excluding categories of seamen from union protection was perhaps easier to negotiate than broadening union conditions to encompass additional sections of the workforce. Successive N.M.B. agreements provided for lower wages for Black and Chinese crews in nearly all cases. While "British coloured" seamen were favored over Chinese they were nonetheless disadvantaged relative to "British white" sailors. As the labor market constricted, the seamen's movement splintered and the union grew increasingly reluctant to confront employers directly, so "British coloured" workers too were sacrificed.[30] For all their denunciations of cheap labor, the National Sailors' and Firemen's Union was deeply involved in perpetuating a race-based wage hierarchy among British merchant seamen.

Throughout the 1920s and early 1930s while the union publicly decried underpaid Black labor, they covertly colluded in its persistence. In the

1930s they complained, "The Union had been working for years ... for the elimination of Chinese, Lascars, Kroo Boys, etc. from British ships." They blamed "the apathy of the public" and shipowners' unpatriotic greed.[31] The ostensible purpose of excluding Black sailors was to constrict the labor supply available for well-paid jobs, thus to provide steady work for union men and perhaps drive wages up. Yet the union also participated in perpetuating the racial stratification that kept most Black labor "cheap," thus more attractive to employers. The union's efforts had the effect, not of eliminating Black labor from the British merchant marine, but of pushing Black seamen out of well-paid jobs at N.M.B. wages and forcing them into low-paid contract labor.

Not only was the union party to the intricate wages hierarchy for Black, white, Chinese, and "mixed" crews written into N.M.B. regulations, but in addition, the N.U.S. had informal agreements with individual companies, who routinely contacted the union for permission to hire and underpay Black crews. In refusing one such request from a company who wished in 1930 to replace their British crews with Africans, the Temporary Management Committee, which assumed responsibility for the union's routine operations on Wilson's death, explained that Elder Dempster was "the only firm allowed to carry West African Natives" and that as the company in question "are not trading solely to West African ports, their application ... cannot be entertained." Some time later, Morrison and Sons approached Assistant General Secretary Mr. Gunning with the plea that as they were Elder Dempster's competitors in the West African trade, they wished to pay lower wages to West African firemen in that trade only, but were "quite willing" to pay standard N.M.B. rates to their West African employees in other routes. Evidence of N.U.S. cooperation in other "special arrangements with reference to non-white crews" appeared in allusions to a "Furness Withy agreement" covering Trinidadian seaman. As the India Office had found in their efforts to regulate seamen's lodgings ashore, the power that these agreements gave the union was largely illusory. In summer 1931 Robert Clouston, District Supervisor for Tyne and Humberside, discovered that Morrison and Sons were in fact underpaying West African "Kroo boys" sailing out of the Tyne, in spite of Mr. Morrison's "promises" to N.U.S. officials Edward Tupper and G. Gunning.[32]

The union also had a vested financial interest in contract labor through the Royal Seamen's Pension Fund. From 1911 on, money for union members' pensions came from joint employer-employee contributions. Lascars and other nondomiciled seamen were ineligible to collect the pensions, but employers contributed two pence per week per man all the same.

The fund relied on having far fewer beneficiaries than contributors. In 1945 the union stated frankly, "The income of the Fund is primarily dependent upon the number of seamen having neither residence nor domicile in the U.K. who are employed in the British merchant marine." In the 1940s the union also became concerned that a postcolonial Indian government would appropriate the "Lascar money" as they called it.[33]

The Lascar fund had political uses. Since most paid-up members were at sea, Havelock Wilson and his successors controlled the union through their influence over its pensioners. Thus the suggestion that ordinary seamen replace Lascars, or that Asiatic and other special articles be upgraded, eroding their financial advantage to shipowners, constituted a threat to retired seamen's pensions and thus to current leaders' power. In 1938, a threat by shipowners to the pension fund stifled union opposition to abolishing latitude limits, a provision putting Lascar crews in direct competition with N.U.S. members in the North Atlantic. As Mr. Snedden of the Shipping Federation warned the union bluntly, "no lascars, no pensions."[34]

It is unlikely that the rank and file knew of the union's active collusion in the institution of cheap Black labor. Arrangements among the N.U.S., the Board of Trade, and the Home Office regarding the Coloured Alien Seamen Order or the Elder Dempster scheme were never fully aired even in the union's Executive Council, much less with the rank and file. Similarly, Henson's sporadic reports on the progress of the Coloured Alien Seamen Order were cryptic and vague. Thus the assumption that union policy was a symptom of rank-and-file racism involves a series of logical leaps. On the contrary, N.U.S. racism was criticized by such insurgent seamen's organizers as George Hardy and J. W. Ford, and by other trade unionists such as Tommy Lewis.[35]

In contrast to their collusion in contract labor, the union devoted considerable energy and publicity to forcing Black men out of jobs with standard rates of pay. Union officials acted as watchdogs on shipping companies and even individual ships, ensuring that Black labor was not substituted for white. In the interwar years local or district union representatives routinely conducted "emergency" negotiations at dockside, to persuade shipsmasters or agents for individual ships to replace their Black crews with all-white ones. Successful cases were reported regularly in the *The Seaman*. The exhaustive nature of these efforts was reflected in officials' minute acquaintance with and concern about the manning of individual ships.[36]

The fortunes of the labor movement vacillated between the wars and it is reasonable to argue that N.U.S. acquiescence to shipowners' racial strategies was an understandable consequence of the union's weak structural position. Part of N.U.S. failure to deal firmly with shipowners, however, stemmed from Wilson's longstanding commitment to "non-political unionism" and "industrial peace." The union's involvement with the National Maritime Board facilitated Wilson's "friendly interview" style of negotiation. In addition, Wilson allegedly "sacrificed all else" to safeguard "harmony" with employers essential to preserve the now-voluntary N.M.B. This entailed discouraging rank-and-file militancy.[37]

Wilson and his cadre of District Secretaries ran the union from the top down, squelching dissent. In spite of occasional outbursts of bellicose rhetoric in *The Seaman*, union leaders appear to have little concerned themselves with grass-roots protests against manpower cuts, speedups, intimidation, overwork, and suicides. Wilson and *The Seaman* deflected criticism of their present inaction with minute disquisitions about "the bad old days" before union-instigated improvements. If N.S.F.U. leaders were insensitive to their Black members, they were also contemptuous of the white rank and file. Wilson vilified rank-and-file militants as ingrates: "a lot of dirty useless rubbish."[38] In the 1920s, N.S.F.U. officials often seemed less concerned to organize the unorganized than to discipline the rank and file and prevent non-N.S.F.U. members or recalcitrant members from working.

Not suprisingly, seamen who were compelled to join the N.S.F.U. only to accept wage cuts were dissatisfied. In spite of the union's privileged position in the joint supply system, many seafarers remained aloof from it, allowing their membership to lapse between voyages, and only "buying" membership in the form of dues arrears as a condition of employment. Rank-and-file insurgency as well as "grisly inter-union conflict" punctuated the early 1920s, including an international wildcat strike in summer 1925 against a union-sanctioned pay cut, and unauthorized support for the 1926 General Strike, for which the N.U.S. withheld strike pay. A series of splinter or rival unions including the British Seafarers' Union, the Amalgamated Marineworkers' Union, and the Trade Union Congress's own Seamen's Section attempted to fill the breach, as did the rank-and-file organizers of the Communist party–sponsored Seamen's Minority Movement.[39]

For the rank and file were not the only parties dissatisfied with the N.U.S. in the 1920s. The union was also weakened by its isolation from the rest of the labor movement. Relations with other unions were often strained as the seamen's union under Havelock Wilson pursued an independent course. In the 1920s the union's prewar legacy of stormy relations with the N.T.W.F. and other unions hardened into staunch independence and antagonism. The most serious rift with the T.U.C. came with the N.U.S. failure to support the General Strike of 1926, which the notoriously undemocratic union boycotted on the pretext of balloting the members. Related instances of scabbing in 1925 and 1926, including the attempt to found a rival coal miners' union on principles of "Industrial Peace," led to the union's expulsion from the T.U.C. It was not reinstated until mid-1929, shortly after Wilson's death. Havelock Wilson also antagonized the International Transport Workers' Federation (I.T.F.) by founding the International Seafarers' Federation (I.S.F.), an organization explicitly opposed to alliances between ship and shore workers, and intended to rival the I.T.F.[40]

Admittedly, Wilson successfully averted major conflicts between the union and shipowners, but he was suspected of selling union members short in these "friendly interviews." This is not the place for exhaustive discussion of the union's internal or interunion politics, but one episode may illustrate Wilson's conciliatory demeanor toward shipowners and contempt for the membership and its impact on Black seamen. In June 1925 Wilson complained that of 5750 seamen currently unemployed in Liverpool, 3,000 were not N.U.S. members. Some may have been members of the Amalgamated Marine Workers' Union who boycotted A.M.W.U.'s merger with the N.U.S. in summer 1925. "Go on board one of those big liners of the White Star Line," Wilson lamented, "You are helpless to prevent any man from getting a job . . . you are immediately surrounded by a hungry mob of scabs."[41] The following month he bargained shipowners a wage cut in implicit exchange for ridding their ships of non-N.U.S. men.

Anticipating wage cuts, Wilson himself suggested that the N.M.B. meet to discuss them: "If there is going to be a cut your duty to the men," he instructed his officials in June, "is to make that cut as small as you possibly can." Meeting with owners Wilson offered a £1 cut, depicting it as "a manly thing." Owners' representatives happily agreed to the £1 reduction, although they deprecated it as "a drop in the bucket."[42]

In addition, N.U.S. representatives offered to discipline their members to forestall a strike, in exchange for extended closed shop arrangements. Although the union had obtained "what amounted to a closed shop" during the war, loopholes remained, widened perhaps by the postwar shipping depression and grass-roots dissatisfaction with the leadership. In 1925 the union was still forced to conclude many closed shop agreements on a yearly basis, company by company and sometimes ship by ship. In the coasting trade, particularly colliers, the union received dues from only 40 percent of the men. The balance were disgruntled by pay cuts and, Wilson declared indignantly, "want to use the union for their own purposes." Wilson tried to persuade shipowners to employ N.U.S. men exclusively, arguing that others would not honor the N.M.B. contract: "There should be no room in your ships for men of that description," he admonished, denouncing them as "a lot of dirty tow-rags" and "danger men" to the Union and owners alike. Wilson warned that such men were likely to "throw in their lot" with striking miners, dockers, and railwaymen in the anticipated General Strike. After the union boycotted the General Strike, the Shipping Federation, Britain's largest employers' cartel, began requiring men to produce a document promising adherence to N.M.B. rules as a condition of work.[43]

Racial divisiveness was integral to these arrangements. Union leaders' credibility with employers was jeopardized by rank-and-file acts of resistance. They invoked the bogey of Black competition to justify wage cuts and to cow restive union members. In 1921 Wilson advised a joint meeting of the Shipping Federation and the I.S.F. not to fear insurgent industrial action: "The coloured element . . . are a great danger and it is doubtful that any strike would be a success." In 1925, again in the context of rank-and-file revolt against the wage cut, he cautioned his officials against militancy: "You have got the Arabs increasing in number in some districts [and] you have got any number of non-Union men."[44]

Union leaders depicted non-European crews on N.M.B. articles as a *prima facie* problem, yet used their presence to better control the white rank and file. Wilson repeated the shipowners' contention that they hired Black and foreign labor because of "indiscipline" among white seamen, urging punctuality, sobriety and diligence on the membership. He defended the employment of Arabs, invoking owners' argument about their "good behaviour." Wilson alleged that "where Arabs had been taken out of a ship," probably at N.S.F.U. behest, "and replaced by white men, [they] had failed to join at the proper time and from other causes given the owners trouble."[45] In defending shipowners' practices and giving credit to their racial arguments, Wilson in effect assisted employers in enforcing labor discipline on their workers.

After Wilson's death, union leaders continued to use these arguments to discourage militancy. In spring 1930, at the height of the N.U.S. anti-Arab campaign in the Tyne, Robert Clouston declared, "Some drastic action should be taken by the Union to discipline such members of the

Union as brought discredit upon the organisation." He recommended "putting the men on the streets for a period of three months"—that is, refusing them the union's PC5 work "ticket"—to punish or deter them from "giving trouble to the Master and Officers" of their ships.[46] The following year Clouston again criticized "white seamen who were put on vessels to replace Arabs, and had not conducted themselves in a proper manner. Thereby having a tendency to nullify the work being done with regard to the replacing of Arab crews with white crews."[47]

Similarly, members of the Executive Council attributed the employment of Chinese and "coloured" labor to the "misdemeanours of the white seamen."[48] Clouston's suggestion was apparently taken, for in 1931 *The Seaman* warned in a front page editorial, "In future, whenever men misbehave themselves... especially when they are displacing coloured crews, we are going to take the names of all such men with a view to denying them employment until they come to their senses."[49] Thus the National Union of Seamen manipulated fears of Black seamen taking their jobs to discourage white seamen from militancy that might jeopardize their accommodation with shipowners.

Union officials attempted to manipulate gender as well as race, hoping that seamen's wives would discourage their husbands from militancy. To impugn the responsibility of militant men, the union sought instead to elicit manly protectiveness toward "the real sufferers in such disputes, namely the women and children," by invoking the very real privations of the working class wife in her role as domestic manager. On the occasion of the 1921 wage reduction the wives of Liverpool men who were absent at sea were balloted in the strike vote. Chris Damm defended the action to the militant A.M.W.U.: "The women folk have got a say in such affairs as it is they that have to suffer.... It is all very well for a single young fellow to come out on strike." Discouraging industrial action after the 1925 wage reduction, Bristol Channel District Secretary Matt Tearle asked rhetorically, "Who is the Chancellor of the Exchequer in your home? Your wife, and what will happen to her and the kids if there is a strike on?" In 1926 the N.S.F.U. sponsored an organization for seamen's wives, the Women's Guild of Empire, for the explicit purpose of combating strikes. In this context, the appeal to women was far from egalitarian. The tactic may not have been very effective. George Hardy recalled that when he read the smuggled report about the 1925 cut to a crowd of strikers at Poplar Town Hall, "The silence in the hall was complete—broken only by the voice of seamen's wives at the back of the hall cursing Wilson."[50]

Yet the union, however grudgingly, did admit Black and Chinese members in the interwar years, perhaps as many as several thousand. Official ambivalence and contradictory practice structured Black seamen's tenuous standing within the union. Union officials showed confusion and disunity as to whether all Black seamen or merely nonunion members should be excluded from work, as to whether Black men should be admitted to union membership at all, and as to whether union membership conferred the same entitlement on Black as on white seamen. Ambiguity about the relative status of aliens and Black British subjects also clouded the issue. Union leaders were inconsistent about the distinctions among these categories, both in the rhetoric propounded through *The Seaman*, and in practice.

In 1919 the N.M.B. Sailors' and Firemen's Panel, for example, considered the question of Chinese and "non-British coloured" seamen in tandem, and debated "as to whether the Board of Trade should in future refuse to register British coloured seamen, including British Chinese." Yet in 1923, union delegates agreed that men who had seen war service or who had married local women should be exempt from proposed employment restrictions. In early 1936, the Executive Council, on a motion by George Reed and Damm, restrained local officials from enrolling new members from among "non-domiciled seamen and other persons from Mandated and Protected Territories, of which there have recently been a considerable influx."[51] Union leaders' "Manichean" interpretation of race seemingly extended to their own Black members. When defending Lascars' employment, the union indignantly stressed their rights as British subjects. When one of these British Lascars sought a job at N.M.B. rates, however, he was transformed, chameleon-like, into a "foreigner."

Union leaders resisted requests for assistance and representation from Black seamen both within and outside the union. Repeated approaches by Black union members seeking a voice in union governance were rebuffed, with the paternalistic answer that union leaders were doing all that was possible or necessary. As early as June 1915 the Executive Council received and rejected a proposal "from S. A. Powell regarding the appointment of a coloured delegate in each port." The body resolved that "no action in the matter be taken at present." This Executive Council included Tom Mann, an active participant in the campaigns against Jewish immigration in previous decades.[52]

In a dispute in 1922, Mr. Straker, a Black union delegate, declared he "did not consider that the coloured men had recieved fair treatment in Cardiff." In response, Mr. Straker was reminded of "what Mr. Henson had done in trying to get the coloured men everything it was possible," and that "the coloured men are getting as good a share of the shipping as anybody else." Henson, after detailing union-sponsored "cases taken up for coloured men," asked rhetorically "if the coloured men left the Union . . . what position they would be in[?]" Finally, Wilson "appealed to the British instinct in Mr. Straker" to forget his grievance. In the same meeting, in response to a Black delegation headed by Mr. O'Connell, Wilson responded to allegations of unequal treatment by enumerating union efforts to obtain "a fair chance" for Black seamen, especially those "who have been sailing in this country prior to 1914."[53]

Shortly after Wilson's death in 1929, the N.U.S. rebuffed another approach from the Black rank and file. On this occasion, a petition from "several coloured members of the Union in London" solicited the appointment of "a coloured delegate . . . to look after their interests." Matt Tearle, London District Secretary, "stated that the Coloured men in London had always been well looked after, and the petition was the first he had heard of their desire to have a coloured delegate." Just prior to this petition, a resolution was routinely adopted and sent to the N.M.B. "re: the closing of the books of the Union to Arabs (New Members) owing to the number of white firemen unemployed"; as well as a resolution calling for an approach through Members of Parliament to the Home Office to restrict "the employment of Alien Coloured and Arab seamen" because "white British seamen" were "being displaced by Malay, Arab and other Alien Coloured seamen."[54] To say merely that the union was insensitive to its Black members thus understates the case. The consequence was that Black seamen within the union, even more than the white rank and file, were rendered voiceless and powerless.

Yet Black seamen continued to pursue union membership and to agitate from within for equal and democratic representation. Like Chris Braithewaite's fleeting interaction with "Jimmie" Henson, these incidents illustrate the paternalistic demeanor of even sympathetic union leaders, and the invidious position Black seamen occupied in the union. That such ambivalent figures as James Henson or Joseph Havelock Wilson could claim with credibility to be their advocates indicates the meager portion allowed Black seamen. Inside the union they were marginalized and silenced, while outside it they were even more vulnerable. For Black seamen, solidarity with the N.U.S. was a one-way street. In spite of this, Black seamen, like white seamen, had little choice but to remain in the union, and they continued to place claims on union leadership.

Just as union leaders rebuffed their Black members, they spurned colonial labor organization. As the major union in a key British industry with branches worldwide, the N.U.S. was strategically situated to forge an international labor and working-class movement, uniting colonial unions with those in the metropole. The union's ill service of the Black rank and file in Britain was part of a broader failure to align with colonized workers.[55]

Yet this too altered over time. In the early 1920s, when the situation was still somewhat fluid, although wary of "the danger of admitting such men to organization," Wilson had professed the hope that Chinese and Indian seamen would unionize independently, eliminating their market advantage over British seamen: "The strike of seamen in Hong Kong would eventually make some difference ... the Lascars were beginning to make demands ... even now shipowners who formerly carried Lascars were beginning to carry white men." On another occasion he expressed the desire to "get hold of the men" by organizing Indian seamen "on this side," although nothing came of it.[56]

In the 1930s, it was the T.U.C. and the I.T.F. who pressed the N.U.S. to link up with and support colonial unions. In July 1930 James Henson submitted the latest I.T.F. initiative pressing the N.U.S. to organize colonial seamen. Henson, then chairman of the Seamen's Section of the International Transport Workers' Federation, invited N.U.S. General Secretary W. R. Spence to "meet Mr. M. Daud, the President of the Indian Seamen's Union and Mr. S. T. Ally" who were founding an "Indian Seamen's Union of Calcutta and Bombay." Damm, Continental District Secretary and architect of the Arab seamen's "rota," a quota system for seafaring jobs, and Mr. Flett, representing the Northeast Coast Engine Room Section, led the successful opposition. In summer 1933 the Management Committee rejected a request by Indian Seamen's Union leader Aftab Ali for an N.U.S. representative to assist union organizers in India. The following year the Executive Council rebuffed a deputation from the League Against Imperialism concerned with "the position of coloured seamen."[57]

By the late 1930s even employers were urging the Government of India to formulate protective measures for Indian seamen as a "bulwark against Left-wing extremists" and "irresponsible trade unionists" in India. In summer 1938 the Executive Committee grudgingly received an Indian T.U.C. delegate sent by Walter Citrine, General Secretary of the T.U.C., to observe the union's methods. With this exception the union continued to ignore requests for assistance for colonial seamen's unionization until the Second World War.[58] In snubbing Indian seamen's organizing effort, union leaders exhibited not only insensitivity but no doubt reluctance to challenge the

Lascar institution subsidizing their pension fund and thus their power over the white rank and file.

Union policies of racial divisiveness continued through the 1930s, 1940s, and 1950s. After Wilson's death the N.U.S. rehabilitated their politics on many issues to bring them more in line with the mainstream labor movement, but their attitude toward Black seamen if anything coarsened after reconciliation with the Transport and General Workers' Union (T.&G.W.U.) and Labour politicians. The first episode in this new relationship was the anti-Arab campaign of 1929–30.

Havelock Wilson died in April 1929 after a long illness. In August 1929 the N.U.S. rejoined the T.&G.W.U., denying that the move was "capitulation." In September the union rejoined the T.U.C. after signing a noninterference agreement with the Miners' Federation of Great Britain and dis-affiliating from the Non-Political Trade Union movement. In January 1931 the union began publicizing its imminent "ballotting on re-affiliation with the Labour Party."[59] These events coincided with the union's anti-Arab campaign.

The anti-Arab campaign of 1929–30 was not a visceral rank-and-file reaction to the Depression. Through the campaign, the union leadership further restricted the jobs available to Black seamen in Britain. The campaign focused on Arab tramp firemen, one of the last groups still working for standard wages.[60] Rather than seeking to organize them, the leadership attacked Arab seamen while extending the union's power over their lives and work.

The anti-Arab campaign featured the revival of tactics used in the Yellow Peril campaign, including deputations to the government, resolutions at the T.U.C., and invective in *The Seaman*. Behaviors attributed to Arab seamen—like the Chinese—reflected the dialectical process of identity formation and "othering": the culprits' identity and the catalogue of their crimes metamorphosed over several months, as the union groped for persuasive arguments. As in the Yellow Peril campaign, racial and cultural images were marshaled to support an economic agenda. Colonial sexual taboos were invoked to inflame prejudice. Fanciful and exaggerated accounts of the methods by which Arabs arrived in Britain and of the numbers involved stirred disproportionate alarm. In the anti-Arab campaign the union directed its ire not only against Black working men but against the multiracial seaport settlements sustaining their presence in Britain, discussed more fully below. It is useful to note here both the rehabilitation of Yellow Peril tactics, and the role the rest of the labor movement played in the campaign.

The anti-Arab campaign began in early 1929. It was actually James Henson, still estranged from the N.U.S. and currently organizing for the T.&G.W.U., who first raised the cry against "Arabs and Lascars," "Somalis," and "Aliens." In February 1929, with Havelock Wilson in failing health, *The Seaman* argued in defense of Black seamen's jobs, reminding Henson and the T.&G.W.U. that "Lascars" were British subjects and accusing them of "colour bar." George Reed rebutted an article in *John Bull* describing Black seamen as "cheap labour," insisting that all men signed through Board of Trade Mercantile Marine Offices received the same wages, and that the union had "no control" over men signed abroad. *The Seaman* also repeated shipowners' racial rationales, including the argument that Black seamen were more "suitable" for tropical voyages and that their low wages were shipowners' compensation for hiring two or three to do one white man's job. The union warned of "wholesale transfer of certain British trades to a foreign flag" if Lascars received equal wages.[61] They insisted indignantly that "the great majority of coloured seamen who sail in British ships are British subjects." The postscript to this statement equivocated, however: "This union is doing everything in its power to eliminate the Alien Seamen, and as far as possible the Lascar, although the latter, as a British Subject, has a perfect right to work on a British ship."[62] Yet by autumn 1929, the union began to invert these arguments, urging Black seamen's elimination from British ships.

The National Union of Seamen's turn from covert racist practices to public efforts to intensify the division of labor coincided with Havelock Wilson's death in April and the union's reaffiliation with the T.U.C. in autumn 1929. Wilson's avowed imperialism, his alliance with employers, and his defense of the prevailing racial divisions in seafaring had kept overtly racial attacks on Black seamen in check. With his death the union abandoned hostility to the T.U.C. and adopted the rhetoric that T.U.C. critics had employed in spring 1929 and that Wilson had deprecated as "colour bar." Under Wilson the N.U.S. had resisted Lascars' overt exclusion, defending them by invoking their British nationality. But Wilson's successors apparently saw his death as the opportunity to intensify attacks on Black men on standard articles.

Once again the politics of race diverted attention from union reluctance to struggle over wages and working conditions. In November 1929 the Temporary Management Committee that replaced Wilson discussed "the present bad state of the shipping industry" and warned of "the danger to the Union and its members of putting forward at the moment any drastic demands to the shipowners." Acting General Secretary W. R. Spence rejected Charles Jarman's suggestion that the union begin formulating a strategy "to bring forward when an opportune time arrived," arguing that "the Union should not press the owners at the moment for any radical changes." As an alternative, he added in the same breath, "There were questions that could be proceeded with, one of which was the Arab question."[63] In short, while agitation for improved wages and working conditions could disunite the union, disrupt its arrangements with shipowners, and quite possibly fail, the anti-Arab campaign was endorsed by the Executive Council and already in progress.

As in the Yellow Peril campaign, *The Seaman* was the medium of N.U.S. rhetoric. "News" items alleging corrupt hiring practices and trafficking in discharge books among Arab seamen set the stage for a December 1929 deputation to the Board of Trade and the Home Office comprising fourteen major N.U.S. officials and six Members of Parliament. While their professed goal was to stop abuse, George Reed's statement to the *Journal of Commerce* betrayed the simple desire to inhibit Arab seamen's access to jobs, demanding stricter enforcement of the 1925 Coloured Alien Seamen Order, and use of the language test for "all coloured seamen." The joint N.U.S./T.U.C. agenda also implied a traffic between unions, for Reed suggested that Black marine firemen be replaced by "redundant workers in the mining areas of South Wales."[64]

"The Colour Problem" was again front page news, as *The Seaman* struggled to express the union's program in acceptable language.[65] Although the original object of vilifaction was the "Arab" or "coloured" seaman identified by the T.&G.W.U., images evoking the Chinese were revived. When critics, including South Shields seamen's boardinghouse keeper Ali Said, objected that many "coloured" and "Arab" seamen were British subjects and paid-up union members, *The Seaman* adjusted its rhetoric accordingly, to target the "Alien" or the "unregistered" seaman, or to explain away his union membership as an unfortunate expedient. Later the emphasis shifted again to the seamen's boardinghouse keeper and the café owner, denounced as an exploitative "crimp," with the Arab seaman as his victim, in need of N.U.S. protection. Finally, after the settlement, the Arab seaman was once again portrayed as "one of us." Even the "married Arab," denounced weeks before as a polluter of the English racial stock, was now solicitously promised the "fair shake" ostensibly withheld by the boardinghouse keeper.

Reinforcing Orientalist images of Black men's "excitability" and immorality, in December 1929 and January 1930 *The Seaman* featured items about "tribal warfare," "Lascar deserters," "the Superiority of White crews," "robbery with violence," "bribery and corruption": the culprits were "Arab seamen" and "Coloured seamen." The front page of 15 January 1930 replied to Ali Said, "We have to make the Arabs union members . . . to allow us to keep our eyes upon them" but professed the union's "anxiety to get rid of such membership by repatriation." Rhetoric confounded "alien" status with race: several times *The Seaman* or George Reed called on the Home Office to review "the credentials of all coloured seamen." At other times *The Seaman* asserted support for "British nationals white or coloured." Union representatives in Hull distinguished between West Africans and West Indians whom they regarded as entitled, and Arabs whom they did not. At times the union asserted that restriction would "benefit" Arab seamen. At other times the union stooped to schoolyard vulgarity, asserting that solicitor Muir Smith found *The Seaman* "a dirty green rag" because it was "soiled by the hands of his dusky clients."[66]

By March and April, apparently stung by accusations of race prejudice, *The Seaman* revised its rhetoric, vilifying the "Alien Coloured Seaman Menace" and insisting "with British Coloured men, Arabs or otherwise, we have no quarrel." Indignation passed from the "Arab seaman" and "coloured seaman" to their settlements and networks ashore. *The Seaman* of 12 March reported the "Scandal of Traffic in Arabs," portraying the seamen as "ignorant men" and "pawns in the game" run by boardinghouse keeper "crimps." Arab boardinghouse keepers were portrayed as "fat lazy parasites . . . out for loot" who were "filching" wages from their country-men. In this argument a man's legal status became moot; as a victim he was a problem regardless of nationality: "The Arab both British and Alien is being shamelessly exploited."[67]

The Seaman also promoted conspiracy theories and rumors, reporting that Arab seamen were "smuggled as stowaways" by a "hidden organi-sation" through "agents in Marseilles," and alleged a "traffic in forged and spurious papers." George Reed claimed that Arabs were "smuggled" into Britain through "bribery," facilitated by the "ease with which registration and discharge papers could be passed among coloured races." The size of the Arab population was also exaggerated—to an implausible 20,000 in April 1930. The union freely admitted they had no proof for their claims, explaining at one point that "the Arab would never admit his fault"; that two witnesses from whom they had obtained "signed statements" had subsequently "disappeared"; and that "the powers that be would not accept the unsupported testimony of an Arab Seaman."[68]

The anti-Arab campaign not only revived tactics first used against the Chinese, but featured their return to the front page of *The Seaman*, in an alleged "Chinese Seaman's Armoury." In May and June, while asserting that "we have no quarrel with British coloured men, it is the alien," *The Seaman* broadened its call for enforcement of the Coloured Alien Seamen Order to encompass Chinese, Arabs, Somalis, and "negroes." *The Seaman's* rhetoric also exhibited a contradictory attitude to miscegenation. After the successful imposition of the rota, callous denunciation of "half-castes" gave place to anxious solicitude for the "married Arab."[69]

This campaign reached beyond the workplace into dockside settlements, impugning interracial families as pathological and Black boardinghouse keepers as exploiters and criminals. Like employers who recognized that shipboard racial stratification must be reinforced by barriers ashore, union leaders may have sought to isolate Arab seamen within the labor pool by undermining the infrastructure of boardinghouses, cafés, and interracial families that sustained them in port. The targeting of South Shields boardinghouse keeper and community leader Ali Said by both the union and local police, and his summary trial and deportation in autumn 1930, suggests that they recognized interracial dockside settlements as critical in sustaining Black seamen's presence in British ships.

The campaign culminated in a "rota" for Arab and Somali seamen in summer 1930, modeled on a system that Chris Damm had designed and implemented on the Continent. Arab seamen were in effect placed on a waiting list, confined only to the number and types of jobs the N.U.S. considered fit for them—establishing a quota and an occupational ghetto. In signing on the rota, men were rendered "independent of engagement through the coloured boardinghouse keepers," but left at the mercy of the union and the authorities for jobs and other assistance. The rota did not eliminate Arab firemen from the least desirable shipboard jobs; in effect it guaranteed them this segment of the labor market. It also enhanced union control over the distribution of jobs, further rationalizing the seafaring workforce. The rota also exacerbated racial and cultural divisions, for employers could now choose among three separate categories, Arabs, Somalis, and the rest, when selecting a crew. Since registers of Arabs and Somalis were not kept in every port, the rota also limited men's mobility. Arab seamen initially boycotted the rota in Cardiff, South Shields, and elsewhere, but were ultimately forced to capitulate. The rota established in summer 1930 appeared to satisfy the union and little was heard of it after autumn 1930. By November a T.U.C. General Council communication concerning "Alien and Undesirable Coloured Labour on British Ships" met an indifferent response. The rota, Spence explained, had successfully alleviated the problem.[70]

Yet, in spite of an apparent shift to heightened racial divisiveness at Wilson's death, N.U.S. officials remained disunited and ambivalent. In mid-1930, while drafting a resolution on Arab labor for the upcoming T.U.C., disagreement surfaced in the Executive Council—among Reed, Damm, Clouston and Spence—regarding the purpose of the rota, thus the rights of Arab seamen. Spence, now General Secretary, reported that the purpose of the scheme was to regulate Arab seamen's employment and to "prevent an influx of unregistered Arabs into the British Mercantile Marine." But its purpose was actually a source of confusion. Spence instructed a representative who was reluctant to accept dues from a long-term Arab member that such contributions should be accepted: the object was to keep out *new* men. Refusal to accept union dues from an Arab member would effectively prevent him from working, at least on a union vessel, exacerbating the problem of Black nonunion labor which the rota was purportedly designed to eliminate. Yet Chris Damm and George Reed, District Secretary for the Bristol Channel, disputed Spence's interpretation.[71] Although some union officials expected the rota to eliminate illicit extra-union activities, others such as Reed, Damm, and the unnamed local official perhaps wished to force Black seamen out of the union and, effectively, into the arms of the boarding master "crimp" who could then be denounced to the police and the Home Office.

Union inconsistency, confusion, and occasional hostility no doubt reinforced Arab seamen's efforts to get jobs outside union channels, principally through boardinghouse keepers. From a Black seaman's viewpoint, grudging admission to the N.U.S. and the rota imposed in 1930 might confer no more benefits than obtaining jobs from the boarding masters, who additionally took responsibility for their boarders when unemployed—something the union did not do: the standard bribe or "backsheesh" of £2 was precisely the price of the PC5.[72]

Such inconsistencies imply that the impetus behind the anti-Arab campaign had little to do with smuggling rings, forged documents, or slaving networks. Nor does the campaign appear to have been a response to the high unemployment of January 1930, for its inception antedated the shipping slump by nearly a year. It was also shorter-lived than the Depression. With the establishment of the rota for "Arab and Somali" seamen in autumn 1930, a device further stratifying the labor market, the union's concern with "aliens" dissipated. In spring 1932, Clouston and Tarbitten alleged evasion of the rota but, when asked for proof, produced only one case. Thus, it is not at all clear that the anti-Arab campaign was a direct response to the Depression, although the effects of the Depression certainly exacerbated the situation, especially for Arab seamen who were, after all, those most affected. The effort expended to "keep our eyes upon" Arab firemen apparently availed the N.U.S. little: they accepted another wage cut in 1932.[73]

The rota for "Arabs and Somalis" remained in force until the Second World War, as part of the National Maritime Board "Joint Supply" system. By 1937 the union reduced its entrance fee in a drive for new members, but did not relax restrictions against Black seamen. Twice in 1938, 350 Black seamen of Cardiff approached the Bristol Channel District Committee to abolish the rota, "so that they could have free access to employment the same as other members of the Union." Union officials responded that "our business could be carried on as at present, as . . . officials in the Channel would give all members a fair deal." Officials reacted to the second approach by calling a special meeting to reinforce the system. The national Executive Council took the same paternalistic approach, declaring the union "satisfied" that the "rota . . . is in the best interests of all concerned."[74]

After 1935, in spite of the British Shipping Assistance Act and attendant publicity, in spite of the Second World War, in spite of or perhaps because of Indian independence and the Nationality Act of 1948, the union remained ambivalent and often unresponsive toward its Black members, and snubbed Black colonial seamen's unionization efforts. The union offered support to the Indian seamen's unions only belatedly. Not until the 1940s did they receive a delegate from the West African Seamen's Union, and only in the late 1950s and early 1960s did they discuss altering the *de facto* racial stratification still prevailing on British ships. Not until the late 1970s, in the industry's decrepitude, did they challenge Asiatic articles.[75]

The union abandoned its early policy of organizing all comers and its professed internationalism in the process of incorporation through the National Maritime Board. The Yellow Peril campaign was the prelude to interwar compromises, as the union borrowed colonial and imperialist racial dogmas to support racial exclusion. Weak and isolated from the rest of the labor movement both nationally and internationally, and reluctant to press shipowners for improvements in wages and working conditions through forceful industrial action, the seamen's union turned in the 1920s to tactics of racial division. In the 1930s these tactics continued to enhance their control over the labor force while commanding the support of the mainstream labor movement. For if the union used racial divisiveness in the 1920s to relieve its isolation from labor's mainstream, its reconciliation with the labor movement did little to mitigate its racist policies.

The history of the National Union of Seamen provides a critical approach to understanding the continuing divisions among British working people along lines of race, gender, age, skill, and geography. In the interwar years the N.U.S. was deeply complicit in the racial subordination within the seafaring workforce. Rather than a necessary sacrifice in defense of the white majority, racial divisions were integral to the National Union of Seamen's compromises. Union efforts did not so much preserve jobs for British seamen as preserve the union's tenuous privileged relationship with shipowners through the National Maritime Board.

Shipowners' patriotic rhetoric of "British men for British ships" obscured the fact they continued to employ vast and growing numbers of colonized contract laborers at a fraction of N.M.B. wages and standards; this was never given play in the pages of *The Seaman*. In spite of their vocal xenophobia, neither employers nor union leaders were really committed to barring Black labor from British ships. The maintenance of the super-exploited Black workforce ensured both the marginal profitability of the shipping industry and the prestige, power, and credibility of union leaders. The implicit threat to replace unionized seamen with Lascars or other contract laborers enabled shipowners to keep the seamen's union at bay. The racial implications, in turn, enabled the union to maintain the tenuous loyalty of the rank and file without jeopardizing their relations with owners. The constant threat of cheap nonunion labor persuaded sailors disgruntled with union acquiescence to nonetheless accept wage cuts and other concessions.

The union also reused employers' racial imagery: the menace of the foreign scab was infused with racial overtones: fear of mythical hordes of "coloured aliens" anxious to replace white seamen in British ships enabled union leaders to discourage militancy that might jeopardize its relations with employers. Exploitation of racial divisions yielded superficial gains for union leaders at the price of a damaging split in the maritime workforce. Like employers, union leaders deflected criticism of contract labor by focusing attention on the small numbers of Black men on standard articles of agreement. Like employers, union spokesmen blurred the distinctions between the two groups, both by stressing their common racialized Otherness, and by misrepresenting their relative numbers in the labor force.

This investigation nonetheless suggests that the seamen's union has been held responsible for racist policies promulgated by governments largely hostile to organized labor, policies whose provisions cut across the union's own admittedly inconsistent stance toward Black seafarers. Union leaders' failure to oppose practices that divided and weakened their rank and file was negotiated with employers and the state from a position of weakness. The union's turn from Wilson's avowed internationalism to policies of racial exclusion appeared to arise from strength derived from the union's position as the seamen's sole representative on the National Maritime Board. In reality, however, policies of racial divisiveness kept unionized seamen, Black and white, vulnerable to the threat posed by unorganized cheap labor. Racial divisiveness impeded rather than aided the N.U.S. in protecting its rank and file.

Union leaders' focus on the small number of Black seamen on standard articles obscured their collusion in the spread of contract labor, the real source of unemployment and poverty among seamen and their families. The ongoing N.U.S. campaign against "foreign" labor resulted in the substitution of Lascars on Asiatic articles for "aliens," and British subjects on National Maritime Board articles, depressing wages and working conditions overall. In the same years, while the proportion of "British" seamen remained fairly stable, the proportion of "Foreign seamen" on standard articles—among whom many Black seamen, British and otherwise, were classed, fell steadily. Having conceded the principle of unequal wages and conditions, the union was powerless to prevent the steady erosion of unionized jobs in favor of contract labor that continued through the 1980s. Thus the argument that white workers automatically benefited from Black workers' subordination is fallacious.

Since the union was both materially and ideologically dependent on the racial division of labor in shipping, it is not surprising that they were disinclined to respond to approaches from Black seamen, whether Lascars or men on standard articles. Since the union represented a global labor force, in capitulating to employers' racist agenda it also abdicated the opportunity to lead a global labor movement.

As the first British union to deal with Black workers in large numbers, the National Union of Seamen established patterns for exclusion and subordination of Black workers, and involved the state, the mainstream labor leadership, and the white rank and file in racist practices, an unsavory legacy for postwar British race relations. Racial exculsion was a learned behavior constructed in conscious if deluded response to a particular structural context. Racial exclusion and animus did not come "naturally" to union leaders: employers steered them toward it. Union leaders' racist practice was tactical: they sought to manipulate rather than reflect rank-and-file sentiment. In addition, both employers and the union sought to extend shipboard racial divisions into working-class settlements in the ports. Their success in doing so is the next question to consider.

CHAPTER SIX

Contesting the Boundaries of Race and Nationality: The Coloured Alien Seamen Order, Policy and Protest

The British Empire has to endure its own black or coloured subjects: it need not extend the same charity to similarly coloured aliens.
—Sir John Pedder, Home Office Aliens Department, 8 April 1925

If we are classed as aliens our brothers who have made the supreme sacrifice on various battle fields of the Great War for the preservation, flag, prestige, honour and future welfare of the British Empire can be termed mercenaries. We know, feel, and believe that every breast was bared in freedom's cause, every eye, heart, soul wish and imagination pointed to the same goal as the truest Englishman that ever lived. Victory for the Allied cause with an honourable peace and as true as we were to Britain in War and danger so true are we and wish to remain in time of peace.
—Letter from 26 West African and West Indian seamen residing in the Barry Dock Mission to Seamen, 30 April 1925

IN SEPTEMBER 1925, Mrs. Mary Fazel, wife of a marine fireman living in Bootle in the Mersey estuary, penned a distressed appeal to the India Office. The previous week, upon disembarking from the SS *Derville* in Cardiff, Mrs. Fazel's husband, Fazel Mohamed, had been registered as an alien by local authorities, who disregarded his war-era Certificate of Nationality as well as his Mercantile Marine book. Mary Fazel turned to the India Office for aid: "Would you kindly inform me if it is correct that the Mercantile Marine book should have been ignored as documentary proof," she inquired, "and if so could you advise me where I could obtain a copy of his birth certificate. . . . I have been married to him seven years, and we have three children, therefore the knowledge that my husband is not a recognized British subject causes me some consternation, as should any-

First epigraph: HO45/12314/476761/5. Second: HO45/12314/476761/17.

thing happen to him in a foreign port his rights as a Britisher would be jeopardized, and consequently my own and our children's."[1] Mrs. Fazel's alarm was not ill founded. The British-born wives and children of Germans and other "aliens" had faced threats of deportation and other hardships during the war, events vivid in living memory. Yet Fazel Mohamed was a British subject who had served in British ships for years. He held a Certificate of Nationality signed in August 1919 by a Mercantile Marine Superintendant.[2] Fazel Mohamed was one of thousands of British subjects unjustly registered in ensuing weeks under the Coloured Alien Seamen Order, and the order itself was only the most notorious instance of ongoing state involvement in racial subordination.

Given the opportunistic flexibility of racial categories as employers defined them, and given continual resistance by Black seamen and their advocates, it is no surprise that the British state had difficulty codifying racial categories or enforcing racial subordination and exclusion. Interwar racial policy was not a product of consensus but of conflict and negotiation, coercion and subterfuge. It did not reflect a unified effort among local and national officials, and other elites, "to tighten up government control within the metropolis as well as a wider economic and political response on the imperial plane."[3] There was no such unity. Between the two world wars, the definition of who was "coloured" or Black, and to what this entitled him was continually contested, thus shaped, in struggle among employers, union officials, and local and central government, and by resistance from Black seamen and their families and allies, from consular officials and colonial governments, and from colonized elites. Black workers' resistance and evasion compelled the British state into increasingly intense supervision of the Black workforce in Britain, of which the Coloured Alien Seamen Order, far from an isolated anomaly, was merely the most visible manifestation.

The Special Restriction (Coloured Alien Seamen) Order of 1925 was the first instance of state-sanctioned racial subordination inside Britain to come to widespread notice. Through the order, the Home Office aliens bureaucracy misapplied its regulatory mechanisms and police powers in an effort to exclude Black seamen from Britain. Many have seen the Coloured Alien Seamen Order as an anomalous portent of the conflicts following the Second World War, and of the state's acquiescence in union-inspired popular racism. These interpretations tend to overestimate the union's role, while investigation reveals that the state and employers took the principal initiative in policy formation.

Until recently, scholars' major sources of information on the Coloured

Alien Seamen Order have been the League of Coloured Peoples' investigation, conducted in 1935; and anthropologist Kenneth Little's study in 1948.[4] Both were based largely on the recollections of Black seamen themselves, ten and twenty years after the event. Contemporaries were unaware of central government involvement and logically blamed overzealous local police for exceeding their charge while enforcing the order. Supporting assumptions about localized popular racism, some have argued that the order, aimed principally at alien Arabs, was only applied to other Black seamen in error.[5]

Identifying local officials or the union as the perpetrators of racial subordination through the Coloured Alien Seamen Order has absolved the central government of its critical role in formulating and enacting this and similar policies. As a result, enforcement of the order has been misinterpreted as an expression of popular will, supporting the view of racial conflict as universal, atavistic, endemic among ordinary people. Evidence subsequently available shows that the Coloured Alien Seaman Order manifested neither a spontaneous outbreak of popular racism, nor simple abuse of power by provincial police and officials. Policies of racial subordination originated and were encouraged at the highest levels of government, in response to converging pressures from historical actors within and outside the state. As Mrs. Fazel's letter suggests, attacks on Black seamen also involved assaults on their families, settlements, and networks in Britain and overseas, and mobilized commensurate resistance.

Scholars are increasingly rejecting the view of interwar British society and politics as either monolithically tolerant or monolithically racist.[6] Within Britain, different agents had entrenched and competing agendas regarding Black workers' rights. The broad and encompassing definition of British nationality, implied by imperial and Commonwealth ideals and rhetoric and reinforced by wartime exigency, suited Black seamen and their advocates in the India Office and the Colonial Office, and was accepted by many local officials in Britain. But a more exclusive view of British nationality, promoted by the Board of Trade, local immigration officers, and union spokesmen, eventually prevailed in state policy.

The mid-twentieth century has been portrayed as a period in which demoralization, decline, and retreat from empire brought forth a narrow and implicitly racial popular definition of Englishness.[7] We have seen, on the contrary, that the reconstruction of racial barriers in the 1920s and 1930s did not reflect a retreat from empire so much as the efforts of an influential section of the metropolitan elite to continue to reap the benefits of empire without bearing the costs. The Coloured Alien Seamen Order was an episode in this ongoing process, and its contradictions reflected the dilemmas of empire in the mid-twentieth century.

In the early 1920s the British state successively shifted and redefined the boundaries of race and nationality in response to competing pressures from employers, the union, local and national government, and resistance by Black seamen and their advocates. The result was the codification of a new political category, and, implicitly, of racial difference itself, in the Coloured Alien Seamen Order of 1925. As the affected seamen continued to contest and resist its effects in the years 1925 to 1932, this category was broadened from an initially small and specific group of "Arab" seamen to encompass a disparate group of workers defined chiefly by their vulnerability in the global labor market and by attributed "racial" characteristics. In the process, racial difference itself became a *prima facie* political disability. This new political category was codified in 1932 in the Special Certificate of Nationality and Identity, a second-class passport for Black workers only, and applied not only in Britain but eventually in the overseas empire.

Racial policy became the province of the Home Office in response to direct and indirect pressure from employers, local officials, the seamen's union, and in default of action by other central government ministries such as the Colonial Office, the India Office, and the Board of Trade. Charged with policing labor and civil agitation, the Home Office also regulated immigration through its Aliens Department. Between 1917 and 1925 the Home Office reluctantly undertook the policing of Black workers in Britain, using aliens regulation against British subjects in breach of the letter and spirit of existing legislation and of common practice. As the ministry in charge of aliens matters, the Home Office first got involved in policing Black seamen who were of genuinely doubtful nationality. For in the course of the First World War, British strategy created a pool of presumptive British Protected Persons in Southern Arabia and East Africa, men who, because their nationality was ambiguous, were subject to inclusion or exclusion as it suited British purposes.

In 1917 local police arrested three men for failure to register as aliens because they lacked birth certificates to prove they were from Aden, a British colony. The Home Office, at Foreign Office and Colonial Office behest, rebuked the police. Arab seamen, they wrote, "never have proper passports.... They are seldom if ever able to support their claim to British nationality by documentary evidence, but unless there is a reason to doubt it, the permits [leave to land] are issued."[8] Major-General J. M. Stewart, the Political Resident at Aden, took an even broader view.

To him, it mattered little whether the men were actually British subjects, or, as he suspected, French Somalis: "Things are in a state of flux and transition. . . . It will be most impolitic at this time when . . . Turkish territories and ours [are] no longer, by reason of the war, clearly defined, to dismiss all trans-border Arabs as beyond the pale of our consideration and to treat them as enemy subjects."[9] "Arab" seamen, in demand due to a manpower shortage in British war transports, were permitted to land in Britain for ulterior foreign policy goals. But seamen so credentialed proceeded to use these documents for their own purposes—to enhance their position in the seafaring labor market by remaining in Britain and seeking jobs under European conditions. Thus in 1917 the convergence of wartime labor demands and British imperial ambitions expanded the definition of who was treated as British and to what that entitled him. Like colonized people generally, the men in question were explicitly offered the prerogatives of British nationality in exchange for their service in the war. But this convergence lasted only until the Armistice. Political boundaries in the Near East, and with them the status of "Arab" seamen, solidified with the peace. Residents of the Aden settlement remained British subjects. Many more were residents of the British Protectorate of Aden, not technically British subjects but still under British jurisdiction through the India Office.[10] No longer potential defectors to be wooed from the Turks, this group of "Arab" seamen of genuinely ambiguous status became the initial focus of Home Office attention.

In traversing the geographical barriers between colonizer and colonized, Black seamen who traveled to Britain to evade colonial exploitation entered the milieu of labor conflict in the metropole. Consequently they occupied the strategic intersection of imperial and domestic political struggles and economic contradictions. After the Armistice, the demand for merchant seamen slackened due to industrial mismanagement and postwar depression, with its attendant labor struggles. Local immigration authorities and police, often influenced by images of colonized peoples' irrationality and volatility as well as class-based hostility to workers in general, increasingly viewed Black sailors, like other unemployed workers, as potential criminals. The Board of Trade, unable to constrain employers' labor practices, supported efforts to confine Black seamen to labor contracts negotiated in the colonies. The Board of Trade, with the union and some local officials, manipulated fears of racial conflict to persuade the Home Office to exclude Black seamen from the ports.[11]

Home Office staff initially resisted policing Black workers in Britain, for most of them were British subjects in the broader sense, technically outside the purview of aliens legislation. In 1920 they countered pressure from the Board of Trade by suggesting that Arab seamen like white seamen be guaranteed repatriation on engagement, removing their advantage in the labor market. In 1921 they discounted James Henson's warnings of "imminent" race riots in the ports, later dismissing him as "the low type of seamen's union agents whom the Newport Chief Constable suspects of fomenting colour riots." In January 1923 the Home Office resisted another effort by the Board of Trade and the N.S.F.U. to draw them into policing Black workers, unmoved by Henson's warnings about "the morality of the East," the use of "razors and knives," "back-sheesh" (bribery), and "bloodshed and all that sort of thing." When the union attempted to appropriate the language of nationality, pointing out that "the Arab seaman is not a British seamen according to the Colonial Office and according to the Home Office; he is an alien seaman," the Home Office confided privately that "the dividing line" between alien and British subject "is narrow and not easy to trace."[12]

The Home Office was not anxious to undertake its tracing in any case. Aliens controls developed before and during the First World War were originally directed against the nationals of continental European states: Russian Jews and, later, Germans. In contrast, seamen from the colonized empire considered themselves British and were commonly so recognized— by local magistrates, for instance, who frequently refused to convict them for breaches of aliens regulations.[13] But since aliens controls increasingly made the right to live and work in Britain contingent on British nationality, postwar political and economic pressures prompted their selective enforcement against new groups, shifting the boundaries and the meanings attached to race and nationality themselves. For in spite of their scruples, in 1920 the Home Office began penalizing undocumented Arab seamen for their officially ambiguous status, using aliens powers on a selective, racial basis. Once created, this racialized and implicitly pejorative political category—"coloured alien seamen"—was broadened to encompass increasing numbers of men—whether British subject or alien, whether seaman or not.

In autumn 1920 the Home Office capitulated to pressure—and dire warnings of imminent racial conflict—from the Board of Trade and local port officials. They directed immigration officers to bar "Arab seamen" without proof of British nationality from arriving as passengers. The measure was designed to exclude all except *bona fide* seamen; the Home Office consoled themselves that it would affect few of the men in question, since most were genuine seamen. Yet this measure was a significant concession to race discrimination, for a discharge book or a discharge sheet—a record of past employment—while still deemed evidence of identity for other seamen, was no longer accepted from Arabs, who, the Home Office well knew, "never have proper passports."[14]

Encouraged by this concession in autumn 1920, the Board of Trade and immigration officers in the ports proceeded to demand Home Office action against other undocumented seamen. In the process the category "coloured alien" broadened to encompass men from Asia, Africa and the Caribbean, British or alien, seaman or not. Like the union's concession to the principle of unequal pay, Home Office capitulation to exclusion further precluded "levelling up" Black seamen's working conditions to remove their competitive advantage in the labor market, instead preserving the disparities between colonizers and colonized. Using aliens legislation for this purpose covertly racialized the definition of British nationality itself.

In December 1920 the Board of Trade warned of "discontent and disturbance among British seafarers," adding, "There is no reason for treating alien coloured seamen other than Arabs differently from Arabs; they are equally undesirable." In January 1921 the Home Office ordered immigration officers to exclude all incoming "coloured" seamen who could not prove British nationality, not just those arriving as passengers.[15] Thus within weeks of their first reluctant policy shift, Home Office scope broadened from putative alien nonseamen to all undocumented "coloured" seamen.

After barring new arrivals—first "Arabs" and then all Black seamen, *bona fide* or not—local authorities and other branches of the central state pressed the Home Office, directly and indirectly, to deport men already in Britain. In spring and summer 1921, India Office and Colonial Office inaction steered local Poor Law officials and the union toward excluding unemployed Black seamen. Unemployment due to "slack trade" had overtaxed local relief efforts in Cardiff and Liverpool. Local Poor Law officials, the Lord Mayor of Liverpool, the secretary of the seamen's union, and the chaplain of the Seamen's Mission in Cardiff, as well as representatives from local charities, initially sought state assistance in providing relief for unemployed Black seamen, "these men who served this country." The Colonial Office and the India Office, financially responsible for stranded colonial subjects, rebuffed their pleas. The sole alternative was deportation, euphemistically called repatriation, which the Home Office proffered only in fear of labor agitation or racial conflict.[16] Thereafter the Home Office responded to reported threats to public order by supporting projects intended to deport unemployed Black seamen, projects that repeatedly failed because Black men refused to be forced back to colonial labor conditions.

Thus in the early 1920s, racial difference, compatible in the eyes of many with British nationality, came through a political process to signify "outsider" status. These events suggest that the institutionalization of racial hierarchy and the codification of racialized definitions of nationality in interwar Britain were not the inevitable manifestation of visceral popular racism or "natural" antagonisms and affinities. Instead they were shaped by the Board of Trade's and the unions' capitulation to employers' racialized labor practices; sporadic pressure from local officials; and Colonial Office and India Office evasion of financial responsibility. In late 1924 several additional ingredients produced the Coloured Alien Seamen Order, requiring all Black seamen in Britain's major ports to establish their British nationality or be registered as aliens.

The pretext that the order was intended to remedy a surfeit of labor in the shipping industry is questionable: unemployment had peaked and was declining by mid-1924. Conversely, the mid-1920s were years of renewed labor agitation in the shipping industry. Insurgent seamen's strategies included organizing across the racial barriers that kept the rank and file divided and vulnerable. In November 1924 the *Western Mail* reported the formation of a multiracial seamen's organization, led by a committee composed of three white, three West Indian, and three Somali seamen, envisioned as the "nucleus of a powerful white and coloured combine of seamen."[17] This report's appearance in Home Office files hints that the Coloured Alien Seamen Order may have been as much a response to the threat of labor insurgency—multiracial insurgency at that—as to a labor glut.

Two other events coincided most immediately with this new policy: Arthur Henderson's installation as Labour's first Home Secretary in January 1924, and budget cuts into the immigration staff in spring 1924. Many in the Labour party, now in power for the first time, had been hostile to aliens regulation since the anti-Semitic campaigns at the turn of the century, and George Lansbury approached Henderson immediately after he took office to modify the system. Immigration staff may have seen the budget cut as a prelude to Labour's outright abolition of aliens controls, proposing in self-preservation "a special system of Police registration" for "coloured seamen." Although the Labour government of 1924 was short-lived, the impetus to control Black seamen proved congenial to the succeeding Conservative administration, which took office determined to vanquish organized labor.[18] Again, racist policy was shaped by political and financial imperatives—both long and short term.

On 18 March 1925, Henderson's Conservative successor William Joynson-Hicks invoked powers under Article 11 of the Aliens Order of 1920, requiring all "coloured" seamen "who cannot produce documentary evidence of British nationality to register with the police as aliens." The order was made in full knowledge that few sailors, Black or white, carried passports, using instead the continuous discharge book which contained a record of previous voyages. The Coloured Alien Seamen Order effectively invalidated the continuous discharge as proof of identity for all Black seamen, even British subjects, while it was still accepted from white seamen, whether alien or British subject. Thus, the order blurred the distinctions between Black aliens and Black British subjects while reinforcing racial hierarchy between British subjects. Upon registration, each man would be photographed, fingerprinted, assigned a number, and issued a small passportlike book identifying him as an alien seaman, and containing demographic data, signature, thumbprint, and photograph. The man's "aliens registration number" was permanently stamped across all personal documents, including his discharge papers.[19]

Not surprisingly, many men disembarking from inbound ships or apprehended on the street by zealous police did not possess documents satisfying the order. The ambiguity of many Black seamen's nationality, of which British authorities took ample advantage during the war, now became a weapon used against them. In the space of a few years, Black seamen went from welcome additions to the empire and particularly to the seafaring workforce, with or without "proper passports"; to undesirables denied entry to U.K. ports or deported when destitute, whether subjects or aliens; to presumptive aliens illegitimately in Britain. At the same time the boundaries of the undesirable target group broadened, from genuinely "alien" Arabs who were irregular seamen, to all undocumented Black seafarers, including men the Home Office knew were British but could not prove it.

The order became the occasion for widespread harassment of Black residents of British ports, both alien and subject, seaman and nonseafarer. Examples of the order's arbitrary application included sixty-three Indian peddlers—neither aliens nor seamen—registered after Glasgow police successfully pressed the Home Office to extend the order to their port; two aged coffeehouse keepers in South Shields, Ali Saleh, aged eighty-three, and Syed Hashim Mahdi, sixty-nine, who were registered as seamen; and William Jacob Berka, whom the Home Office refused to register under the order on the grounds that he was not a *bona fide* seaman, when the order was ostensibly designed for irregular seamen. In the course of enforcing the order, many Black British subjects were registered as aliens and threatened with deportation. Others saw their British passports and other documents confiscated or altered by local police.[20]

Contemporaries as well as historians have interpreted the latter as an examples of police excess, but it was actually central government policy: the Home Office planned to treat expired passports issued in London or single-journey passports as no proof at all of British nationality, and to register the bearers as "coloured alien seamen" after impounding their documents. In the aftermath, some British subjects remained registered as aliens indefinitely, suffering additional hardship in 1935 when alien sailors were excluded entirely from state subsidized vessels as a condition of the British Shipping Assistance subsidy. Yet as the Home Office had feared, the order proved a blunt instrument in effecting the conflicting purposes for which it was designed. The ports covered by the order and the small numbers of men registered in spring 1925 bore little relationship to the scale or distribution of unemployment in the industry.[21]

The enduring result of the Coloured Alien Seamen Order was the codification of a hierarchical definition of British nationality dependent on race, class, and occupation, a definition shaped by the demands of the shipping industry, by the vagaries of the interwar economy, by local and national politics, and by state policy. The 1925 order was not a simple reflection of popular racism arising from a self-evident or "natural" distinction between white and Black. It was not a matter of bringing law and policy into conformity with custom and practice defining Black seamen as "archetypal strangers." Legal and policy changes violated custom and practice, giving birth to new definitions of the relationship between race and British nationality. Indeed, the creation of racial hierarchy preceded the redefinition of who was Black, a definition that was continually contested—thus shaped—by Black seamen's resistance.

Resistance to the order took various forms, from simple evasion to collective public protest. Black seamen's continuing subversion of the mechanisms of control prompted increasingly convoluted measures from the Home Office, and created an ever-widening network of race discrimination involving an increasing number of public and private actors. In turn, fear of colonial disaffection stimulated opposition from the Colonial Office, the India Office, and British consuls and officials overseas. The result of the ensuing conflict and negotiation was the adoption of the Special

Certificate of Nationality and Identity—a second-class passport for all Black colonial subjects.

By defining the right to work and live in Britain in terms of nationality, state race policy shaped the nature and content of Black seamen's resistance around a discourse of Britishness and military service. For British nationality itself was a product of interpretation and custom; as the treatment of the Adenese in 1917 suggested, its ambiguity and elasticity was intrinsic to Britain's global dominance. The terms of the order cut across claims to nationality and loyalty to the sovereign and the Mother Country that colonial governments had cultivated among the "martial races" of India and other colonized people—most recently rearticulated in the First World War. Black seamen's sense of betrayal was complemented by the use to which they put the ideology of empire. Appropriating the imperial rhetoric of fair play, equality, and rights earned through military service and allegiance, they fashioned from it a competing definition of British nationality and pressed the state to support it.

Immediately after the order came into effect, in April 1925, the India Office and the Colonial Office received protests from Adenese, West African, West Indian, and Indian seamen harassed by local police in South Shields, Barry, and other ports. These complaints indicated that local officials were using the order against men who were obviously British subjects, and against non-European seamen generally rather than just "Arabs." In April 1925, only a few days after the order's promulgation, George F. Willett, solicitor for the Cardiff Adenese Association, conveyed Adenese seafarers' objections to the order in a cluster of arguments characterizing Black protest throughout the interwar years. While they approved of the effort to stop trafficking in discharge papers, the men were offended by the word "Alien" appearing on their papers: "They consider themselves to be very much British indeed," wrote Willett, "and they ask what flag are they supposed to be under if they are not under the British one." Adenese sailors' war service, they asserted, entitled them to treatment as British. "They fought as British subjects during the war, and have lost many of their friends." Home Office personnel assured him the men had "no way out" of the order but offered a cosmetic concession, altering the stamp on Adenese seamen's documents to "Arab seaman." The word "Alien" remained on their registration cards, and as the Home Office recognized, "The fact that they have to represent themselves to every Aliens Office at the various ports . . . rankles them very badly."[22]

Willett and his clients were isolated, thus easily silenced or intimidated,

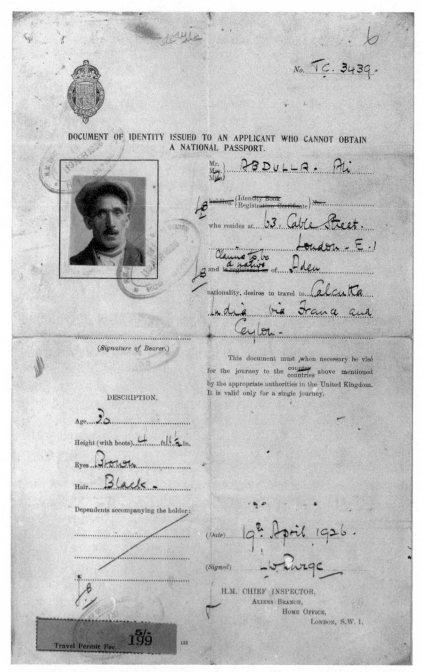

No. TC. 3439.

DOCUMENT OF IDENTITY ISSUED TO AN APPLICANT WHO CANNOT OBTAIN A NATIONAL PASSPORT.

Mr.
Mrs.   ABDULLA. Ali
Miss

holding {Identity Book} No.
         {Registration Certificate}

who resides at 53. Cable Street.
                         London - E.1

and is registered Claims to be a native of Aden

nationality, desires to travel to Calcutta
India via France and
Ceylon -

(Signature of Bearer.)

This document must ,when necessary be visé for the journey to the country/countries above mentioned by the appropriate authorities in the United Kingdom. It is valid only for a single journey.

DESCRIPTION.

Age 25

Height (with boots) 4 ft.1½ in.

Eyes Brown

Hair Black -

Dependents accompanying the holder:

(Date) 19th April 1926.

(Signed) Purge

H.M. CHIEF INSPECTOR,
ALIENS BRANCH,
HOME OFFICE,
LONDON, S.W.1.

Travel Permit Fee 5/-
199

4. Identity document issued to Adenese seaman in lieu of a passport, 1926. Reproduced by permission of the Controller of Her Britannic Majesty's Stationery Office.

but soon the Home Office faced more powerful adversaries in the India Office and the Colonial Office. In April 1925 the Colonial Office forwarded a protest from twenty-six West African and West Indian seamen, residents of the Mission to Seamen in Barry Dock in the Bristol Channel. Invoking the links the imperial government itself had forged among British nationality, war service, and the right to work, they sought in turn to place claims on the state. "If we are classed as aliens," they wrote, then "our brothers who have made the supreme sacrifice" during the Great War "can be termed mercenaries." stressing that D. J. Smith, one of their number, was permanently injured in a mine explosion at sea during the war, they concluded, "We sincerely believe that our government will rectify what we believe to be a mistake."[23]

The India Office and the Colonial Office, indifferent to Black seamen's distress a few years before, came to their aid in 1925 because they feared that the order would create controversy among colonized elites, threatening imperial credibility. An India Office Minute declared, "The Home Office policy of worrying coloured seamen is being pushed to indefensible limits."[24] In law a Lascar seaman should never have been expected to produce credentials, for he remained on articles while ashore. Beyond the illegality of breaking a labor contract, Indian British subjects had every right to be in Britain. From May and June 1925 through early 1926 the India Office reinforced their protests with the threat to issue the men passports. This was tactical, for on June 9 Turner had confided: "It is not certain that the Home Office will wish this office to help actively in substantiating the claims of coloured seamen to British nationality, because . . . if an individual seaman's British nationality is certified by giving him a passport . . . he is more likely to make his presence felt in ways that the authorities here might not like." In short, by subtly threatening to issue passports wholesale, the India Office hoped to hold the Home Office at bay. This was also an assertion of authority. Turner identified "this possibility of offering to help these men in proving their British nationality" as the "only convenient way of replying to the contention of the Home Office that we are not concerned with them."[25] Citing continued Home Office opposition to passports, India Office personnel mused, "The ostensible ground of their objection . . . is quite likely . . . fear that such a step would knock a large hole in the administration of the Order of 1925."[26]

Furnishing every Indian sailor with a British passport was the last thing the Home Office wanted, when their current efforts were to discourage Black migration to Britain and to keep the men ignorant of their rights as British subjects. These unguarded comments exposed the contradiction in the registration scheme itself, for registration eventually ceased to be a deterrent, and instead became desirable, signifying aliens' legitimacy in Britain. It also spurred increasing numbers of Black seamen to seek passports or other means to secure their position in Britain.[27]

The India Office was not motivated by altruism. In addition to considerations of imperial credibility, there were practical reasons for pressing colonized subjects' rights: Turner explained that should they be prevented from working, the Secretary of State for India became financially responsible for destitute Indian subjects in Britain. Delays could be expensive.[28]

After 1925 the India Office became a clearinghouse for Coloured Alien Seamen Order matters; they forwarded letters and copies of documents to the appropriate parties, inquired of the Home Office about particular cases; and reassured alarmed Indian subjects. In the absence of modern facilities, documenting a claim to British nationality required direct correspondence with local officials in a man's birthplace. At best the process took weeks and months, and this was complicated by inconsistent practice by the Home Office and local officials. The India Office would contact the local British governing authority, such as the Government of India in Simla or one of its outposts, or the Political Resident at Aden. The central goverment would then correspond with a village headman or other local authority to establish the man's nativity. Such communication could involve a journey by camel into the hinterland of Aden of upwards of one hundred miles, and could take weeks or even months.[29] In the meantime, the India Office, much less the men in question, were powerless to accelerate the process, in spite of urgent and sometimes desperate appeals, spurred by pressure from local police.

The variety of these appeals in the course of 1925 suggested that the order had already begun to acquire a life of its own: local officials were applying it to men who were obviously British subjects. Divergent police practices were illustrated by the case of West Indian seaman Alexander Givvons. Although Givvons resided in Newport, he had landed in Cardiff for the first time after the order's promulgation and was compelled to register there. Arriving at Newport he was registered again, with Home Office approval. Conversely, some local police were reluctant to register, thus legitimate, nonlocal men, so that while Alexander Givvons was registered twice, other men in the same situation were refused registration in both Salford and Manchester. Other local police frankly wished to broaden the order from seamen to all Black workers, and beyond the original thirteen ports.[30]

The first tally of men registered under the order by October 1925

suggested that the Coloured Alien Seamen Order was ineffective in accomplishing the admittedly conflicting agendas for which it was designed.
Of 7,408 registrants, most from Cardiff, South Shields, and Barry, the
bulk were not aliens at all but claimed to be undocumented British subjects.
In addition, as even the Home Office admitted, registration had limited
deterrent value, for it implied official approval of a sort. The contradiction
in such credentials, Home Office personnel noted, was that registering
men without proof of leave to land would legitimize their presence in the
port, yet "if registration is refused, they cannot be got rid of . . . there will
be no sort of control." As early as October 1925 some local officials realized
this and ceased registering men they viewed as newcomers, instead pros-
ecuting them as illegal aliens. In turn they demanded broader powers from
the Home Office precisely because they tended to lose such cases in English
courts.[31]

By winter 1925–26, Home Office staff themselves were abetting a new
policy of "deferred" registration, rendering men unemployable in hopes
that they would be forced to request repatriation assistance. By the late
1920s they had apparently ceased registering new men altogether, and the
India Office commented ironically on their refusal to register Gulam Rasul
on the pretext he was not a *bona fide* seaman when the order was developed
explicitly for irregular seamen. Faced both with resistance from Black
workers and seamen and their official advocates, and with the internal
contradictions in the policy itself, the Home Office might have rescinded
the order, about which they themselves maintained grave reservations.
Instead, they proceeded in an effort to close the loopholes through increasingly intensive policing and coercion of an ever broadening category
of men. They unilaterally extended the order to all U.K. ports in January
1926.[32]

With the new year the situation was complicated as debate spread into
Parliament and ultimately to the colonies. In turn, struggle intensified in
Whitehall. On 19 December 1925 protest against the order had reached
the House of Commons in the form of a "unanimous resolution" by the
Cardiff Coloured Association "to the effect that the registration of Coloured British subjects in Britain as aliens is undesirable and unjust."[33] In
late 1925 and 1926 newspaper cuttings and excerpts from parliamentary
questions began to collect in Home Office and India Office files.

The India Office was mortified when a protest from Glasgow reached
Indian newspapers. Immediately upon the order's extension to Glasgow
in January 1926, Chief Constable Smith rounded up some sixty-three
peddlers of whom the bulk were British subjects and only two seamen,

registering them as aliens. The men appealed to the Indian Union of Glasgow University who contacted the India Office, the Indian Legislative Assembly, and the Indian press. The story appeared in the Madras newspaper *New India* under the banner headline "Agitate for the Commonwealth Bill," and later in the Calcutta *Forward* accompanied by discussion of the "colour bar" in Glasgow cinemas and dancehalls.[34]

In January 1926, Hugh Alex Ford, British Consul in Colon, forwarded a clipping from the *Negro World*. Expressing outrage that Black British subjects were "treated in Great Britain as aliens," its author incorporated the themes of war service betrayed, race discrimination in Britain, violence, and anticolonialism into an ominous mix. Ford was worried by the resultant "perturbation" among "loyal British West Indians in Panama," and feared that such reports would be "exploited by the disloyal element" to discredit the British empire. Public outrage in the colonies about racial conflict in Britain raised the specter of colonized elites making common cause with their working-class compatriots. By mid-1926 Foreign Secretary Austen Chamberlain demanded a resolution to the current situation, lest adverse publicity in the colonies "serve as a peg on which to hang anti-British propaganda."[35]

Protests in Britain also continued. On May Day 1927 a "mass protest of Indians" in Cleveland Square, Liverpool, denounced the use of the "Alien Certificate for Indians," called on the India Office and Home Office to formulate an identification document for Indian seamen, and announced the formation of the Liverpool Indian Association led by Mr. N. J. Upadhyaya, "for the defence and promotion of the political, social and economic rights of Indians." Perhaps most alarming to the authorities, the newly formed organization called on the Indian National Congress to investigate their complaints and assist in their redress.[36]

Resistance from Black seamen and their allies first prompted the Home Office to retreat, but ultimately to redefine British nationality itself along racial lines. By winter 1926 numerous loopholes were apparent. Men's principal means of resistance was to obtain passports or other credentials, whether legally or illegally, that identified them as British. Men could still get British passports and papers in many of the colonies before embarking. After Asiatic articles were imposed on Red Sea ports men simply traveled as passengers to Britain, obtaining British consular documents in France that British and French officials not surprisingly accepted as evidence of British nationality. In the course of the late 1920s and 1930s, registrations under the order gradually diminished, as increasing numbers of men established their status as British subjects. When in 1930 British officials began confiscating passports and Certificates of Registration from men returning to Aden, Adenese seamen wrote to friends and relatives in Britain, "warning them that they had better not bring their registration certificates to Aden." Even forcible deportation was ineffective: "When the Shipping Federation supply [repatriants and deportees] with tickets to Aden, they get into France and destroy or sell the Marseilles portion." Then they sought to return to the United Kingdom.[37]

In June 1926, after the India Office again threatened to give them passports, the Home Office agreed to exempt British Protected Persons from the port of Aden from the Coloured Alien Seamen Order. This relieved the India Office of financial responsibility for stranded men, but they remained classed as aliens. Enforcement of the order also disrupted arrangements with foreign governments. When men holding hitherto valid consular documents were rejected by British immigration officers and returned to France, British consuls and French officials, not to mention the men themselves, were astonished and outraged. The Home Office in turn wished to constrain consuls from issuing Black seamen any documents at all, but consuls protested this was unworkable. In order for a Black British seaman to get work on a French ship, for instance, he needed a document stating he was "free to engage under another flag." If consuls withheld such a documents the men, unable to ship out, were likely to end up in "grave distress."[38]

In the 1930s the Home Office began replacing Black seamen's passports with a Special Certificate of Nationality and Identity, a document whose validity for travel within the British empire was restricted on grounds of race, class, and occupation. The Home Office developed the Special certificate in explicit response to India Office threats to issue Indian subjects passports; to Colonial Office plans to encourage colonial subjects to carry passports to the United Kingdom; and to Indian and colonial subjects' continued migration to Britain using passports and other credentials obtained legally. The Special Certificate of Nationality and Identity represented the admission that excluding Black seamen was untenable without redefining British nationality itself along racial lines, simultaneously redefining the meanings and implications of racial difference.

The India Office had squelched a proposal in 1925 to issue West Indian and Indian British subjects Certificates of Nationality. They feared that the Home Office wished to alter the validity of these documents once issued, which was precisely what they did. Since the war, the Home Office had been grappling with the problem of subjects of British Protectorates who possessed British passports. Although technically aliens, such men

NOTICE TO SEAMEN.

In accordance with the law now in force in the United Kingdom it is necessary that all coloured seamen who are being discharged from vessels in the United Kingdom shall have in their possession a Certificate clearly proving their identity and stating that they are of British Nationality.

Coloured seamen not in possession of this Certificate on being discharged from a vessel in the United Kingdom, will be registered as aliens and suffer considerable inconvenience accordingly.

Seamen belonging to British Guiana can obtain these Certificates on application to the Harbour Master's Office, Public Buildings, Georgetown, and they are strongly advised to do so in their own interests.

H. de B. TUPPER, Commander R.N.,
Harbour Master.

Harbour Master's Office,
Public Buildings,
Georgetown,
13th March, 1926.

5. Notice issued by the Harbour Master in Georgetown, British Guiana, advising seamen to carry identity documents when sailing to Britain, 1926. Reproduced by permission of the Keeper of the Public Records.

were regarded as British by local authorities and other officials.[39] The strategy adopted for this "second problem," the ambiguous status of British Protected Persons, was to substitute the Certificate of Nationality and Identity for their passports. Again, this special provision became a model, eventually broadened to encompass all Black workers.

In July 1930 the Foreign Office directed authorities to confiscate passports and Certificates of Registration under the Coloured Alien Seamen Order from men returning to Aden from Britain. Thereafter they would receive documents of limited validity at the discretion of British officials in Yemen. This innovation was soon extended beyond Adenese seamen. In October 1931 passports of all "coloured British seamen" of India, Africa, East Asia, and the West Indies were revoked and replaced with certificates of Nationality valid for five years. In 1934 the Certificate was extended to "Coloured persons or natives belonging to the Union of South Africa or South West Africa and to "coloured seamen belonging to Southern Rhodesia.[40]

Like the Coloured Alien Seamen Order, the Certificate of Nationality blurred the distinction between British subjects and Protected Persons while creating a starker demarcation between Black and white British subjects. It consummated the process, begun in the 1920s, of systematically depriving Black British subjects of the rights other subjects enjoyed. Yet the special certificate acknowledged the Britishness of its holders, including Protected Persons. At the stroke of a pen, racial difference was no longer a marker of presumptive alien status; instead it marked a version of British nationality explicitly detached from the prerogatives of other British subjects.

The most successful effort to resist these policies again illustrated the mutability of racial definitions and their susceptibility to political and economic pressure: this was the process that exempted Maltese seamen from the certificate. Soon after the order's promulgation, in autumn 1925, L.B. Freeston of the Colonial Office had successfully persuaded the Home Office to exempt West Indian seamen, who were obviously British subjects, from the regulation. Immigration officers would classify West Indians not as "aliens" but instead as "coloured seamen," a category now implying a particular political status.[41] Freeston also complained that Maltese seamen were encountering harassment under the order. C. D. C. Robinson of the Home Office assured him that Maltese were not included in the order— were not classed as "coloured"—but would need to prove they were Maltese in order to be exempt. A man's race would in this instance be

determined not by his physical appearance, an apparently self-evident signifier, but by his nationality, a legal and political mechanism.

In 1935 the Home Office attempted to apply the special certificate to
Maltese seamen, but were again dissuaded by political pressure. Malta
depended heavily on migration to relieve underemployment and over-
population. A man identified as a "coloured alien seaman" by his own
government would be rendered virtually unemployable abroad. The "special seamen's certificate issued in England to coloured seamen," argued
Edward Mifsud of the Office of the Lieutenant Governor, "would place
[Maltese seamen] at a disadvantage for employment" especially in "France,
Algeria, Tunisia, Morocco, Egypt and the U.S.A." The men would also
have "serious difficulties" if they "attempted to return overland to Malta
without proper passports." While the India Office and the Colonial Office
resisted the order only on tactical grounds, the Maltese government had
a concrete stake in Maltese seamen's employability, and perhaps this is
why they prevailed.

After months' delay, the Home Office relented, allowing Maltese seamen
to continue carrying passports, and assuring Mifsud that "no steps need
be taken in the meantime to extend the issue of special certificates of
nationality and identity to white colonial seamen." Maltese seamen, to
their advantage, were now classified as white—provided they could prove
they were Maltese.[42] With this decision the Home Office radically altered
the life opportunities of the men in question; their status in the eyes of
foreign governments and their own; their international mobility; and their
ability to get a livelihood and to provide for their families. Thereafter the
deployment of the special certificate somewhat arbitrarily signposted the
fluid and unstable boundaries between Black and white: in April 1936 other
"white colonial seamen" such as "natives of Cyprus," Seychelles, Gibraltar,
and Mauritius, who "did not appear to be 'coloured' seamen" were permitted "passports of limited validity."[43]

The Coloured Alien Seaman Order was renewed in 1938 and again in
1942, and soon thereafter it was abolished to make British Protected
Persons eligible for conscription.[44] The end of the Coloured Alien Seamen
Order was consistent with its promulgation—a measure designed to move
Black working men to meet the needs of the imperial system whether in
war or peace. The definitions of who was welcome to live and work in
Britain, and with it the definitions of race and nationality—of "Coloured
Alien Seamen"—were shaped by domestic and international economic
forces, political considerations, and institutional actors. These definitions

could change in the space of a few years or even a few months from broadly inclusive to narrowly exclusive.

The order originated in the central government's effort to resolve conflicts created by intensified racial segmentation in the maritime workforce. It did not orginate with white working people. Employers, the Board of Trade and the National Union of Seamen isolated Black workers, identifying them as targets for hostility and exclusion. Local officials followed their lead in an effort to act visibly against poverty and social dislocation whose sources were beyond local control. State policy and the categories of race and nationality it implied were formulated in struggle among different elites and nonelites, by government, industry, labor unions, pressure groups, and individuals, acting collectively or individually, sometimes in concert and often in conflict.

To the Home Office fell the unenviable task of attempting to mediate these conflicts. Ultimately they resolved them only through redefining British nationality itself. This showed in the language of various Home Office communications, frequently opposing "British" to "coloured" with no reference to nationality.[45] Defining all Black seamen as presumptive aliens, lacking the rights accorded British workers, effectively reimposed the vulnerability and subordination the men had sought to shed by traveling to the metropole and claiming rights as British subjects. Rather than a retreat from empire—a decolonization, as some scholars would have it—the Coloured Alien Seamen Order, by legitimating extraordinary control over Black workers in Britain, actually amounted to their recolonization in Britain.

Yet other branches of the state responded differently to Black resistance, depending on whether their primary concern was colonial or domestic politics. Local officials and the Home Office in their racially exclusive practices actually worked at cross purposes to the India Office, the Colonial Office and consuls abroad. Content to let Black seamen starve in silence in 1921, the India Office and the Colonial Office later opposed overt subordination in Britain because it exacerbated colonial disaffection and disrupted customary arrangements with foreign states and nationals. Policy based on imperialist ideologies of racial inequality and incompatibility conflicted with the imperialist promise of equality and unity within the empire.

In this process of struggle, well-meaning outsiders, white or Black, took little part. Emphasis on well-intended "middle opinion"—"central, informed" popular thought—as the counter to "the extension of systematic racist doctrines" is misplaced.[46] The idea that informed public opinion prevented overt racial subordination in twentieth-century Britain is flawed. The Home Office simply avoided confronting public opinion, concealing their activities even from other branches of government. The Coloured Alien Seamen Order, for example, was an Order in Council rather than a publicly debated piece of legislation, and opponents such as the India Office and the Colonial Office, like the Black advocacy group the League of Coloured Peoples, could only speculate about its origins. Even its implementation smacked of subterfuge, taking the form of a confidential letter from the Home Office to chief constables.[47] In the 1920s and 1930s the Home Office publicly disavowed race discrimination among British subjects. When he was questioned in Parliament in December 1925 by Captain Arthur Evans, for example, Joynson-Hicks declared that "no British Subject is required to register" as an alien.[48] For the same reason, the union's impact on the content of specific policies in the 1920s and 1930s has been overestimated. Official racism was "unofficial" between the wars, thus the Home Office was not accountable to the British public for the Coloured Alien Seamen Order or other covert measures.

It is therefore difficult to argue for popular sanction either supporting or opposing racial subordination. The most powerful force mediating, shaping, and subverting official policy was resistance by Black seamen. Throughout the interwar period Black seamen fought to preserve their livelihood, through collective and individual protest. Only pressure from Indian and colonial seamen compelled the India Office and the Colonial Office to resist the Home Office. Incidents of organized protest help to repudiate Black workers' all too common depiction as isolated and politically naive. Indian, Adenese, African, and West Indian seamen and their families well understood their rights as workers. They were aware of their prerogatives as British seamen and subjects, and of the perilous implications of losing them. They obtained legal services, appealed to state ministries, and took direct action. Appropriating the language of fair play and the reciprocal obligations of military service and patriotism, they pressed the state to reconcile their demands with imperialistic rhetoric.

The history of the Coloured Alien Seamen Order not only shows the institutionalization of racial subordination in British state policy and practice, but also demonstrates that race itself is not simply a natural attribute but a political category whose boundaries have been shaped by historical forces. Racial boundaries were contested terrain in Britain in the 1920s and 1930s, and where they were drawn was a question of power.

CHAPTER SEVEN

"The Honour to Belong":
Black Workers and Interracial
Settlements in Interwar Britain

If there is to be further trouble these are the men who are likely to be the
cause as they have made the U.K. their home, they have formed attachments
with white women and are prepared to stubbornly defend what they call their
rights.
                    —Cardiff Chief Constable to the Home Office, 18 June 1919

The capitalist press, including the *Daily Herald*, gave an account which
showed Arabs attacking white men honestly seeking work and the police
coming on the scene to defend the white men. This is a deliberate distortion
aimed at fomenting race riots. . . . The facts are that 2000 seamen, both white
and coloured, were united in a common struggle for better conditions. . . . I
do not stand here to defend myself, but to indict the shipowners, the N.U.S.,
the Labour Government and the Police.
                    —John Dowell, unemployed miner and Seamen's Minority Movement
                    organizer, at the trial *Rex v. Ali Said*, November 1930

ALTHOUGH EMPLOYERS, the state and the union sought in the interwar
years to bar them from Britain, Black seamen continued to migrate and
settle in dockside neighborhoods, forming social networks and institutions
and marrying into local families. The persistence of these interracial settlements posed a tacit challenge to the racial divisions in the maritime
workforce and in the empire as a whole. Bound by personal ties, residents
of these enclaves proved resistant to the imposition of hegemonic racial
barriers, as well as to more overt intervention.

Many white Britons first became aware of the Black population among
them during the seaport riots of 1919. This occasion of widespread pub-

First epigraph: HO45/11017/377969/20 f89. Second: National Union of Seamen
Mss175/L/E/105, 11–13.

licity served to identify Britain's interracial settlements with the ill consequences of the war that ended Britain's global dominance and to reinforce
images of violence, volatility, and irrationality inherited from the colonial
experience. The publicity that accompanied the riots illuminated these
hitherto obscure settlements, and crystallized and articulated attitudes
shaping the state's response to Black working people for the balance of
the century.

The seaport riots of June 1919 occurred in the context of widespread
civil turmoil following the First World War. In Liverpool and the Bristol
Channel ports, Newport, Cardiff, and Barry, crowds of white men and
women invaded racially mixed neighborhoods, pillaging homes, putting
several people in the hospital and a pair in the morgue. In one of the
uglier incidents, Black Navy fireman Charles Wooten was chased from his
home in Upper Pitt Street, Toxteth, to the Queen's Dock, where he was
pushed or fell into the Mersey and drowned amid cries of "Let him
drown!"[1]

Black residents of Britain responded to the violence by reasserting their
rights to live and work in Britain unmolested, premised on their British
citizenship and their participation in the first total war. In the wake of the
riots, "a number of representatives of the coloured men in Liverpool
headed by Mr. D. T. Aleifasakure Toummanah, Secretary of the Ethiopian
Hall," appealed to the people of Liverpool for tolerance and gratitude and
to the British state for protection.

> The coloured men have mostly served in the Forces, Navy and transport.
> They are largely British subjects, and are proud to have been able to have
> done what they have done for the Empire.... The majority of negroes
> at present are discharged solders and sailors without employment....
> Some of us have been wounded, and lost limbs and eyes fighting for the
> Empire to which we have the honour to belong.... We ask for British
> justice, to be treated as true and loyal sons of Great Britain.[2]

Similar meetings were held on the Cardiff docks by a body of Arabs,
Somalis, West Indians, and Egyptians led by an elected spokesman, Dr.
Rufus Fernell, M.D.; and in Hyde Park by London's Society of Peoples
of African Descent, led by Mr. Ellred Taylor.[3]

The aftermath of the riots yielded the first albeit incomplete census of
the Black population of one city, Liverpool, showing that by 1919 Black
workers were already a longstanding presence. The official response included efforts to uproot Black residents from Britain by persuasion or

compulsion, presaging those in London and other ports in the early 1920s, in South Shields in 1930, and in Cardiff and Liverpool again in 1930 and 1931.[4] Black Britons' protests were also echoed in subsequent episodes: invoking their service in the Great War, they refashioned imperial rhetoric to defend their rights as British subjects, defining these rights to include freedom from violence, from exclusion from Britain, and from racial subordination, and to support claims on British resources—not least on the state itself. Thus the 1919 conflicts were neither the beginning nor the end of Black settlement in Britain, but a well-publicized and well-documented episode in Black Britons' struggle to maintain and assert their economic and political rights.

In the wake of the riots, for example, and in spite of countervailing evidence, police and other officials concluded that conflict was the result of Black men and white men competing for the same jobs, housing, and women. Their solution was to remove the source of "irritation," as Liverpool's Lord Mayor John Ritchie put it, by removing Black working men from Britain.[5] The Home Office agreed to deport "those who are not British subjects." As for the rest, "while it is not possible to deport compulsorily any coloured men who are British subjects . . . so far as possible all unemployed coloured men should be induced to return to their own countries as quickly as possible."[6] A state-sponsored repatriation campaign began. Local committees formed to facilitate the collection of men willing to leave the United Kingdom.[7] The Ministry of Labour agreed to provide a £5 resettlement grant and £2 to defray U.K. debts, and solicited voluntary contributions as supplements. Authorities attempted to obtain ships and "persuade" men to board them, efforts in the end only meagerly rewarded.

The repatriation campaign was not very effective. An impediment to wholesale repatriation was Colonial Office reluctance to accept financial responsibility, in particular for spouses: "It was generally agreed that there can be no question of providing a passage at government expense for the European wife of a coloured man." While fiscal stringency was the fundamental reason, the decision also suggests a paternalistic attitude toward white women—incredulity that they might choose the society and culture of their Black husbands. No doubt the authorities also feared that the appearance in the colonies of state sponsored interracial couples might undermine colonial race stratification. In the absence of shipboard facilities, women's departure was delayed indefinitely.[8]

Most significant was men's widespread and emphatic refusal to leave. By 19 June only 50 of the 240 places on the SS *Batango* had been filled, and three vessels painfully extracted from a reluctant Ministry of Shipping proved impossible to fill. The Cardiff Chief Constable was only able to persuade five West Africans to take up the offer and, lest they change their minds, was "escorting them to Liverpool tonight." Of the hundreds of men enumerated in the Liverpool tally, only 59 West Indians were actually repatriated, while of the 450 Cardiff men who originally expressed interest, only 205 had actually embarked by July. Some of them claimed they remained in Britain because of financial arrangements with boardinghouse keepers. With the failure of voluntary repatriation, the authorities contemplated compulsory measures. The Home Office recognized that the men could not be compelled to go in the absence of "special legislation." The police bemoaned the lack of "penal conditions" to use against men "who, having drawn the [maintenance] allowance ... refuse to return home."[9] Depriving a man of relief if he refused repatriation became a common technique of "persuasion" in the 1920s and 1930s.

By 30 July, "some 600 men had actually been repatriated" and the Home Office judged the effort "successful, as apparently the situation was now quiet and there was not rioting." Yet in September they commented in frustration, "These coloured seafaring men prove to be exceedingly difficult to deal with. Anxious to please they willingly signify their desire to be repatriated, but when the opportunity occurs they decline to sail." Their changes of heart were attributed to "the uncertainties of shipping movements," but also to the fact that the men were British subjects. "On this they pride themselves, as also on the knowledge that, as British citizens, they have a right to be and to stay where they please within the Empire."[10]

This pattern continued not only in summer 1919, but in the 1920s and 1930s: however desperate and impoverished, even with terrifying memories of white violence fresh in their minds, few Black men who had any hope of employment in Britain or any means of support opted for "repatriation" to colonial exploitation and subordination. The publicity surrounding the riots also illuminated the social institutions holding Black men in Britain: boardinghouse kin networks; marriage and family ties; social institutions such as the Ethiopian Hall; feelings of patriotism, cultural affinity, and political entitlement. In spite of reports that demobilized "American sailors" and other "outsiders" first brought violence into interracial settlements, official fears of racial violence by white working people were repeatedly invoked in subsequent years, by local police, the Home Office, and even the seamen's union to justify racially repressive measures.[11]

In the 1920s and 1930s, defying intensifying state and union efforts to define and exclude them as outsiders and strangers, Black working men continued to find refuge in British ports. The resultant culturally and racially diverse settlements were not enclaves of transients, as they have been depicted, but were held together by bonds of kinship and personal obligation, impermeable to secular authorities. For precisely this reason, employers, the union, and the state saw interracial settlements in Britain as a threat to the inequalities that sustained the industry's profitability and indeed the imperial system. Justifying official scrutiny and interference, British authorities defamed them as illegitimate and deviant, mobilizing gendered and class-specific as well as colonialist images of moral, racial, and cultural degeneracy.

But as their collective response to the riots suggests, Black Britons did not view themselves or their cultural practices as external to British society or irreconcilable with those of their white workmates, neighbors, and kin. Instead they expressed complex notions of allegiance, belonging, and place that repudiate teleological models of assimilation or monolithic and reified views of ethnicity, nationality, and Britishness. Their identities and loyalties could be plural and overlapping, and could change over time and in response to racial attacks. They articulated an alternative, counterhegemonic and pluralistic vision of Britishness that linked imperial incorporation and military service to political and economic rights.[12] From all these they marshaled resources to resist racial subordination and exclusion. By the 1920s and 1930s, because the authorities ignored their diversity, treating them as monolithically "Black," these disparate networks began to coalesce into a united front against racial attacks and in defense of their rights. At particular historical moments their experience as workers in the same industry and as people resisting racial subordination in British society called forth a sense of common interest that transcended kin and culture but was more complicated than class consciousness alone—a racial identity.[13]

The origin of Black settlement in Britain is obscure, but interwar port settlements probably assumed their modern form in the late nineteenth century, shaped by the labor demands of the mercantile marine. Black men arrived from the colonies both voluntarily and involuntarily. Black seamen might be discharged or abandoned when ill, or deliberately stranded in Britain by employers. Others traveled to the United Kingdom by perfectly legitimate means, whether by working one-way passages or arriving as passengers. Suffering longer periods of unemployment due to race discrimination in the labor market, some moved inland to nonseafaring jobs such as peddling, navvying, coal mining, and factory work.[14]

All of Britain's larger and more familiar interwar Black settlements formed in working-class dockside neighborhoods. The largest settlement, numbering several thousand, was Butetown in Cardiff—also notorious worldwide as Tiger Bay—but substantial settlements, numbering in the hundreds, existed in several other ports. These included Toxteth in Liverpool; Mill Dam and Holborn in South Shields; Stepney, Poplar, and Limehouse in the East End of London; Barry Dock and Newport in the Bristol Channel, and Kingston-upon-Hull.[15] They were near the docks because so many Black working men were or had been seafarers. In addition, dock neighborhoods' historical transiency and disrepute perhaps made them more hospitable to newcomers than "respectable" and more settled neighborhoods inland.[16]

The composition of individual settlements was probably determined in the first instance by the ports of call of various shipping lines. Few Indian seamen landed in Barry or Liverpool in the early 1920s, for example, while Elder Dempster seems to have accounted for Liverpool's West African settlement and, according to social workers, its poverty. Yet the decision to stay in a particular town or locale was a personal one. Black settlers clustered in dockland enclaves, analogous to the Little Italies and Chinatowns in American cities, linked or defined by kinship, culture, language, religion, or other common bonds. Here they had access to shops, cafés, clubs, and boardinghouses run by fellow countrymen: "If the sailor is making his first visit to Stepney...he will be sure of a welcome by the coloured people connected with the local cafe life."[17] In 1912 *The Seaman* fulminated, "Liverpool, as everyone knows, has its Chinatown, a populous community, it has its organizations for the welfare of the cheap labourers from the East, the dark skinned Lascar and the Yellow Oriental."[18] In 1932 Liverpool social investigator David Caradog Jones identified, in addition to Welsh and Scottish "colonies" and "a Jewish ghetto in Brownlow Hill," "racial colonies" including "Chinese in Pitt Street" and larger enclaves of "negroes" in Pitt Street and Upper Canning Street, all in Postal District 8, also known as Toxteth, the cosmopolitan district bounded by the southern docks. "Arabs and Lascars" also lived nearby.[19]

In Butetown, Cardiff's peninsular docklands, Black and "foreign" residents also clustered in ethnic enclaves. Reported the Chief Constable in 1919:

> The coloured men comprised principally West Indians, West Africans, Somalis, Arabs and a few Indians. They live in boarding houses kept by coloured masters in an area bounded on the north by Bridge Street, the east by the Taff Vale Railway not very far distant, on the west by the

Glamorganshire Canal, and on the south by Patrick Street. Some of the Arabs and Somalis live in the northernmost portion of this area but the majority, particularly the West Indian negroes, live in the southern portion. The area is divided by a junction of the Glamorganshire Canal to the West Bute Dock which has two bridges, one in Bute Street and one at East Wharf.

In 1920 the settlement also included Berbers, Egyptians, and Adenese.[20] In South Shields, Adenese and Somalis inhabited the Holborn district adjacent to the maritime district called Mill Dam. Enumerations under the Coloured Alien Seamen Order show that between 1925 and 1939 the distribution and cultural configuration of Black enclaves in particular ports remained relatively stable. These figures, although highly incomplete, suggest a Black population of several thousands, distributed among six or eight major ports and dozens of smaller ones.[21] Many of these neighborhoods, like Liverpool 8 and Stepney, remain centers of Black settlement today.

Perhaps the most important institution in these settlements was the boardinghouse. Unmarried Indian and other Black seamen tended to live in dockside hostels or boardinghouses established especially for seamen, often operated by charities. While most claimed to minister to men regardless of race, nationality, or religion, many Black and especially Islamic seamen felt unwelcomed by other patrons, feared proselytization, or were put off by the presence of games and other activities offending their religious scruples.[22] In practice many Black seamen relied on social networks for housing and maintenance between voyages.

As in Britain, seafaring in India and many of the colonies was a kin- and community-based occupation. Indian and Asian seamen often worked in gangs or crews composed of kinsmen or covillagers, while the West African Kru were a seafaring people. In Bombay men who had wives and families inland lived in seamen's clubs or lodging houses in the port. The *kur*, or Goanese lodging house, served as a sort of mutual benefit club for villagers; a man's "rent" payments sometimes continued while he was at sea, entitling him to "concessions" including death benefit and low-interest loans.[23]

These practices were imported with modifications to Britain. A Somali, West African, or Indian seaman arriving in a British port might seek out a boardinghouse or café run by a man of his nationality, who might also be a kinsman or covillager, and who would find him work, circumventing union race discrimination, and support him through periods of unemployment, evading deportation. These houses offered compatible and familiar company and environment, facilities for religious and dietary observance, and a haven from a sporadically unsympathetic host society. Reported Ministry of Labour investigators B.R. Hunter and G.K. Pollard in 1939, "The Moslem seaman usually resides in communal fashion at an Arab boarding house. He does on occasion obtain a meal at one of the other organisations patronised by white seamen but the recreation amenities which are provided there do not attract him and he prefers the company of his own race and facilities for practising his own religion."[24] Some of these boardinghouses appeared to function more as mutual benefit societies or clubs than businesses. Somali seamen in Cardiff contributed £1 per voyage to a mutual benefit fund, and in 1930 police in Barry reported of the Habr Owal Somalis there, "This tribe as a rule assists one another, whatever money is earned is divided among the whole of the tribe at home, in addition they have a common fund into which they place money for the aid of the sick, and help others in case of need."[25] James Evans, a Ministry of Health investigator, corroborated the practice of "communal feeding" and pooling of resources by "fellow tribesmen" in Cardiff boardinghouses: "These establishments are usually run by persons of their own nationality, the prop.[rietor?] being recouped when the men have secured employment."[26]

In the frequently lengthy periods between voyages, many such boardinghouse keepers permitted their clients, with whom they might have personal or kinship bonds, to remain beyond the exhaustion of their resources, deferring payment until they found employment. A destitute man in a charity hostel would have been turned over to the authorities and quite possibly deported.[27] Thus in attacking boardinghouse keepers the union and the state undercut a critical source of sustenance to Black seamen ashore.

Boardinghouse keepers had a financial stake in their clients' employability and sometimes assisted them in negotiation with employers, acting as employment agents: "One of the Arab boarding house keepers would board the vessel and see the Chief Engineer or the second Engineer, and see whether he could supply a crew." There was imputedly "competition" among the Arab boardinghouse keepers for these commissions. Boardinghouse keepers provided a variety of other services, including processing nationality credentials through the Home Office and the India Office, and interceding with various authorities on their clients' behalf. Like the Italian *padrone* system in America or "crimping" in East London's Jewish community, these networks and institutions could have an unsavory side. Some

boardinghouse keepers had arrangements with employers for direct payment of their clients' wages.[28] Thus arose the possibly accurate but abusable
image of the Arab boardinghouse keeper bleeding his tenants while in
port to keep them in perennial debt to him at sea. Arab, Indian, and
Chinese boardinghouses were a particular target of official ire, denounced
by the state and the union alike.

Charges that boardinghouse keepers were enriched or that Black seamen
were particularly exploited through this system must be weighed against
the customary obligation to keep clients through periods of unemployment, frequently prolonged by race discrimination in the labor market.
Several houses went bankrupt during the depressions of the early 1920s
and the 1930s, and the authorities took the opportunity to deport—
"repatriate"—their unemployed residents.[29] Union membership was com-
mensurately costly and conferred none of these benefits.

Critics charged, perhaps with some justice, that boardinghouse keepers
encouraged Lascars' desertion to jobs at standard rates or as peddlers,
miners, or ironworkers in South Wales or Scotland. Lurid fantasies apart,
the authorities correctly perceived boardinghouses as the medium through
which men gained access to employment and other resources in Britain.
Because the union discouraged the employment of "coloured" men at
standard rates, many quite likely felt compelled to circumvent the normal
channels in order to get work at all. One Mrs. Nairolla, wife of a London
boardinghouse keeper, told authorities in 1923 that "representatives of
the house were . . . set on board ships carrying natives in order to induce
these men to come to the house i.e. encourage the men to desert." The
men did not stay long with Mrs. Nairolla, but "found ships . . . at European
rates of wages . . . and their advance notes taken as payment."[30] This benefited ships' officers and agents who were free to offer them low wages
since they were engaged unofficially. When the alternative was race discrimination through the N.M.B. labor supply system, the boardinghouse,
although possibly exploitative, provided services and a measure of security
to Black seamen ashore in Britain.

The recollections of Harriet Vincent, daughter of an interracial couple
who kept a boardinghouse, indicate that the view local people held of
boardinghouse keepers diverged widely from the image of disrepute and
criminality the authorities held. Mr. Vincent was a Black Nova Scotian of
West Indian descent; Mrs. Vincent a local Welsh woman, daughter of a
ship's pilot. Mr. Vincent had begun shore employment selling confec-
tionery and bakery from a handcart. By the time Harriet was a child her
parents operated a substantial boardinghouse for West Indian seamen, and

sold tea and hot soup to the neighborhood from an attached cookshop. Harriet Vincent's parents, as local merchants and as partners in a "successful" racially mixed marriage, were leaders and role models in Edwardian Bute Town. Mr. Vincent was Grand Master of his local Friendly Society lodge. Their sense of a reputation to uphold was reflected in the strict, "respectable" upbringing they gave their daughters.[31]

Not all boardinghouse keepers and racially mixed marriages may have attained the popularity and good repute the Vincents enjoyed. Yet their marriage, family, and business provide a useful foil to the negative images outsiders promoted about dockside neighborhoods. Their function as community leaders perhaps explains the frustration of union and state officials whose interest in keeping Black men rootless, mobile, and deportable was thwarted by Black boardinghouses and by interracial marriages.

For in addition to these institutional networks, local women helped sustain interracial settlements in Britain. The support of families ashore was critical to men who spent months and years at sea, reflected in the inclusion of wives as nonvoting members in the National African Sailors' and Firemen's Union of Liverpool. In 1935 a defense committee composed of "Malays, Arabs, Somalies, West Indians and Africans" formed to resist the British Shipping Assistance Act, which effectively barred Black seamen from state subsidized ships, boasted of "the unanimous support of the women as well as the men." Wives were more likely to be literate in English and conversant with British institutions and cultural practices and, like Mary Fazel, might assist their husbands in negotiating the treacherous terrain of life ashore. Women were also active in the dockside service sector, acting as informal agents for boardinghouses, and operating cafés, clubs, brothels, and other local businesses: "The cafes can be classified into groups, each group being used by a different section of the coloured community, such as the Muslims or the Negroes, but they are all used by the white women." In the 1940s Stepney's "West Indian club" was managed by a white woman.[32]

In addition, marriage or cohabitation with either a Black or a white woman conferred concrete benefits. The authorities treated single Black men as transients in spite of their presumptive British nationality, seeing their destitution as the opportunity to deport them. But through founding a household a man established domicile in the United Kingdom. This not only freed him to seek better paid work but entitled the family to relief. Especially after the embarrassing John Zarlia affair, such men were also somewhat impervious to deportation, due to "the disinclination of the

Home Office to insist upon the removal of men who, though without British passports, have married white women in Liverpool, or are living with white women and have children by them." Such dependents, if a man was deported, might require relief. Marriage might also integrate a man into local kin networks, giving him resources when unemployed and eroding the social barriers reinforcing racial divisions at work. Social investigator Nancie Hare reported to Britain's League of Coloured Peoples in 1937, "Most of the men have married women from the dock areas, people whose families have lived there for some time and usually the children of docks."[33]

Repudiating assimilationist models of Britishness, interracial marriages exhibited signs of syncretism between husbands' and wives' cultural practices. While some interracial couples encountered social ostracism, others were accepted, even living in the same houses with the wives' parents, a common British working-class residential pattern. Both of Harriet Vincent's maternal aunts were also married to West Indian seamen. The three sisters and their parents lived near each other and visited frequently, consistent with working-class custom. The flexibility of racial identities was reflected in Hare's report that many white wives identified with the Black community: "They take sides with them; they include themselves in the category of 'coloured,' and talk of 'we'" as well as joining Black social organizations. Black fathers had a reputation for spending more time and money on their wives and children and less in the pubs than white working-class men. One of Hare's informants amused her by exclaiming, "I wouldn't change my husband for fifty white men!"[34] Such evidence suggests that Black and white working people could be as bound together by marriage and kinship as divided by race, and that Britishness could coexist with a variety of cultural practices.

Owing to a scarcity of Black women, couples typically comprised a Black husband and a white wife. Still, there were some Black women in Britain's seaport neighborhoods, and as in other racially mixed societies Black men married them when they were available. Although numerically small, their presence serves as tacit repudiation of the stress on Black and white men competing only for white women, racist in its view of Black women as less desirable, and sexist in its view of all women as passive in gender relations. Although silence has all but blotted these women from the historical record, what we know of their experiences suggests that the boundary between Black and white could shift from generation to generation, and that kin ties cut across and problematized racial barriers.

Women of color in interwar Britain were as disparate as their menfolk.

At the time of the Liverpool riots, the Chief Constable reported a Jamaican and a Liverpool-born Black wife among Black seafarers and their families applying for repatriation to the colonies. David Caradog Jones found six British-born "half-caste" women over forty-five years of age in his 1939 survey. In Stepney in 1942 the survey team enumerated twelve "coloured" women, including Malayans, West Africans, and two of mixed race, including a "half-caste Indian".[35] Indeed, the most visible and well-documented women of color in interwar Britain were the racially ambiguous daughters of interracial couples.

Social workers and observers had difficulty classifying children of interracial couples in Britain's racial hierarchy. Nancie Hare reported, "In appearance they vary from completely white to almost completely coloured. Usually the mixture of blood is obvious and noone would think most of the children were either pure Negro or pure white." In 1939 Caradog Jones somewhat tentatively defined "coloured families" as "the families of West Africans or West Indians who marry white women." A 1942 survey described all of the 136 children in their sample, including the 116 with white mothers, as "coloured" or "Colonial children."[36]

The story of Harriet Vincent is again pertinent, for as the offspring of an interracial marriage, Harriet was one of the children outsiders disparaged as "half-caste," and for whom they predicted a dire fate. As children of local merchants and community leaders, Harriet and her sister and brothers were raised in a strict "respectable" style; well fed, clothed, and shod to middle-class standards and expected to maintain "polite" norms of etiquette and behavior. Their father, a teetotaler and ardent Nonconformist, kept his daughters away from the male boarders and closely supervised Harriet's dates. In the Vincents' family life, class status overshadowed racial difference, reflecting these settlements' reputed interracial harmony. Yet Harriet's individual experience as she matured fits observers' accounts of Black women's and girls' disadvantaged lives in interwar Britain a generation later. Her neighborhood friends were white girls, but race affected girls' employment prospects: "very dark ones couldn't get a job." When Harriet herself married, both times it was to Barbadian seamen.

Harriet's own identity was founded on the racial tolerance her parents taught and she herself embodied: "Well I can't call one black nor I can't call one white. My father was black, my mother was white, and I had to respect both." Still, what Paul Thompson correctly saw as Harriet's downward social mobility, from a comfortable upbringing as the daughter of local businesspeople, to marriage into working-class adulthood, was also downward mobility within Britain's racial hierarchy. In the course of becoming a woman she had become Black in British eyes and in the eyes of her community.[37] As the experiences of British girls and women of mixed race illustrate, kin ties transgressed racial boundaries from generation to generation, confounding rigid definitions of racial difference and their attendant disabilities. Racial positioning could shift in the life course of individuals, shaped by age, gender, family, and economic relations. Black women in small numbers and white women in larger numbers not only sustained Britain's interracial settlements, but were critical participants in the breakdown of racial barriers.

Dozens of religious, fraternal, and social networks, some culturally homogeneous, but others multicultural, also sustained Black people in Britain. Although in some ports such as Hull, Black and white seamen and residents shared the same facilities, most ports featured institutions and organizations established for and often by specific Black religious, cultural or kin groups.[38] In the late 1930s the Islamia Allawia Friendly Society, for instance, located at 216 Bute Street, Cardiff, "formed for the purpose of providing a meeting place for Moslem seamen. . . . [and] aims at uniting all members of the Moslem community in the port."

> One large room on the ground floor . . . is carpeted and furnished in Eastern style. Arab newspapers and copies of the Koran are provided. There are no facilities for games or any other form of recreation as these are understood to be contrary to the true practice of the Moslem religion. At the rear of the premises a large room is used for religious services and a priest is in attendance at various times during the day.

Apart from this large facility, four other Cardiff boardinghouses provided prayer rooms: "A Moslem priest or mufti resides in the district and he and his two assistants conduct services daily at each of the five boarding houses." In spite of assaults on its integrity in the 1930s, the Islamic community appeared to be burgeoning in 1939, having "acquired four houses which they propose to demolish and, when funds permit, to build a mosque at which all Moslems can attend."[39] Local organizations were also knit together by a number of national bodies such as the Somali Association of Great Britain; the Islamic Association of Great Britain, which came to South Shields seamen's aid in 1930; and the London-based League of Coloured Peoples.[40] This less-politicized institutional infrastructure supported the numerous organizations formed over the years to defend Black settlers from official assaults.

In addition, many facilities, such as missions and institutes, were provided by British charities and churches. Outsiders tended to view Black people's use of such institutions as evidence they lacked their own institutional structure, as well as to draw spurious distinctions between the Black resident population and seamen who, as transients, they excluded by definition from any sort of community. Yet London's Black residents explicitly appropriated one such seamen's hostel, identifying sojourning seamen as their own.

Since the 1850s the Strangers' Home for Asiatic Seamen in West India Dock Road, Limehouse, had housed Indian seamen ashore in Britain. In 1935 its British sponsors, the Asiatic and Overseas Society, closed the facility, citing lack of funds and "lack of patronage and support over a period of years." The Jumait-ul-Muslmin (Muslim Association) of East London protested the closing, articulating a complex sense of identity, place, and entitlement. Identifying the organization as "the representatives of the peoples of Asia resident in Aldgate, Poplar and other parts of East London," they appealed to the High Commissioner for India. They expressed "grave concern" at the prospective "disappearance of a place of refuge for the peoples of Asia in London," and asked to participate in discussions designed to keep the home open. They legitimated their sense of proprietorship by reminding the High Commissioner that money from Punjabi Prince Victor Daleep Singh had built the facility. Their suggestion that the home be made available to "seamen of other parts of Asia and Africa" implied recognition of a common need for "a place of refuge" from the unreliable hospitality of the Mother Country.[41]

Although unsuccessful, this effort by the Jumait-ul-Muslmin indicates Asian seamen, even if they lived in a hostel like the Strangers' Home, were accepted as part of the larger Asian community. Hostile observers' perception that Black residents of Britain were a transitory "problem" arising inadvertently and regrettably from the vagaries of the shipping industry is contradicted by the evidence of how they saw themselves—in this case as residents of Aldgate and Poplar; as part of an Asian community in London. As this episode illustrates, Black people in interwar Britain, like many other migrants, held overlapping allegiances to neighborhood; to birthplace, to networks in London, and to global networks of Black seafarers and of colonized people. Their identities similarly overlapped: as seafarers, as imperial subjects, as natives of Aden or Bengal or Lagos, as residents of Poplar, as members of local organizations and families. The oversimplified view of the migration and assimilation process presupposing a gradual transformation from a monolithic allegiance to traditional cultures to indistinguishability from what scholars optimistically call "the host culture" slights the complex subjectivities of living people, each with personal as well as collective identities. Such evidence complicates homogeneous and static models of ethnicity in general and Britishness in particular.

The incident also shows that Asians, Africans, and other colonized people in London understood their common relationship to the white residents of the city and indeed of the empire; they saw themselves, if not as a unified Black community, at least as people with common problems, related to race. In each port, indeed, enclaves of Chinese, Arabs, Africans, West Indians, and Asians coexisted, each possessing individual character and autonomy and social and religious functions, yet prepared to unite politically against actions based on a monolithic racial definition imposed from outside, as well as to join with white working people to resist labor exploitation.[42] For white working people's understandings of racial difference, belonging, and Britishness were as complicated, inconsistent, and contested as those of Black port residents or of the white elites who made imperial policy. Residents of racially mixed dockside neighborhoods exhibited an admittedly parochial definition of entitlement to work in which race was only one among a range of factors, such as longevity in the trade and the locality, defining a man's right to live and work there. It appears that explicitly racial conflict was brought to these settlements by outsiders, including employers, the union, local officials, police, and social workers—and by the policies of the central state. Harriet Vincent reported that violence entered Edwardian Butetown with weekend football crowds, for example, whereas demobilized war veterans were prominent among the rioters of 1919.[43] In the 1930s as in 1919, the flashpoints of conflict illuminated the workaday contours of interracial relations in the ports.

The imputed incident of racial conflict in Salford resembled another alleged "race riot" in North Shields in May 1930: conflict arose when employers attempted to sign Black seamen from a distant port in Shields. A scuffle in Hartlepool in February 1930 occurred when local men sought to repel South Shields Arabs. In each case the objections of the rank and file, Black and white, were against the importation of nonlocal men of any race or nationality to take jobs while local men were unemployed. The migration or importation of white seamen from distant ports also prompted complaints. In each case it was apparently N.U.S. officials, the local press, and employers who provoked racial conflicts or interpreted the incidents in racial terms. Even George Reed, N.U.S. District Secretary for the Bristol Channel, alleged that "riots" in Barry had resulted from "the importation of seamen from Cardiff to sign in various ships."[44]

From Salford police testimony and what we know of the division of labor in seafaring, moreover, men deprived of jobs by nonlocal Arabs would likely have been local Black men, probably Arabs, not white seamen at all. Still, white seamen stood in solidarity with local African and Arab seamen in Salford. Even though the National Union of Seamen used incidents like these to promote anti-Black propaganda, they actually suggest a localistic moral economy in which white and Black seamen's main objection was to nonlocal men.[45] This bias was muddled with racial difference by the union and by shipboard racial divisions. It was intensified by owners' maintaining their preference for crews who could be paid less by N.M.B.-enshrined "custom": importing Black stokehold crews from a distant port if insufficient Black seamen were available locally, employers paraded them before unemployed local men to the National Maritime Board offices. Thus it appears not merely the scarcity of jobs but the manipulation of racial divisions that provoked violence.

These and similar incidents suggest that among working people, and particularly within interracial dockside settlements, racial difference was but one of several considerations affecting a man's entitlement to work. Some authorities may have been inclined to interpret violence and protest in the ports as interracial conflict because it affirmed their own agendas and lent credibility to policies such as the Coloured Alien Seamen Order and repatriation to which, however ineffectually, they were already committed. The incidents also cast doubt on the reliability of press interpretations of interracial incidents, filtered as they were through a lens of relative power and privilege.[46] They compel us to look beyond visceral popular racism or even simple competition for jobs and scarce resources to explain racial conflict, to the powerful institutional actors who structured scarcities along racial lines.

Interracial networks did not exist in a political vacuum. Their very formation constituted defiance of imperial hierarchies, but, in addition, as we know, from 1919 some local authorities and the central state cooperated in attempts to prevent additions to interracial settlements and to dismantle those already existing. In addition to seafaring, in the 1920s and 1930s Black working men were integrated into seaports in a variety of occupations. Yet even when Black men were not seamen the authorities assumed they once had been, viewing them as stowaways, deserters from labor contracts, drifters, and potential criminals. A common though conspicuously unsubstantiated charge was trafficking in discharge papers, the seaman's work credential and record of service. Men in shore occupations, café proprietors, and peddlers were also criminalized. Many authorities treated all Black working people as an anomalous presence who rightly belonged in the colonies and who ought to be "repatriated." Yet as constraints on state efforts to remove them only clarified, if they were subjects they were legally entitled to remain. It is little wonder that a Somali, Adenese, or Bengali might choose to live in the United Kingdom where he could sign on European articles for several times the pay of a labor contract negotiated in India or Aden. We have seen that immigration authorities were repeatedly frustrated by local magistrates' reluctance to convict accused "deserters" and "stowaways" or holders of allegedly forged documents, in the absence of evidence and on the assumption they were British subjects.[47]

There were more repatriation campaigns in 1920 and 1921.[48] The "offer" of repatriation was extended not merely for the men's protection but to serve purposes congenial to the state. Efforts in 1919 were nominally designed for genuinely stranded men, but as years passed the authorities grew increasingly hostile to Black British residents. Intensified intervention in interracial settlements may have reflected the limits of policy such as the Coloured Alien Seamen Order and the Elder Dempster Agreements as well as heightened disaffection in the colonies and corresponding bargaining and ambivalence in the metropole.

In addition, the fortunes of merchant shipping had an influence. With the Depression competition for jobs intensified, as did employers' efforts to maximize profits through racial divisions and the union's to manipulate these divisions to enhance its credibility. Invigorated N.U.S. efforts to replace Black with white crews prompted the rota and other efforts to control Black workers by undermining their self-sufficient institutions. Deportation of Black workers appeared a panacea for economic distress. Jobless Black seamen's visibility embarrassed local authorities, while their imputed threat to civil peace renewed Board of Trade and Home Office concern. Removing a small number of Black workers did little to solve the fundamental problems of global depression and moribund industry, nor did it significantly diminish numbers of unemployed maritime workers. Yet repatriation schemes were a means by which local and national authorities could be seen to take action, at little cost, and without threatening the union or employers.

Overt intervention in interracial settlements focused on the very institutions that enabled Black men to survive in Britain institutions already under stress due to the Depression. The central government deliberately withheld financial assistance from local authorities, boardinghouse keepers, and individuals who requested it, until men were so desperate they would accept repatriation.[49] Thus in the acute economic crisis of the early 1930s,

Black settlements in such places as Liverpool, Cardiff, and South Shields were eroded as the unemployed were starved out and shipped off to the colonies.

By July 1930 the Chief Constable of Cardiff reported a desperate situation prevailing among Somali seamen in the port: "A year ago there was £400 in a fund which this tribe had built up for mutual help in time of difficulty but this had now been exhausted. Some of them are drawing unemployment relief. Generally they object to parish relief which they regard as charity and in one or two instances institutional relief which alone can be offered to single men has been refused."[50] In Cardiff and Barry Somali seamen refused to apply to the Public Assistance Committee for indoor relief, as it would preclude seeking work: Yusuf Mohamed, who had served in British ships since 1925, declared "he did not want relief, only an opportunity to follow his occupation as a marine fireman." Mohamed Ismael, spokesman for the Habr Owal Somalis in Barry Dock, appealed to the Shipping Federation and the union, explaining that "our faith will not allow us to beg" and rejecting repatriation: "All we want is work, . . . all we ask is to be given a fair chance when we are endeavouring to get a ship." By mid-July 1930 Cardiff Poor Law authorities were prepared to offer limited relief payments, as they had in 1921 and 1923. As Cardiff was one of few South Wales municipalities prepared to relieve Black workers, unemployed men converged on Cardiff and became ghettoized there, unable to seek work or relief elsewhere in South Wales.[51]

The rota, instituted in summer 1930 in South Wales, Hull, and Tyneside, only aggravated unemployment, further straining boardinghouse keepers' resources. From October 1930 the Home Office simultaneously restricted access to peddling licenses, one of Black seamen's principal options for shore employment. Protests against the rota by Arab and Somali seamen and boardinghouse keepers changed the sympathy of some local police to alarm. In Cardiff, Arab seamen boycotted the rota, and Cardiff boardinghouse keepers hired a solicitor and planned a deputation to the Home Office. As in the 1920s, the central government, when approached for assistance by local relief authorities and boardinghouse keepers, offered only repatriation.[52]

In this context, the official image of Black boardinghouse keepers deteriorated from sympathetic and legitimate community leaders to impediments to Black workers' removal.[53] The actual role of the boardinghouse keeper was largely obscured by the 1930s in a barrage of innuendo. The seamen's union likened him to the nineteenth-century "crimp," depicting the union as the champion of the exploited Arab seaman, "slave" to the

Mr. ALI HAMED DELHI,

SEAMEN'S BOARDING HOUSE AND
REFRESHMENT HOUSE KEEPER,

95 and 103, West Holborn, South Shields.

Mohamed Silam, Debt. he owes me ... £45 0 0	Mathana Rajeb, Debt, he owes me ... £71 10 0	
Saleh Hassan. Debt. he owes me ... £33 0 0	Guide Hassine. Debt, he owes me ... £34 10 0	
Naser Assam. Debt. he owes me ... £30 0 0	Mohamed Said, No. 3. Debt, he owes me £47 0 0	
Abdul Milek. Debt. he owes me ... £20 0 0	Hassen Ahmed. Debt. he owes me ... £53 0 0	
Abdulla Salim, Debt. he owes me ... £35 0 0	Guide Said, Debt, he owes me ... £21 0 0	
Ahmed Mahomed, Debt. he owes me ... £31 0 0	Ali Ahmed. Debt. he owes me ... £46 10 0	
Mohamed Ahmood. Debt. he owes me ... £51 0 0	Redman Guide, Debt, he owes me ... £60 0 0	
Hassan Mohamed, Debt, he owes me ... £49 0 0	Maldi iSaid. Debt, he owes me ... £41 0 0	
Said Fada, Debt, he owes me ... £29 0 0	Mohamed Murshad. Debt, he owes me ... £35 10 0	
Mohamed Ali, Debt. he owes me ... £39 0 0	Dnifulla Mehsen. Debt. he owes me ... £69 0 0	
Saleh Mohamed. Debt. he owes me ... £42 10 0	Nag Saleh, Debt, he owes me ... £30 0 0	
Saleh Hamed, No. 1. Debt. he owes me £61 0 0	Ali Mohamed, Debt. he owes me ... £41 0 0	
Nassar Ali, Debt, he owes me ... £41 0 0	Mohamed Hussen, Debt, he owes me ... £43 0 0	
Said Saleh, Debt, he owes me ... £34 0 0	Ahmed Mahomed, Debt. he owes me ... £40 0 0	
Mohamed Said, No. 1, Debt. he owes me £36 10 0	Ali Hamed, Debt. he owes me ... £45 0 0	
Saleh Messen, Debt. he owes me ... £41 10 0	Mohamed Abdulla. Debt. he owes me ... £39 0 0	
Mohamed Hassan, Debt, he owes me ... £51 0 0	Mohamed Shemson. Debt. he owes me ... £75 0 0	
Ali Ahmed, Debt. he owes me ... £61 10 0	Ali Mohamed, Debt. he owes me ... £30 0 0	
Ahmed Hassen, Debt. he owes me ... 47 10 0	Ali Mosleh, Debt. he owes me ... £29 0 0	
Garnum Chuman, Debt. he owes me ... £81 10 0	Mohamed Newmann, Debt. he owes me £48 0 0	
Sala Hamed. No, 2. Debt, he owes me ... £39 10 0	Zaid Abdulla. Debt. he owes me ... £29 0 0	
Krist Mohamed, Debt, he owes me ... £48 10 0	Saleh Nasser. Debt. he owes me ... £51 0 0	
Mohamed Said, No. 2. Debt, he owes me £49 10 0	Salah Abdulla. Debt, he owes me ... £29 0 0	
Ahmed Saleh. Debt, he owes me ... £35 10 0	Mohamed Abdula. Debt. he owes me ... £33 0 0	
Ali Batash. Debt. he owes me ... £24 10 0	Wais Abdul Kader, Debt, he owes me ... £61 0 0	
Mohamed Mosley, Debt. he owes me ... £69 10 0	Hamood Alwa, Debt, he owes me ... £71 0 0	
Ahmed Alwen. Debt, he owes me ... £51 0 0	Ali Ahmed, Debt, he owes me ... £81 0 0	

SIR,   WEDNESDAY, 10/9/1930.

Enclosed list of Arab Seamen unemployed, and the debt they owe me only, up to the present date, all are in the National Seamen's Union, paying 1/- per week ; unemployment being due to this Rota Scheme brought forward by the National Union for Seamen and the Federation Officials.

The Arab and Somali refuse to take the Rota Scheme, because it is not justice to number the said two races of Coloured Seamen. and not every other coloured race, namely. Malaya. Chinese, Indian, African, and not to mention the Foreigner, such as Maltese, Greeks. Norwegian, Danish. Swedish, and many others.

This list of Arab Seamen's names are proved British Subjects, or Protected persons, their proofs having been forwarded from Aden through the Colonial Office. London, and therefore are entitled to all help and aid a Britisher can give them in or out of England.

This only refers to the said mentioned Arabs, and does not include any other Arab or Somali who has taken the Rota Scheme or intends to do so in the future.

This tribe of Arabs mentioned are natives of Dheli, Towahi, Aden, Arabia. and wish to seek employment on British Ships in the old way and not under the Rota System. as early as can possibly be done, as some of them have been idle over one year, or more, and any funds of any description will be gladly received. or the last resource for the N.U.S. to pay all the said mentioned Debts, and send the men to their own home.

Signed, yours,
ALI HAMED.
born Mehakum, Dheli,
Towahi, Aden,
Arabia.

Present address :—103. West Holborn, South Shields.

6. List of debtors published by boardinghouse keeper Ali Hamed Dheli, protesting his clients' unemployment induced by the rota, 1930. Dheli's name was misspelled by the typesetter of the placard. Reproduced by permission of the Keeper of the Public Records.

Mephistopholean boardinghouse keeper. Although the union produced no evidence to substantiate its charges of smuggling rings and enslavement, the images acquired credence among police and civil servants, in particular Home Office personnel, who routinely assumed that boardinghouse keepers engaged in criminal activity.

By far the most serious instance of official interference in a Black settlement occurred in Tyneside in August 1930, where the techniques successful in Cardiff backfired. In Tyneside the Seamen's Minority Movement successfully linked Arab and Somali seamen's boycott of the rota with their ongoing campaign against the hated PC5. In summer 1930 they held a series of rallies on the Mill Dam in front of the union and Shipping Federation offices. Some local union officials supported them, embarrassing the national Executive Council. In union leaders' view, successful imposition of the rota was critical and "the crux of the whole position lay in South Shields." General Secretary W. R. Spence visited South Shields three times in late summer 1930 and missed the T.U.C. Annual Conference to man the N.U.S. Head Office during August.[54]

The Home Office too was alarmed by this interracial movement. They cooperated with South Shields police and the Board of Trade to divert South Shields boardinghouse keepers Ali Said and Ali Hassan Dheli, whom they scorned in racialized terms as "these brave warriors . . . on the warpath," from their intended visit to Whitehall. They hoped that "if this move is frustrated . . . the new system will be accepted by the coloured Colonies on the Tyne." The events of summer and autumn 1930 show a convergence of interest among these different parties. The state's interest was evident in an intense correspondence between the Home Office and South Shields before and during the August 1930 disturbances.[55]

In August 1930 a confrontation on the Mill Dam between Arab seamen and Seamen's Minority Movement activists on the one hand and police and union officials on the other became violent. A melee ensued when two white men, alleged *agents provocateurs* shouting racial epithets and brandishing weapons, declared their intention to sign on jobs vacated by boycotting Arabs. In addition to several Minority Movement activists, a number of Arab seamen were arrested and deported. Among them were boardinghouse keeper and community spokesman Ali Said and Minority Movement Treasurer George Verschelde, although witnesses testified neither was on the Mill Dam during the violence. The union and police recognized boardinghouse keepers such as Ali Said as local leaders. Ali Said had been an antagonist of the N.U.S., who denounced him as "one of the 'shining lights' of the Arab Boarding House Keepers' Fraternity in South Shields." In the trial at Durham Assizes, a South Shields police constable testified, "In all cases where we have had trouble with the Arab community, Ali Said has been at the bottom of it.... He is a cute, crafty man." All of the defendants denied participating in the violence and evidence against several was purely circumstantial. Both the prosecutor and the judge appeared ignorant of trade union politics and from the beginning to the end of the trial were unable to identify individual defendants in the dock before them or to recall previous testimony.

The Home Office hoped the harsh sentences meted out in Durham would have the "salutary effect of convincing coloured alien seamen generally and their white accomplices and instigators that disorder will be firmly dealt with."[56] Of the Tyneside seamen now blacklisted from the rota, the Home Office commented, "So long as they remained an incubus on the coloured boarding house keepers, the sooner the system under which many of them had no doubt gained admission to this country would be destroyed."[57] Because boardinghouses offered support and an alternative to the union, local and national authorities wished to detach Black seamen from them. The events of late 1930 reveal pressure on boardinghouses, whether financial, as in Cardiff, or forcible, as in South Shields, that undermined the larger networks of which they were a critical part.

For the same reason, throughout the 1920s and 1930s official and unofficial assaults on Black working men involved attacks on the women and families who sustained them. In spring 1932 the Board of Trade responded to unemployment in Liverpool with unilateral action. Since men's access to passports made them immune to deportation, the authorities decided to eliminate their passports. First they ceased issuing passports or Certificates of Nationality at the source in West Africa, making them available only to men domiciled in the United Kingdom and, incidentally, depriving British subjects in West Africa of the means to prove their nationality. Second, after December 1932 passports were replaced by special certificates of limited validity, rendering men virtually unemployable, for shipmasters were reluctant to hire undocumented men whom they could not discharge in foreign ports. The only men now immune from deportation were those who had fathered children in Britain. Men lacking passports or "family ties" were termed "removable men," to be deported from Liverpool within the month. To prevent them establishing domicile in the interim, Immigration Officer P. N. Davies suggested they ought to be incarcerated: "Unless the men are held in prison, several would set about establishing domicile by formal or informal marriages." Davies reluctantly discarded this idea, fearing "an outcry both here and on the Coast."[58]

However callous, such remarks acknowledged women's centrality to interracial port settlements. The authorities viewed Black men's efforts to form families and settle into the wider society with alarm. Outsiders focused on racially mixed couples because these partnerships transgressed the race and gender boundaries upholding British imperial power, as well as the racial stratification in the shipping industry. Union spokesmen, employers, and civil authorities denounced Black men's marriages with white women as deviant and ignored Black women's existence. They impugned dockside settlements as sites of race and gender disorder. The press interpreted the riots of 1919, for example, as the legitimate reassertion of white male authority over women and Black people in response to its perceived erosion in the war: "A foolish woman and a negro may easily cause a serious riot, for the white man will not put up with it."[59] Invective against white women who married Black men accompanied overt constraints on Black men's freedom to live and marry in Britain.

Slanders against Black boardinghouse keepers were echoed in the lurid language describing Black and interracial families in interwar Britain. The authorities' ample material reasons for opposing interracial marriages were reinforced and justified by the ideologies of moral and racial inferiority, sexual degeneracy, and eugenics inherited from the colonial experience but adapted to immediate uses. The recurrent motif of many a shipowner's or union spokesman's jeremiad was the peril of sexual relations between Black men and white women. Government officials parroted their complaints. Thus in 1926 when pressing Elder Dempster's case on the Home Office, E. N. Cooper wrote, "Mr Fudge, who has now acquired a very intimate knowledge of the workings of the native mind, assures me that the height of ambition of the native West African is to get a white woman, preferably with children, to live with him and to qualify for the dole. These women are generally prostitutes of a very low type."[60]

As Cooper's remark suggests, the defamation of interracial couples involved portraying both partners as unfit, in class-based and gendered terms as well as racial ones: idle, unproductive, unmanly men, and women of mean estate, easy virtue, and dubious maternal qualities. Ideological and cultural factors apart, the principal reason the authorities mistrusted Black and interracial families and networks in British ports was because these institutions impeded them from disposing of Black workers as they wished. The construction of a norm of racially endogamous heterosexuality and its denial to Britain's Black working men, impugning the homosocial milieu of the seamen's boardinghouse and labeling interracial families deviant, reinforced overt assaults on Black men's political and economic status. Thus Black settlements' persistence must be appreciated in the context of repeated attacks, both overt and covert, by local and national authorities, police and other outsiders.

For in addition to kin networks and to cultural, religious, and social organizations, Black residents of Britain formed numerous organizations with explicitly political agendas, to defend themselves against attacks on their livelihoods and their claims on British resources. By the 1920s and 1930s many of these organizations were multicultural in character, incorporating Africans, Asians, West Indians, and Arabs, catalyzed by intensifying intrusion by employers, the union, local governments, and the central state. The National African Sailors' and Firemen's Union (N.A.S.F.U.) was an early example of an organization incorporating social, political, and trade union agendas.[61] Founded in 1920, and composed principally of West Africans, the N.A.S.F.U. was based in Liverpool 8, the city's historically Black neighborhood. The organization's constitution reflected political and social as well as strictly bread-and-butter issues. Membership was open to "all coloured persons" engaged in any aspect of seafaring and honorary membership was available to other interested parties, including "unlimited members of persons of both sexes." One N.A.S.F.U. goal was "to promote amity and a better understanding between the coloured races and others of a different race." The union's founders apparently recognized racial conflict as prejudicial to the promotion of their "pure" trade union goals, such as affiliation with other unions, improvement of wages and working conditions, and the seamen's franchise.

In spite of its ambitious beginning, the N.A.S.F.U. succumbed to problems endemic to seafarers and especially Black ones. Unemployment and mobility, two forces always hampering seamen's organization, crippled the N.A.S.F.U. By June 1923 all but four of the original dozen or so officers had returned to Africa. Of the three remaining in Liverpool, one, Tom Orrama, now worked elsewhere in the city. Only General Secretary S. S. Ross was currently at sea. The union president, Mr. A. O. Ezenwaighhebu, had been imprisoned in Lagos after journeying there to set up a union branch and allegedly misappropriating union funds.

The brief, poignant history of the N.A.S.F.U. illustrates the problems Black seamen faced in attempting to organize in defense of their rights as workers and British subjects. Seafaring took a man away from his home for lengthy periods, subjecting him to shipboard discipline of the most arbitrary and unfettered nature, and often as not discharging him in a distant port to wait indefinitely for a berth on a home-bound ship. Unemployment might drive a man temporarily or permanently from seafaring into another trade.[62] The difficulty of appealing to workers in the colonies from the United Kingdom was compounded by the hazards of returning to the homeland with its repressive colonial administrations hostile to political and union activity.

Yet by the 1930s organizations founded by and for Black seamen and other residents flourished in many of Britain's interracial settlements, some in explicit response to the enhanced repression accompanying the Depression. The Seamen's Minority Movement, a white-dominated rank-and-file movement, whose leader, George Hardy, was a former Wobblie turned Communist, organized rallies in Poplar, a seafaring district of East London, attended by Black and white Londoners protesting global racial issues such as the Scottsboro case in the United States and the Abyssinian crisis. But Black workers were galvanized to political action by immediate threats to their livelihood posed by such measures as Cardiff's "colour-bar" means test, which paid Black-headed households less relief than white-headed ones; and the British Shipping Assistance Act of 1935, which effectively excluded Black seamen from subsidized ships.[63]

The Cardiff Coloured Seamen's Committee, headed by longtime N.U.S. activist Harry O'Connell, formed in 1933 to combat the union's burgeoning anti-Black campaign. A rank-and-file trade union organization, the committee was in contact with both *The Negro Worker*, a publication of the Red International of Labor Unions, and the self-help organization the League of Coloured Peoples (L.C.P.). It was the first to draw L.C.P. attention to the British Shipping Assistance Act. In the late 1930s its successor, the Colonial Defence Association, aided by the L.C.P. and W. Arthur Lewis in particular, successfully challenged the colour bar in Cardiff's means test. In mid-1934 the Coloured Nationals Mutual Social Club formed in North Shields. Comprised "chiefly of West Africans, West Indians, Indians and Malays," the club welcomed "coloured Nationals . . . irrespective of creed or religion." On 27 May 1935 the club and "other coloured seamen of North and South Shields" heard impassioned speeches by Shapurji Saklatvala, Communist M.P., denouncing the discrimination accompanying the British Shipping Assistance Act.[64]

In London the British Shipping Assistance Act prompted the formation of the Coloured Colonial Seamen's Association of "Indians, Negroes, Arabs, Somalis, Malays and Chinese." Founded in mid-1935, and led by

President Chris Jones (a.k.a. Chris Braithewaite) and Secretary Surat Alley, an Indian labor organizer, the association remained active in the late 1930s. Arnold Ward of the Negro Welfare Association was also apparently associated with the organization. In November 1935, perhaps under pressure of events, the Negro Welfare Association too broadened its appeal to "non-Negroes who agree with the aims and objects of the Association." In November 1936 the First Annual Convention of the Colonial Seamen's Association met in London. Attended by fifty-one delegates including representatives of the Negro Welfare Association, the Indian Swaraj League, the League Against Imperialism, the Cypriot Club, and the League of Coloured Peoples, the conference denounced the colour bar and the British Shipping Assistance Act, invoking Black seamen's and subjects' service in the Great War.[65]

In this way, a multicultural Black political identity emerged among working men in interwar in Britain, catalyzed by official actions such as the closing of the Strangers' Home, the racially discriminatory Cardiff means test, and the British Shipping Assistance Act. This nascent Black British identity coexisted with but transcended religious, cultural, and linguistic diversity. It formed not only because of monolithic race discrimination by national and local authorities, but in spite of employers' and unions' efforts to "divide and rule" through such devices as the rota and other labor control measures. Official racial divisiveness backfired. Black workers responded by organizing to resist, invalidating both elites' divisive efforts and scholarly assumptions that racial violence was the inexorable consequence of heightened economic competition.[66] Thus "racial" identity formed in a process of struggle analogous to but not identical with class formation; instead, "racial" identity overlapped and intersected with Black working people's identities as part of both a global and a local British working class.

This evidence challenges the conventional view of Black people as outsiders to the British working class, and conflict as a product of their differences. Instead, it seems more sensible to understand working-class culture as diverse and fluid, complicated by patterns of global migration, formed through global as well as local processes of labor exploitation. Black people in interwar Britain enjoyed a measure of integration into or at least mutual toleration with the white working people among whom they lived, worked, and married. This mutual toleration was not unproblematic. Class, cultural and religious divisions and even conflicts remained, but violence was neither endemic nor ineluctable. As Black settlers asserted their identity as British, their sense of belonging was not uncontested, but we must pay greater attention to who took part in these struggles and to their goals and methods before the "intolerance" of British working people can be assumed.

In spite of repeated assaults between 1919 and World War II, Black people remained part of local port populations. Their ability to survive and resist lay in their capacity to organize across barriers of culture and race. Thus in the course of the 1920s and 1930s a multicultural Black British identity emerged, in a process of struggle against assaults by white elites, built from the raw materials of social institutions and kin networks in which Black and white women played a critical role. Black workers and multiracial settlements, if embattled, persisted, until the return of global war brought them once again to prominence.

CHAPTER EIGHT

"Getting Out of Hand":
Black Service and
Black Activism in "The People's War"

Mr. Lall impressed on me that it was absolutely essential that in these times the officers of vessels carrying lascar crews should treat the lascars properly and above all should listen patiently to what the lascars had to say. Mr. Lall is convinced that if the lascars are properly treated by their officers it will be possible to get them into a reasonable state of mind, and even to appeal to them on patriotic grounds.
—Board of Trade Mercantile Marine Department, 1939

If we are fighting for liberty, we cannot set the bounds to the advance of other races which look to us for their welfare. We must avoid any reproach that, when we blamed Hitler for his poisonous doctrine of the Herrenvolk, we had a similar doctrine lurking in our own hearts.
—Lord Moyne, Secretary of State for the Colonies, 1941

WORLD WAR II enhanced Black seamen's and workers' bargaining position, and like other British working people, they sought to apply the painful lessons of the Great War to secure lasting benefits. The empire's vulnerability to low morale and adverse publicity and Black workers' importance to the war effort enhanced their leverage with employers and the state. But the expansion of opportunity presented by the Second World War, like that of the first, was temporary and in many ways illusory.[1] Improvements in Black seamen's pay and working conditions, like other wartime concessions, were granted only under relative duress. Meanwhile, established patterns of paternalism, deception, and manipulation continued and even intensified.

First epigraph: Internal Minute, entry no. 10, September 1939, MT9/3150 M.12623/39. Second: 28 October 1941, quoted by Arnold R. Watson, *West Indian Workers In Britain* (London: Hodder & Stoughton, 1942), 14.

Perhaps the most important wartime concession was official recognition of Indian seamen's labor organization, motivated by the demands of war, the fear of offending the Indian public, and the desire to forestall radicalization among Indian seamen. On the eve of the Second World War the British merchant marine employed an estimated 33,000 to 40,000 Indian seamen, 45,000 according to the Government of India. This figure climbed to 40,000, one quarter of Mercantile Marine personnel, by December 1941 and to 59,000 by February 1943.[2] The most subordinated section of the Black labor force, men on Asiatic articles, were the first to seize the opportunity. In autumn 1939 Lascar seamen struck, refusing to sail without a wage increase and some security for their dependents should they be killed. By December the strike had spread from London, Glasgow, and Liverpool to South Africa, Australia, the West Indies and elsewhere. Hundreds of Lascar seamen were imprisoned in the United Kingdom and the empire for "breach of contract."[3]

Indian seamen's militancy was enhanced by a context of broken promises. In the anxious weeks before the declaration of war, local agents in India had assuaged reluctant recruits by promising war bonuses and wage increases of the sort European seamen would receive in the event of war. As local labor organizers were already active among potential recruits, the Shipping Master in Calcutta warned, "any breach of faith with Indian seamen at the present stage would have disastrous results."[4] The perils of alienating Indian seamen were heightened because the All-India Trades Union Congress (A.I.T.U.C.) supported the Indian National Congress' boycott of the war.

Employers were forced to grant crews' immediate demands to fulfill their wartime obligations to the state. On 30 August 1939 eleven major companies including the P.&O., Coan, Anchor, Ellerman, Harrison, and Brocklebank lines, agreed to pay a 50 percent "war bonus" from the outbreak of hostilities to all crews sailing from Bombay and Calcutta, while the Clan Line agreed to double wages on the *Clan Macallister* while on government service. Demands escalated and by mid-September Asian seamen generally demanded double wages (an amount still far short of N.M.B. standard) and in some cases improvements in working and living conditions: "The Board of Trade thought that the Lascars' demands for 100% increase, plus in one case £10 extra for the voyage, plus 2 new suits, plus a bar of soap, were quite unreasonable"[5]

These events provoked alarm at the Board of Trade, which suggests that the men on Asiatic articles had chosen the proper moment to apply pressure, when the state and shipowners were most vulnerable. In the 1920s and 1930s the economic imperative to keep colonial wages low conflicted with the political impulse to conciliate colonized people. Because the war made the second motive paramount, the Board of Trade and employers were compelled to meet Indian seamen's demands. Yet they disagreed about who ought to absorb these higher costs.

Shipowners initially attempted to deflect seamen's demands with the excuse that the board of Trade intended to "standardize" wages in the event of war, but the board resisted official increases as reminiscent of industrialists' First World War "profiteering." Still, they insisted that war transport continue uninterrupted, whatever the short-term cost: "Although the Government will not pay a war bonus, . . . crew must be obtained at once, even if this means doubling the Lascars' wages." Although the Board of Trade insisted it was not the "Government's business to attempt to stop an increase of Lascar wages or any other wages that might perhaps be low," they became involved because some employers' responses threatened to escalate the conflict. They also had an interest in wages on requisitioned ships, and a history of intervention in such disputes.[6]

The state and employers discussed deterrents such as replacing Lascars with white crews, prosecution for desertion or breach of articles, and even a show of force through summoning police or troops. Yet state officials and all but the most intransigent shipowners realized such methods were "impolitic" because the goodwill of Indians generally and Indian seamen in particular was essential to prosecute the war. The Board of Trade explained, "If in fact the requisitioned ships must be got away to a programmed time the Department and the owners acting for the men were in a weak position." The P.&O. suggested calling in troops but the India Office demurred for political reasons. To the suggestion that Lascars be prosecuted for breach of contract, the Board of Trade warned that prosecution "under articles opened in peace time" would be rejected by the courts, and "use of force . . . might have awkward repercussions in India."[7]

On 28 September 1939 the first opportunity to "make an example" of striking seamen was taken, and the crew of a hospital ship was fined for refusing a 25 percent increase. Yet Indian High Commissioner Firozkhan Noon and F. H. Norman of the Board of Trade agreed that prosecution should not be pursued for fear of public reaction in India. Noon asserted some of the men, afraid for their lives and their dependents, would probably rather go to jail, or back to India, than man the ships. He warned lest others discover that those who had not caused "trouble" were denied increases given those who had. Hoping to revive and exploit the notion of British "fair play," the High Commissioner "evidently attaches great importance to trying to preserve in the Lascar the feeling that he could rely on decent treatment while serving in the Mercantile Marine." Noon's subordinate Mr. Lall warned that punitive measures would yield "more and more trouble." He remained "convinced that if the Lascars are properly treated . . . it will be possible to get them into a reasonable state of mind, and even to appeal to them on patriotic grounds."[8]

Even increases of 100 percent or more were stopgaps, and some employers held out for a permanent settlement of 25 percent above the prewar rate, hoping to buttress their position with a show of force. Yet shipowners were disunited. Some had persuaded crews to sail with no increase and were reluctant to agree to any wage rise, hoping to forestall industrial action through intimidation. One of their techniques remained racial divisiveness. The crew of the SS *Birchbark*, demanding a 200 percent increase, was given "tomorrow to sign at ordinary rates and if not they will be replaced with white men."[9] Shipowner Harold Cayzer, just "down" to Glasgow from his "shooting season in the North," was outraged to find his requisitioned ships paying a 100 percent increase over prewar wages and a £10 war bonus. Citing his firm's sixty years' experience "looking after lascar crews," he proposed a stern remedy: "We intend to send one ship on Sunday to Liverpool . . . and leave the crew ashore, who will be left on the quay and left to the authorities as deserters. We consider this might put the wind up on our other five ships in Glasgow."[10] Yet Ellerman's Captain Kipper realized the flaw in such a strategy: although the Calcutta Commissioner of Police was prepared to prosecute men for breaches of agreement, "if the crews are in gaol, we will be no nearer a solution." Punitive measures assumed a particularly ugly aspect when in October 1939 an ill seaman died when the Bibby Line cut off food and heat to a striking ship.[11]

Both the board and employers resisted dignifying Indian seamen's activism as formal or informal labor organization. Shipowners impugned the legitimacy of Indian seamen's demands, blaming union agitators for the strikes. Harold Cayzer denounced industrial action as *"profiteering of unskilled British lascar labour of the worst sort"* (his emphasis). The Board of Trade was adamant that any extra payment, however necessary to get requisitioned ships to sail, should not establish a precedent for war gratuity or bonus payable by the state, characterizing such payments as "black mail or bribe" won by individual ships.[12]

Their reluctance arose in part from disunity among Indian activists themselves. London organizer Surat Alley, a communist, was disliked by Indian nationalist V. K. Krishna Menon and his minion Tahsil Miya, while the All-India Seamen's Federation (A.I.S.F.) was reportedly a "one-man show," dependent on strongman Aftab Ali. Yet as shipboard conflicts escalated, the state overcame longtime suspicion of Ali. Failing to locate him on short notice, the Board of Trade negotiated with striking seamen through the High Commissioner for India. Firozkhan Noon proved happy to aid the authorities in cowing Indian seamen, proposing to "persuade" them with the threat of high unemployment in India. Apparently sharing the authorities' fears that industrial action might escalate, his efforts to thwart communication among Asian seamen grew comic: when representatives of two striking crews converged on India House at the same time, Board of Trade personnel noted with approval, "The High Commissioner was anxious that these two Lascars should have no contact with other Lascars whom he had waiting in another room."[13]

State officials decided to recognize the A.I.S.F. as well as the Calcutta-based National Seamen's Union of India "as representing Indian Seamen" for two reasons. First, Surat Alley, Aftab Ali's sometime ally and organizer, cooperated with the authorities, engendering goodwill and, as Noon's emissary, compelling recalcitrant shipowners to work with him. Second, the authorities found it difficult to bargain with Indian crews who had no official spokesmen and no entity such as the N.U.S. to impose agreements on the rank and file. Negotiating with representatives of two requisitioned ships, Atur Miah of the *Clan Ross* and Abdul Majid of the *Clan MacBrayne*, for instance, the Board of Trade was disconcerted when the two men, whom the board wanted "tied immediately" to the terms discussed, demurred. Sailors Atur Miah and Abdul Majid personally accepted the offer, but warned they could not vouch for their shipmates. Hope that the A.I.S.F. would impose discipline was reflected in discussion accompanying the wage settlement of 30 November 1939: "The unauthorised stoppage is strictly forbidden." The Board of Trade hoped to undercut a more militant "rival union" by recognizing the A.I.S.F. The Government of India recommended that "for harmony in industrial relations" shipowners too should recognize the A.I.S.F.[14]

Throughout autumn 1939 the situation remained unstable. Private ships were commonly paying 100 percent over the prewar rate, and requisitioned ships usually an additional £10 war bonus. Crews hired in India at a 25 percent rate were disturbed to find wages four times that on their arrival in Britain, and they often demanded more. Strikes were met with prosecutions, and as late as mid-December hundreds of men were still imprisoned.[15]

Eventually the threat to already tenuous Indian loyalty forced the state to bargain. By late November and early December the India Office became concerned because reports were finding their way to India, where public opinion was strongly sympathetic to the strikers. Concern about imperial unity mingled with the impulse to "protect them [Indian seamen] from the influence of disaffected persons who took advantage of their ignorance." On November 30 an agreement was concluded providing for a 25 percent increase of wages and an additional 25 percent war risk bonus.[16] The Board of Trade was anxious that this settlement be widely publicized in the United Kingdom.

Although the strike was not officially over, to minimize further publicity the state would "act toward the lascars as though it was," for the approximately 150 employees of the Clan Line and the B.I.S.N. still imprisoned in Brixton and Liverpool constituted an embarrassment to the India Office. They wished to get these men out of prison and back on their ships before December 14, when the question would be raised in the House of Commons. In addition, "the Home Secretary had been approached on behalf of the imprisoned Lascars not only by Mr. Suhrawardy [H. S. Suhrawardy, Commerce and Labour Minister of Bengal], with the support of his colleagues and the Governor of Bengal, but also by others whom it was most desirable to prevent from receiving any credit for the men's release." Although some shipowners remained reluctant to recognize Aftab Ali's union, the state wished to settle so that the High Commissioner and shipowners rather than "labor agitators" got public recognition for it. F. H. Norman of the Board of Trade was congratulated for containing a situation that had shown "every appearance of getting out of hand."[17]

By December, most of those imprisoned had been released on the intercession of the High Commissioner and had returned to work. Their release was accompanied by a December publicity campaign describing the "valuable" and "faithful" service of the 30,000 men, one-fifth of merchant navy personnel, currently serving on Asiatic articles. As some authorities feared, the success of the strike, while limited, enhanced Asian seamen's self-confidence. Mr. Todd of the Mercantile Marine Department at Tilbury Dock, observing Clan Line crews' jubilant reaction after successful negotiations, reported in consternation that the announcement had a "bad effect on the discipline of the crew.... The men were running about," he wrote, "and the officers had no control over them."[18]

The question of wages and war bonus was no sooner settled than the Shipping Federation complained seamen on Asiatic articles were demanding extra wages if shifted to voyages beyond their customary routes. These transfers, while technically illegal, had been routinely written into

Asiatic articles much as illegal clauses are sometimes written into landlord-tenant agreements. Asian seamen were now seeking compensation for consenting to these transfers. Shipowners wanted the Merchant Shipping Act amended to permit "disciplinary action . . . if men refuse to transfer without additional wages." The Board of Trade, the India Office, and the Government of India argued instead that the men were within their rights and advised shipowners to bargain. Shipowners agreed in September 1940 to increase their war risk bonus.[19]

As the state's reluctance to support maritime employers suggests, the war, by making Black seamen's loyalty an issue of imperial security, enhanced official solicitude for them. Yet reforms were not actively pursued until autumn 1941. Even these were consistent with the bias of interwar policy, deepening colonized workers' estrangement from white working people by segregating them and treating them as sojourners.

A Ministry of Information press release in December 1941 signaled official concern for Indian seamen. Authored by Miss E. M. Booker, the fulsome description of Indian seamen's role in the war was consistent with the Ministry of Information's and the India Office's campaign to assuage Indian public opinion. Extolling the Merchant Navy's "vital and varied" role in the war effort, Booker admonished, "it should not be forgotten that Indian seamen are making their contribution in the same great task under equally hazardous conditions."[20] Public praise for Indian seamen would reassure the Indian people that their sacrifices would be appropriately recognized and appreciated. It alerted the British public that they, too, should be kinder to Indian subjects in their midst since the empire relied on them once more for military service.

A 1943 radio broadcast by Sir M. Azizul Huque, now High Commissioner for India, again portrayed Indian seamen as strangers and sojourners deserving English sympathy: "Sturdy sons of India. . . . These silent, unobtrusive men, the very conditions of whose service on our behalf often make them forgotten men." Linking the provision of a hostel in Hull and of other clubs and amenities for Indian seamen to the "victory over human failings," the message appeared designed to urge racial tolerance on the British people. References to the "brotherhood of man" linked military service to racial equality, suggesting a broader effort, as in 1914, to convince Indians that their long-deferred reward was near.[21]

Of more concrete benefit, perhaps, were the numerous hostels and other facilities established at the beginning of the war for Black and white workers by the state, private charities, and employers. In 1941 the Government of India and His Majesty's Government inaugurated death and disability payments for Indian seamen, to be supplemented privately by the King's Fund. The High Commissioner for India provided Indian Welfare Officers in London, Liverpool, and Glasgow while the Ministry of Labour established Port Welfare Committees and a central seamen's Welfare Board in London. Private charities intensified their activities. Ameliorative efforts were of course not confined to Indian seamen. These provisions were consistent with the upgrading of workplace facilities such as toilets and canteens accompanying the wartime rationalization of industry.[22] Such steps were taken to both placate workers and enhance their productivity by providing for their physical well-being on the job.

As we have seen, comfortable and sanitary accommodation for Indian seamen, long a goal of the L.C.C., the International Labour Organization (I.L.O.), private charities, and Indian seamen themselves, had been effectively stalled by state reluctance to expend the necessary resources and by employers' resistance to accountability for the methods by which their workforce was recruited, maintained, and replenished. The war saw a rapid reversal of this position. Numerous hostels and other facilities were established in the various ports including "colonial hostels" for "Colonial seamen" and age-segregated facilities. There were some gestures toward maintaining such improvements after the war. The wartime Committee on Seamen's Welfare recommended that the recently higher standard for "Indian and Chinese" seamen remain; and the Ministry of Labour suggested the shipping industry be taxed to maintain seamen's facilities. But the temporary and contingent nature of most amenities was explicit.[23]

Indian seamen's lives ashore, subject to neglect or desultory intervention in the 1920s and 1930s, became critical when their loyalty as well as their labor was again in question. The I.L.O. and other reformers had long demanded welfare officers, recreation centers, and hostels, but in wartime Britain these seemingly benevolent measures were accompanied by the same coercion and surveillance that were part of the rationalization of wartime industry. While Azizul Huque and Miss Booker extolled the "sturdy sons of India," the India Office and other state ministries were engaged in deception and manipulation of the men they professed to protect. Their response to Indian labor organization illustrated this.

In contrast to Booker and Azizul Huque, Surat Alley of the All-India Seamen's Federation repudiated the suggestion that Indian seamen were adequately provided for. In an article in the *East London Advertiser* of 20 December 1941, Alley dismissed the much-touted welfare provisions, which he argued "do not touch the fringe of the problem," which was inadequate wages. While Indian seamen's wages had averaged 35s per month from 1919 to September 1939, he asserted, the A.I.S.F. "had been representing the case of Indian seamen to the Shipping Federation of Great Britain, but without any effect." By December 1940, after A.I.S.F. agitation and Suhrwahardy's intercession, pay had risen to 70s (£3 10/) a month, while N.M.B. wages ranged between £9 and £12. Alley argued this was not "a living wage." Indian seamen were still not compensated for overtime, injury, disability, or unemployment. A "meager" lump sum was provided in lieu of old age or widow's pensions. A man's pay stopped when he went ashore into a hospital and he could not collect compensation unless he returned to India. Alley's organization demanded double pay and a war bonus of £10, the same bonus as other seamen. In a letter that skillfully appropriated wartime rhetoric and paternalistic notions of mutual obligation while playing on official fears of Indian disaffection, Alley concluded: "During the last war 3000 Indian seamen lost their lives. In this war many 1000s have already been killed or wounded. . . . Indian seamen want to be useful in this fight against the force of evil. It is for the authorities and shipowners to take advantage of this eagerness by making things easy for them."[24] Alley's letter signaled renewed A.I.S.F. efforts to seize the opportunity presented by the war, for he was already engaged in negotiations with shipowners and the Ministry of War Transport (M.W.T.).

By 1940 there were eleven major seamen's unions in India, representing more than 31,000 Indian seafarers from Karachi, Bombay, and Calcutta. The largest were the National Seamen's Union of India, with 20,000 members based in Bombay, and the All-India Seamen's Federation (A.I.S.F.) comprising five unions including at least 8,500 members in Karachi and Calcutta. These organizations continued to agitate in India and Britain for a wage increase of 50% of the prewar rate to meet the cost of living; the elimination of corruption through rationalized recruitment of Indian seamen by a joint Employment Bureau; fixed working hours and provision for overtime; establishment of a welfare fund for old age; provision for immediate compensation in the event of accident or injury; and arrangements for accommodation in ports and on board and for canteens.[25]

In December Alley had presented these demands to the Shipping Federation but was rebuffed. Employers resisted the government's recommendation that they recognize the A.I.S.F. and were reluctant to treat Surat Alley as its legitimate representative in Britain. Some refused to deal with a plural adversary, insisting on a union representing all Indian seaman and able to impose discipline. Others were particularly chary of the

A.I.S.F., although the Ellerman and Clan lines judged Alley "reasonably satisfactory to deal with." Meanwhile negotiations continued in India.[26]

As in 1939 the Board of Trade was drawn into labor negotiation to avert imminent strife. In early 1942 the government declared Alley's demands "reasonable" and rediscovered they had recognized the A.I.S.F. in 1939. Yet the Shipping Federation insisted on containing negotiations in India. In Spring 1942, after one rebuff, the International Transport Workers' Federation (I.T.F.) succeeded in getting seamen's representatives a hearing before P. J. Noel-Baker, Parliamentary Secretary to the Board of Trade. Attended by Charles Jarman of the N.U.S., H. Oldenbroek, Acting General Secretary of the I.T.F., and Surat Alley, the meeting ended inconclusively.[27]

Afterward, the Board of Trade advised shipowner Sir William Currie that owners should "make a gesture" to forestall Indian seamen's increased demands and should "be prepared to act generously." Later that spring, an agreement in India to raise wages by 75 percent, to £5 17/ monthly, prompted an exchange of telegrams between shipowners in London and their representatives in Calcutta. The British Government of India was reportedly "greatly perturbed" by the implied increase in Royal Indian Navy wages, fearing this might raise the expectations of other Indian workers. But this fear conflicted with the central state's imperative to prosecute the war without disruption. As the M.W.T. explained to the India Office, they "could not afford to have ships laid up with crew troubles," and since 25 percent to 30 percent of their personnel were Indian seamen, who were still cheaper than Chinese or other merchant seamen, they must be placated to forestall mutiny, "particularly with so many India manned ships now proceeding to U.S.A. where we would get no assistance if there was trouble." Even after this increase the M.W.T. continued to observe Indian seamen anxiously, aware that they were still paid far less even than Chinese seamen and fearing "discontent." They urged flexibility on the Government of India to "forestall by timely action any agitation."[28]

In spite of shipowners' and state efforts to contain negotiations in India, stalling on the pretext of workers' disunity, Surat Alley and the Indian Seamen's Union of Calcutta continued to organize in Britain. In September 1943 an All-India Union of Seamen Centred in Great Britain formed in Liverpool, and affiliated to the T.&G.W.U. Composed of men on Asiatic articles, by 1944 the organization also had branches in Glasgow and London. The union's first meeting was in the British Council House in Barnett Street, Liverpool, on 12 September 1943. Through the intercession of Mr. Hudson, a M.W.T. superintendant, and the cooperation of the British

Council, Mr. M. J. Bukht, the Seamen's Welfare Officer for Liverpool appointed by the India Office, attended to spy on the meeting. Mr. Bukht returned with a sample union card and a report.[29]

Attendance at the meeting suggests the All-India Union of Seamen in Great Britain enjoyed belated but broad support from other trade unionists and from the local Asian community. The ninety men who attended the meeting heard speeches by Surat Alley, N.U.S. District Secretary Percy Knight, Oldenbroek of the I.T.F., and Mr. Braddock, a trade unionist and member of the Liverpool City Council, as well as representatives of the Dutch and Chinese seamen's unions. Tea was supplied by the local Indian community, led by a Mr. Abbas, of whom Bukht observed sourly, "He calls himself an eye specialist but has no recognized qualification."[30]

"The main theme of all the speeches," Bukht continued, "was that the shipowners were taking great advantage of the Indians because they were not united. Their only way of Salvation lied on [sic] joining this Union or Centre." The rank and file quickly raised concrete issues, such as greater equity with European seamen in wages, hours, shipboard and shore accommodation, medical care, and wage advances. Bukht's activities did not end with observation, but extended to clandestine sabotage: "I ascertained later that evening that Mr. Surat Ali [sic] was using the Indian Seamen's Club as his headquarters. I have been in touch with Reverend Evans and his activities there will no doubt terminate instantly."[31]

The newspapers reported Percy Knight's remarks at length: "These were days when white and coloured seamen should have a common purpose in view—that of fighting for better conditions in ships and better lodging conditions in their ports of call." Knight added, "Seamen are going to have more say in the government of this country after the war, "but warned that the time to organize was now, during the war, "when the world is saying what wonderful men they are." Mr. S. E. Teh of the Chinese Seamen's Union asserted that the reason for "ill-treatment of Indian and Chinese seamen was lack of unity between them."[32]

These events provoked anxious correspondence among the India Office, the Government of India, and the High Commissioner regarding the legitimacy of the Indian Seamen's Centre in Great Britain, and Surat Alley's role. The Government of India did not object to the union's recognition, as long as it was accorded no real power: the organization must be "consulted only on matters of purely local interest. Larger questions of policy such as pay, bonus, hours of work, etc should continue to be decided in India." India Office Undersecretary Algernon Rumbold concurred in their advice to recognize the union and "avoid giving the Centre a grievance, on the ground that they were being cold-shouldered, which they could exploit."[33] Recognition was no real victory for Surat Alley, however, since A.I.S.F. power to negotiate over major issues was still undercut in favor of centralized negotiation in India.

Percy Knight's presence at the September meeting signaled his union's tardy support for Indian seamen. They joined an I.T.F. deputation to the High Commissioner, now Sir Samuel Runganadhan, on Friday, 7 January 1944.[34] The members of this deputation made strange bedfellows indeed: they included D. S. Tennant, Secretary of the International Mercantile Marine Officers' Association (I.M.M.O.A.); H. Oldenbroek of the I.T.F.; Charles Jarman, Acting General Secretary of the N.U.S.; J. C. Esveldt of the Dutch Seamen's Union; and Surat Alley. Opening the discussion in ominous terms—"We are anxious to discuss Indian seamen's welfare and the question of wages and conditions before they come to a head"—Jarman linked Indian seamen's welfare to their low wages. They "have to buy at the same shops as I have to buy with an infinitely higher wage." Jarman invoked the familiar theme of seamen's loyalty to the empire: "Indian seamen have played a part, . . . in standing out against practically the All-India Congress on the question of loyalty to the Empire and the war effort . . . if for no other reason they ought to be able to command our support."

Jarman argued for a wage increase for Indian seamen and the same war bonus as European seamen. "I can never see the reason why an Indian, just because he is an Indian—he is risking his life as any other seaman— should not receive the same war bonus as a white man. . . . They were good seamen before we thought of going to sea." He concluded his remarks on a truculent note: "If we cannot get the owners to meet us, it simply means that we must go ahead on a militant policy and try and force the issue."

Oldenbroek pointed out that Indian seamen were disadvantaged, not only relative to white European seamen, but even in comparison with other non-Europeans. Alleging that the Dutch provided "three times as good" for Indonesian seamen, he concluded "The Indian seaman is the worst paid seaman in the world. The Indians from West India [*sic*] are in a much better position. They have been very loyal seamen . . . more loyal than the British." Oldenbroek challenged British authorities' refusal to negotiate except through the Government of India, impeding British unions from representing men working and living in Britain: "We do not know where we are . . . if we address ourselves to a certain government, they say 'this is a matter for the Indian government.' If we approach such members of the Indian government as we can get into touch with, we are told, 'it is not a matter for us.' A large number of Indian seamen do not go back to their country and cannot be looked after there." Oldenbroek concluded. "We want to move before something happens . . . this is not a threat."

Jarman warned that the absence of a Chinese seamen's union in Britain had enabled the Communist party to form a Chinese branch in London. He pleaded, "At least tell us what we can tell the men. They are seething at the moment." He added hastily the N.U.S. goal was "not equality, there is a lot of misunderstanding when we talk about equality." In Jarman's words, they would prefer "to say we are starting negociation, rather than go and tell an atrocity story to the press." Moreover, once the "equality" principle was agreed to, negotiations could pass to India, relieving the I.T.F. of responsibility.

Civil servants were unimpressed by the belated solidarity of the N.U.S. with Indian seamen. The union's history of racial divisiveness, well known to the Board of Trade and the India Office, diminished their credibility. Rumbold wrote, "They are interested parties in that the higher the wages of Indian seamen the more employment there will be for white seamen." Alley's request for a second meeting was granted "Merely to allow them to blow off steam." Jarman's presence could be dismissed: "my information is that the N.U.S. are not very interested in the wages of Indian seamen" and the I.T.F. was "not a very influential body." In the second meeting, on 23 February 1944, the India Office again evaded substantive issues, deferring to the Government of India. Captain Tennant, a labor representative, retorted that "the ball bounced between India and London and they seemed never able to catch it." Still, the I.T.F. pledged in this meeting to support Indian seamen in the event of a strike, prompting Lord Munster, the India Office delegate, to advise his colleagues to "press shipowners with headquarters in the U.K. to negociate."[35]

While negotiations continued, Indian seamen engaged in direct action: "In the port of Glasgow, forty-two Indian seamen were arrested for refusing to work unless the very bad food they were getting was changed." The Government of India reported that a wage increase was imminent, but there would still be no discussion of conditions and benefits. As negotiation of substantive issues was confined to India, and recognizing that the underpaid "Indian seaman had a miserable time ashore" and "cut a sorry figure," the India Office sought to blunt their militancy through "welfare provision." "A man who is well fed will be slow to grumble whatever his Trades Union leaders may say."[36]

These responses to Indian seamen's formal and informal labor organization demand reconsideration of "managed" unionism and the agendas and outcomes that accompanied wartime welfare provision. Although more independent of employers than in peacetime, much state intervention in Black seamen's lives and work continued to reinforce colonial exploitation and subordination. Containing labor negotiations in India—even though most employers were British—helped to disassociate Indian seamen's wage levels from those of the British seamen with whom they worked and lived, and helped to define them as foreigners. Efforts to delegitimate or thwart labor militancy were still informed by a paternalistic view of colonized people as childlike and unmanly, impressionable, and incapable of responsible action.[37] These events also suggest that had the N.U.S. genuinely supported Indian seamen earlier, they might have had greater success, for the state disregarded Indian seamen's demands until they were backed by the wider British labor movement. Only after decades of evasion did the British state and British labor acknowledged Indian seamen's organization. In December 1945, George Reed, Assistant General Secretary of the N.U.S., and longtime antagonist of Black seamen, departed for India to help organize a National Maritime Board there. Once Indian labor organization appeared inevitable, the union and the state sought to control the process, efforts that were prefigured in wartime Britain in the "Bevin Training Scheme."[38]

The structures developed over decades to control Black British seamen shaped the experience of other groups of Black working men imported from the colonies to Britain during and after World War II. Because their arrival was fodder for propaganda, their well-publicized presence in Britain during and after the war overshadowed the fact that Black workers and interracial settlements had been in Britain all along, reinforcing popular notions of Black people as newcomers and sojourners. Moreover, in spite of the philanthropic rhetoric surrounding these schemes, they recapitulated Black seamen's treatment in their paternalistic, manipulative, and exploitative aspects.[39]

An example was the much-publicized and heavily stage-managed Bevin Training Scheme that supplied Indian factory workers to British war industries. Between 1941 and 1946 more than 800 young factory workers were brought from India to live and work in Britain for periods of five to eight months. Although the principal purpose of the scheme was to train them in industrial techniques in order to boost Indian munitions production, "a subsidiary fruit . . . should be to inculcate in Indian workers an appreciation of the British methods of industrial cooperation"—an effort to counter "the extreme Left" in India. State sponsors of the scheme sought to ensure that the trainees "make the right contacts and are kept away from the wrong ones" and discouraged from "undue political activity." Accordingly, wardens of the men's hostels confiscated political "pamphlets and other literature" and warned them against attending Indian nationalist "meetings and other functions" in Britain. The Government of India cooperated to prevent adverse publicity surrounding the men's resultant protests from reaching India. Unlike Black seamen, the Indian trainees were handled gingerly and kept as much as possible in a hermetic environment to perpetuate the illusion of class and racial harmony in the empire. Yet, just as the introduction of Black seamen in shipping aggravated the pangs of a declining industry, the placement in Lancashire of Black industrial trainees coincided with depression in the textile industry, heightening tension along racial lines.[40]

A similar but less-publicized episode was the importation of skilled workmen from the West Indies to the factories and shops of Merseyside's war industries. Starting in February 1941, hundreds of "West Indian Technicians" were brought to Britain, a source of desperately needed skilled labor who challenged the system less, for instance, than women workers, who demanded "part-time employment or wartime Nurseries." Like the Bevin scheme, there was also hope that the experience would be "educative" for the men, who might return to "influence the pattern of Society in their homeland." By early 1942, before the arrival of the Jim Crow U.S. Army, these Black workers had already experienced race discrimination by British employers and unions.[41] The solution to conflict was sought and found in a combination of job security and state intervention, not, as in the 1920s and 1930s, to enforce colonial racial subordination by controlling Black workers, but to mediate disputes and enforce equal pay, preventing racial stratification in the labor market. This, according to Welfare Officer Arnold Watson, had produced "an important thing—the day-by-day elimination of racial discrimination . . . on the basis of jobs for all. . . . Remove the fear of the white worker for his job, and you then get a chance to build." Whatever the motives of the scheme, alleviating economic pressure on Black and white workers and regulating employers' attempts to lower wages facilitated relative racial harmony in wartime Merseyside.[42]

The Second World War like the first was affected by and influenced peacetime race relations in Britain and the empire. As these episodes illustrate, race relations cannot be divorced from the economic and political structures that positioned Black and white workers in relation to one another and to employers and the state. We can neither that say Black workers' situation was improving in the late 1930s nor that the interwar years were free of the racial conflict that dogged Britain after the war. The weakness of Black workers' labor organization and their consequent vulnerability was linked to their transience: this transience was enforced by legislation and policy and by official insistence that problems resided in India or the West Indies, or other colonized areas rather than Britain— even though most employers were British. Because the state distinguished between British subjects on the basis of race, Black British seamen found their cause a "ball" that "bounced" between Britain and the colonies, impossible to resolve with either the state or with shipowners and largely ignored by U.K. labor unionists.

Yet these events belie the view of Black workers as passive, exploitable, unorganizable. Black seamen who in peacetime constituted a marginalized labor reserve found that wartime demand made bargaining possible. They used their resources, however limited, to negotiate with employers, the state, and the N.U.S. Surat Alley and his All-India Union of Seamen recognizing the strategic moment, seized and exploited their bargaining position. Their actions reflected a sense of urgency that reforms must come before their services became superfluous, the consciousness of prior betrayals, the recognition that British and Chinese seamen had used similar methods in the previous war, and their sense that their war service in defiance of the Indian National Congress and the A.I.T.U.C. entitled them to place demands on the imperial state. They profited by their own and others' experiences, recognizing that concessions could only be extracted from the authorities under pressure: what they had earned they must yet fight to get.

With the war, official demeanor toward Black workers altered. As in the First World War, Black workers who supported the war effort were welcomed as heroes, at least officially. The strategic demands of total war, the need to placate the colonies and by extension Black and colonized people in the United Kingdom, compelled the British state to intervene in labor conflicts to manage racial confrontation and disparities in wages and working conditions. But as the experiences of Indian seamen and other Black war workers show, "business as usual" for the state and private industry incorporated routine racial subordination only partially curbed by the demands of war. Most state concessions were intended to be only temporary; in spite of wartime wage raises, Indian seamen still earned less than regular British seamen; and segregated housing became part of the reform and rationalization process. Thus wartime reforms hardly signified long-term improvement for Black workers or seamen in Britain. Because the war deepened colonialism's inherent conflicts between economic imperatives and political unity and loyalty, Indian seamen and other Black workers were nominally successful for its duration. But because in peacetime economic exploitation took precedence over political unity, such gains rapidly dissipated with the peace. A return to racial subordination greeted the Black workers arriving in or returning to Britain after the war.[43]

The postwar "influx" of Black workers from the Caribbean and later from India and Pakistan is customarily identified as the catalyst for racial conflict in postwar Britain. But the problems of racial stratification and conflict that took many Britons by apparent surprise in the postwar decades were plain for all who wished to see in the years between the wars. These problems were rooted in the imperial past, and structured by the conflicts of the interwar years.

Conclusion

THROUGHOUT THE TWENTIETH CENTURY, the British working class has remained global and multiracial, and even after formal decolonization, labor exploitation on a worldwide scale has continued, accompanied by a continuing division of labor and racial hierarchy, and continuing conflict over migration. The Second World War altered the size and distribution of Black settlements in Britain, as men from the colonies came to industrial centers to do war work or dispersed to the countryside like the "Honduranian" lumberjacks who harvested timber in Scotland. Thus began the postwar pattern of Black migration to Britain's industrial cities as well as the ports. Yet interracial port settlements remained, and became social centers for African-American and colonial troops, and other Black war personnel.[1]

By the late 1940s Black people's lives in Britain were in transition, as legal migration from the Caribbean and other colonized areas resumed. In 1948 British nationality was recodified, extending citizenship to all Commonwealth subjects. Frequently dated to the arrival of the migrant-laden ship *Empire Windrush* in 1948, the reconstitution and evolution of Britain's Black settlements was actually an ongoing process. Since the Second World War the bulk of Black migrants to Britain have come from the Caribbean, Pakistan, India, Bangladesh, and East Africa. In the 1950s only a few tens of thousands per year arrived, and even today with their children they constitute less than 4 percent of the British population. Yet their presence has provoked disproportionate alarm. As in the interwar years, Black people's socioeconomic disadvantage, shaped by their position in the global as well as the local economy, has been attributed to racial and cultural difference. Again Black British subjects' access to Britain has

178

been progressively restricted through a series of immigration and nationality statutes in 1962, 1968, 1971, and 1981. As in the interwar years, each of these shifts occurred in the context of intense negotiation and struggle, not simply between Black and white working people, but among workers, employers, unions, and the state.[2]

The evidence presented here problematizes the assumption that racial or cultural difference is simply a natural attribute and a natural source of conflict. We have seen that the definition of who was Black and to what this entitled him was shaped by domestic, labor, and imperial politics. Understanding how Black workers were recolonized in Britain through the reconstruction of colonial racial categories should encourage us to seek material and historical bases for racial conflict. We must understand racial difference as a product of structural inequality, and racial conflict as one of many forms of conflict—along lines of gender, class, age, skill—that *result* from inequality rather than create it.

State policy in the 1920s and 1930s aimed to keep Black workers available to shipowners without allowing them to settle in Britain, constituting a threat to the racial hierarchies that undergirded the imperial system. Thus, policing and exclusion were in the first instance a reaction to Black workers' migration, itself an act of resistance to imperial inequalities. The result was the creation of a virtual "guest worker" system manned by British subjects.[3] Developed in response to the dislocations that the First World War and the faltering interwar economy accelerated, Black workers' subordination intensified with the Depression, jeopardizing their settlements in Britain. The apparent proliferation of Black workers' organizations in the 1920s and 1930s, a progressive contribution to the global decolonization process, paralleled a workers' movement on the defensive in response to attacks on their livelihood and legitimacy in Britain—attacks consistent with the illiberal response to world economic and political disorganization. For the reconstitution in Britain of colonial racial hierarchies was challenged and its force was blunted by Black workers' resistance and protest.

These men derived leverage from their strategic position at the intersection of global and domestic politics. A dynamic tension existed between colonized workers' political status and their economic position. The authorities had difficulty in reconciling the imperial legacy of racial inequality and the ideology of cultural and racial superiority with the liberal and racially enlightened values espoused in Britain itself. The conflicts among different branches of the state and between the state, the union, employers, and white and Black seamen illustrate the contradiction between British rhetoric of liberty, justice, and fair play and the demands of imperial economic extraction. Thus it is correct to argue that interwar race policy did not reflect a "cohesive racial ideology," less because of the moderating influence of "middle opinion" than because different sections of the governing classes were engaged in intense internal conflict about racial difference and its meanings.[4] Black workers were able to manipulate this political tension to their advantage.

Indeed, the ideology that accompanied and justified the imperial project, rather than an immutably oppressive "tradition of intolerance," was itself a terrain of struggle. Throughout the twentieth century, Black British subjects as well as white racists helped to define the meanings and implications of British imperialism and nationality, albeit with radically unequal power at their disposal. Black workers appropriated and refashioned the terms of imperialist rhetoric into a "reverse discourse," appealing to employers, the union, and the state in familiar and credible language.[5] Their demand for British justice embodied a claim to British nationality implying freedom from violence, from exclusion from Britain, and from race discrimination, and supporting claims on British resources—including the state itself. Their relations with white working people and the occasional success of such appeals to the union and the state suggest that these claims had broad support.

Race politics in interwar Britain developed in response to Black migration, organization, and activism. Through the act of migration itself, and through protest against and evasion of official restrictions, Black workers exercised the minimal choice and power available to them, influencing the form that race policy took. Their continued challenges to authority prompted increasingly harsh and elaborate measures of exclusion and repression. Yet in spite of official efforts, Black working people established the nuclei of contemporary Black settlements in Britain, and left a legacy of protest and resistance to modern Britain and the decolonizing world. Postwar Black settlements have persisted and flourished, enriching British cultural life and fostering Black people's collective demands for a greater voice in the decisions governing their lives.[6]

Evidence of the historical construction of racial difference and racial subordination is meant to challenge the view of Black working people as outsiders to the British working class and conflict as a product of their difference. Demonstrating the availability of an antiracist alternative is not intended to deny the racism prevalent in British society; rather it enables us to hold historical actors responsible for their conscious decisions to engage in racist practices. Rethinking explanations for racial conflict should prompt a shift of focus to the ways racist power structures have oppressed white as well as Black working people, albeit in different ways. We must investigate and understand whose purposes were served by racist practices, and who participated in formulating racial categories. Then it becomes clear that racism is not a universal human frailty, but a power structure that oppresses all people regardless of race.

Race and racism in twentieth-century Britain were shaped by relations of power and interest integral to the historical process—not independent of it. Twentieth-century racism was not a lingering atavism easily dispelled through reason, education, or right thinking. The fundamental causes of racial subordination and conflict were the same forces impelling other types of historical change.[7] In the 1920s and 1930s British employers, the state, and trade union leaders found intensified racial stratification useful in efforts to preserve their position in the face of domestic demands for a redistribution of power and wealth and colonized people's demands for a measure of political and economic autonomy. Their racialized response to these challenges enhances our understanding of twentieth-century politics and specifically the use of race as well as class and gender to perpetuate power relations.

The debates among different branches of government, employers, and the union enhance our understanding of the conflict and accommodation among "governing institutions"—capital, labor, and the state—during and after the first total war. In formulating racial policy the state sought to exert control over employers but failed: employers easily evaded account-ability for the social costs of their labor practices, while the interwar state, starved of cash and devoid of coercive power, was forced into a policing rather than an advocacy role relative to Black workers and their families. Twentieth-century British race politics further problematize the customary identification of interest among labor leadership, the working rank and file, the Labour party, the labor movement, and what is called "the working class movement."[8]

The policing of Black workers also illuminates relations between the twentieth-century state and the British public. State bureaucratization, originating in the early 1900s but accelerated during the First World War, removed much of the exercise of state power from public and parliamentary oversight. Consequently, in the 1920s and 1930s state race policy was hidden from antiracist British whites as well as colonized elites who might have opposed and perhaps mediated it.[9] Its covert nature facilitated the denial of institutional racism, shifting blame to white working people, local officials and police. Investigation has done little to mitigate the dim view of petty officials, the union, and the press that Kenneth Little first enunciated. But local officials' racist practices, however reprehensible, were encouraged and abetted—if not compelled—by employers and the state. Interwar policies of exclusion and harassment were instigated by employers in the first instance and abetted by the state in the second. Only in default of less harsh solutions they became the method favored by the union and local officials in the ports. Racial conflicts among British working people were the result, not the cause of this process.

One need not "romanticize" the working class to recognize that racism is a learned behavior acquired in the same context of unequal power that has shaped other forms of conflict. Evidence suggests that the sources of racial conflict in interwar Britain were not the inherent viciousness of white or Black working people; nor did conflict stem from an inherent antipathy between people of different races or cultures. When it occurred it was the response to a particular structure of political and economic power, often because employers, union leaders, and even the state pitted white sailors against Black ones in a struggle for jobs and other social goods in particular historical settings—not merely in some abstract sense. Scholars have missed the point of episodes of imputed racial confrontation, mistakenly conflating rank-and-file conservatism with the racially divisive agendas of labor leaders and employers. Most recently Ron Ramdin has blamed "trade unions, the Labour Party and the British working class generally" for creating an oppressed Black "class" in twentieth-century Britain.[10] Yet the agendas of these three were far from identical. As the incidents in Salford and South Shields and others like them suggest, ordinary seamen, Black and white, defined the right to work differently that did either employers or the union.

Indeed, the definitions of "belonging" formulated by the state, employers, and the union conflicted with each other and with popular definitions held by rank-and-file Black and white workers, as well as by Black elites. Historical investigation shows definitions of belonging and entitlement were never matters of consensus or of "common sense"; they were responses to historical pressures and interests, defined by particular people within the state and outside it.[11] Mechanisms of racial subordination were formulated in struggle among employers, the union, and the state, both central and local. Black workers in Britain were recolonized, not at the initiative of working people, Black or white, but of British elites attempting to preserve their power or wealth from twentieth-century challenges. The reconstruction of colonial racial hierarchies facilitated the continued super-exploitation of a section of an exploited global and multiracial workforce.[12]

Whether imperial racial inequalities benefited white working people remains debatable. British society itself was internally stratified; no recent scholarship suggests that the wealth extracted through imperial processes was distributed equitably among the metropolitan population. On the contrary, shipowners and other industrialists, unconstrained by nationalist loyalties, have continued to reinvest their wealth in the economically rational pursuit of maximum profits. These profits continue to be most easily realized where the legacy of formal and informal empire has perpetuated the structural subordination of populations now detached from political claims on the imperial state.[13]

This evidence leads us to reconsider the notion that racially based definitions of British nationality reflected a retreat from empire, or indeed that definitions of nationality have been products of natural affinities and antipathies. In the hands of employers and the Home Office, reversion to a race-based definition of British nationality may not have been a reflection of retreat at all, but rather an effort to reinforce the inequalities that made the empire profitable for influential sections of Britain's elite. Such an interpretation carries implications for the pattern of Black migration and of state control in late twentieth-century Britain, when the relationships among race, nationality and migration remain fraught with conflict and contestation.[14]

For racial conflict in Britain was and is a legacy of imperialism. Discounting the imperial experience when examining British race relations perpetuates the view of Black British subjects as outsiders to the system, rather than recognizing them as a section of Britain's global workforce kept structurally separate to ensure their enhanced exploitability. Black migrants were simply attempting to shift their position within this global system, and it was this that made their presence in the United Kingdom especially threatening. In addition, ignoring Britain's ongoing imperial project in the early and mid-twentieth century effectively absolves elites, who dominated both national institutions and imperial structures, of their critical role in constructing racial categories through economic and political as well as cultural practices.[15] Excluding this wider context and confining the focus to relations between Black and white working people in Britain perpetuates the view that conflict is a product of difference alone.

Indeed, examining the effects of migration only within the boundaries of one country excludes the more extensive global structures within which that migration occurs. Labor migration itself must be understood as a form of agency and resistance to global economic imbalance, as well as a response to the deterioration of the traditional order or the simple pursuit of employment.[16] Within a globally stratified system in which wealth is systematically appropriated from the peripheries to the core through formal or informal mechanisms of domination and exploitation, workers who migrate in turn from periphery to core, far from illegitimate intruders, are simply pursuing the fruits of their labor, whatever personal circumstances or agendas may move them.

The debates accompanying these processes also articulated the hitherto unclear relationships among colonialism, imperialism, and British racism. While the rhetoric and the economics of Britain's global empire demanded integration across geographical barriers, making nonsense of notions of "belonging," the capacity to divide and exploit workers both at the core and in the periphery demanded the formulation of artificial barriers to full integration. State race policy aimed to keep colonized labor cheap by enforcing imperial racial hierarchies in the workplace and ashore in Britain. Even after formal decolonization, the subordination of colonial and post-colonial societies by metropolitan economic and political interests has continued, ensuring continuing economic and political imbalance on a world scale. These inequalities have been reinforced by barriers to labor migration, "guest worker" systems that disenfranchise workers of the fruits of their labor, and "trade zones" and contract labor systems that guarantee employers privileged access to labor reserves without responsibility for their social reproduction.[17] In this sense the super-exploitation of colonized workers has continued unabated even after formal decolonization; and, as the events of the postwar decades suggest, the demand for British justice has yet to be fulfilled.

APPENDIX ONE

Lascars

LASCARS WERE DEFINED by a type of work contract, first codified in 1823.[1] Because they were originally concentrated in "cargo and passenger liners trading East of Suez," the rationale for paying them less was conformity to local wage levels.[2] The terms of the original agreement were commercial, not explicitly racial, enabling the East India Company to pay lower wages in those areas comprising its jurisdiction in exchange for keeping their employees off the English rates, but the work and with it the term gradually acquired a racial definition.[3] In a clarification of various men's eligibility for Lascar contracts in 1901, the Government of India insisted that Eurasians—as men of mixed European and Indian parentage were called—should be eligible to serve either on European or on Lascar articles, and that their status regarding the rights to claim repatriation or to stay at the subsidized Asiatic Seamen's Home would depend, not on their "race" but on their work contract. A man's status as a Lascar was determined by "a combined test depending on nationality and employment."[4] In Britain the term "Lascar" was often applied to any Indian seaman, but in India it originally referred to a category of laborer, analogous to the Chinese "coolie," and only gradually came to denote seamen. Like the term "coolie," in the mouths of the British it carried pejorative connotations.[5] In the early twentieth century a man could be engaged on "Asiatic" articles only "as a member of a crew organized under a headman" composed of "natives of British India or . . . of such frontier races as substantially extend into British India," and only for round-trip voyages beginning and ending in India and nowhere else.[6] The Merchant Shipping Act of 1894 provided that Lascars were not to be carried beyond "limits of 60 degrees North and 50 degrees South latitude; not around Cape Horn, not between 1 October and 31 March; not in the Baltic, or the American East Coast North of 38 degrees."[7] Latitude limits were abolished in 1939 (see chapter 4 above).

Appendix Two

Chronology of the
Anti-Chinese Campaign

1908   Language test of alien seamen: specifically targeted Chinese

1916   Labor Deputation to the Board of Trade

1916   Labor Deputation to the Admiralty; T.U.C., Triple Alliance resolutions re: Chinese

1917   Labor Deputation to the Prime Minister

1918   Labor Deputation to the Ministry of Reconstruction

1919   Nationality and seamen question referred to N.M.B.; Board of Trade represented on N.M.B. when this question discussed

1919   April, N.M.B. resolution against non-British Chinese and Alien coloured seamen

1919   2 May, Controller, refusal to register non-British Chinese and Alien coloured seamen: "Board of Trade has been advised accordingly and it is understood that registration is being refused to Chinamen if they cannot prove British nationality."

Source: National Union of Seamen Correspondence on the Chinese question, Mss175/3/16/1–4.

A Note on Archival Documents

THE MAJOR archival collections consulted in the course of this project can be found in the following locations:

India Office Library, London
  Economic and Overseas Department, L/E/7, L/E/9
  Military Department, L/MIL/5
  Information Department, L/I
  Political and Judicial Department, L/P&J
Public Record Office, Kew
  Home Office Aliens Department, HO45
  Board of Trade Mercantile Marine Department, MT9
  Colonial Office, CO
Modern Records Centre, University of Warwick
  National Union of Seamen Collection, Mss175
  International Transport Workers' Federation Collection, Mss159
The British Cabinet Papers, CAB24, GT, etc., were obtained in the United States through University Microfilms, Ann Arbor, Michigan.

Notes

INTRODUCTION

1. Salford Police Constable Thomas Cleminson to Chief Immigration Superintendant, Salford, 4 June 1930, Ho45/14299/562898/1; and see report in the union's newsletter, *The Seaman*, 4 June 1930, 2–3, which reported that "Englishmen banded with ["the blacks"] to try and prevent ships engaging Arabs who were not registered locally as unemployed." The National Sailors' and Firemen's Union (N.S.F.U.), formed in the late nineteenth century, merged in 1925 with the Cooks' and Stewards' Union to become the National Union of Seamen (N.U.S.). In the 1990s the N.U.S. merged with the Railway and Transport Workers to become the National Union of Rail, Maritime, and Transport Workers (R.M.T.) For most purposes and for most of the century the union has been known as the N.U.S. The reader can assume the N.S.F.U. and the N.U.S. are the same union, but I will use N.U.S. unless I am discussing union activities specific to the period before 1925.

2. The phrase "archetypal strangers" is Michael Banton's, most recently articulated in the "Correspondence" column of *Race* 15 (1973): 111–14.

3. For discussions of this interactive process, see Frederick Cooper and Ann L. Stoler, "Tensions of Empire: Colonial Control and Visions of Rule," *American Ethnologist* 16 (November 1989): 609–21; Douglas Lorimer, *Colour, Class, and the Victorians: English Attitudes to the Negro in the Mid-Nineteenth Century* (Leicester: Leicester University Press/Holmes & Meier, 1978); Leonore Davidoff, "Class and Gender in Victorian England: The Diaries of Arthur J. Munby and Hannah Cullwick," *Feminist Studies* 5 (Spring 1979): 87–141. On earlier Black settlement, see Peter Fryer, *Staying Power: The History of Black People in Britain* (London: Pluto, 1984); Jagdish Gundara and Ian Duffield, eds., *Essays in the History of Blacks in Britain: From Roman Times to the Mid-Twentieth Century* (Aldershot: Avebury, 1992).

4. Approaches that stress popular culture include John Mackenzie, *Propaganda*

and Empire: The Manipulation of British Public Opinion 1880–1960 (Manchester: Manchester University Press, 1984); John Mackenzie, ed., *Imperialism and Popular Culture* (Manchester: Manchester University Press, 1986); and several contributions to Raphael Samuel, ed., *Patriotism: The Making and Unmaking of British National Identity* (London: Routledge, 1989); Paul Rich, *Race and Empire in British Politics* (Cambridge: Cambridge University Press, 1986). For broader discussion of imperial inequalities, and an argument for the identity of imperial and metropolitan elites, see P. J. Cain and A. G. Hopkins, "Gentlemanly Capitalism and British Expansion Overseas, II: New Imperialism, 1850–1945," *Economic History Review* 2d series 40, I (1987): 1–26; Lance E. Davis and Robert Huttenback, *Mammon and the Pursuit of Empire: The Economics of British Imperialism* (Cambridge: Cambridge University Press, 1988).

5. Access to labor power without responsibility for its reproduction is a benefit of "guest worker" and migrant labor systems. For the best articulation of this process, see Claude Meillassoux, *Maidens, Meal, and Money: Capitalism and the Domestic Community* (New York: Cambridge University Press, 1981); also Paul Gordon and Danny Reilly, "Guestworkers of the Sea: Racism in British Shipping," *Race and Class* 28, 2 (1986): 73–82; Gary Cross, *Immigrant Workers in Industrial France: The Making of a New Laboring Class* (Philadelphia: Temple University Press, 1983); Pan-European Conference of Migrant Workers (Beekbergen, 21–24 November 1974), "Statement of the Preparatory Committee," *Race and Class* 16, 2 (1974): 207–13.

6. The quote is from E. P. Thompson, *The Making of the English Working Class* (New York: Vintage, 1966), 11; also see Michael Omi and Howard Winant, *Racial Formation in the United States: From the 1960s to the 1980s* (London: Routledge & Kegan Paul, 1986). This is not to endorse all of Omi and Winant's arguments. On aliens restriction, see Paul Gordon, *Policing Immigration: Britain's Internal Controls* (London: Pluto, 1985), 8–9; Bernard Gainer, *The Alien Invasion: The Origins of the Aliens Act of 1905* (London: Heinemann, 1972); John Garrard, *The English and Immigration 1880–1910* (London: Oxford University Press, 1971); David Feldman, "The Importance of Being English: Jewish Immigration and the Decay of Liberal England," in David Feldman and Gareth Stedman Jones, eds., *Metropolis London: Histories and Representations since 1800* (London: Routledge, 1989), 56–84; and the memoranda of the Joint Standing (Aliens and Nationality) Committee, 1917–26, H045/19966/374304; L/E/7/1214/702. On the status of Black British subjects in the Dominions and elsewhere, see Robert Huttenback, *Racism and Empire: White Settlers and Coloured Immigrants in the British Self-Governing Colonies, 1830–1910* (Ithaca: Cornell University Press, 1976); Partha Sarathi Gupta, *Imperialism and the British Labour Movement, 1914–1964* (New York: Holmes & Meier, 1975), 51–56, 172–87 and passim. On imperial politics, see Nicholas Mansergh, *The Commonwealth Experience: From British to Multiracial Commonwealth*, vol. 2 (Toronto: University of Toronto Press, 1982); Algernon Rumbold, *Watershed in India, 1914–1922* (London: Athlone, 1979).

7. Rights themselves have been defined only through contestation. See "The Rule of Law" in E. P. Thompson, *Whigs and Hunters: The Origins of the Black Act*

(New York: Pantheon, 1975), 258–69. On the relationship between political and social citizenship, see J. M. Barbalet, *Citizenship: Rights, Struggle, and Class Inequality* (Milton Keynes, U.K.; Open University Press, 1988), 37–40, 97; and T. H. Marshall, *Class, Citizenship, and Social Development: Essays by T. H. Marshall* with an introduction by Seymour Martin Lipset (Garden City, N.Y.: Doubleday, 1964), 111–19.

8. For a discussion of racial ideology as a dialectical unity of belief and practice, see Barbara Jeanne Fields, "Slavery, Race, and Ideology in the United States of America," *New Left Review* 181 (May/June 1990): 95–118; also Patrick Brantlinger, *Rule of Darkness: British Literature and Imperialism, 1830–1914* (Ithaca: Cornell University Press, 1988), x.

9. See, for example, Michael Banton, *White and Coloured: The Behaviour of British People toward Coloured Immigrants* (New Brunswick: Rutgers University Press, 1960); Michael Banton, *The Coloured Quarter: Negro Immigrants in an English City* (London: Jonathan Cape, 1955), 14, 17–19. For a critique of the "culturalist" approach, see Jenny Bourne with the assistance of A. Sivanandan, "Cheerleaders and Ombudsmen: The Sociology of Race Relations in Britain," *Race and Class* 21, 4 (1980): 331–33.

10. Such ideas were reflected in Margaret Thatcher's notorious prediction that Britain would be "swamped by people of a different culture," quoted in A. Sivanandan, *A Different Hunger: Writings on Black Resistance* (London: Pluto, 1983), 132; and in Enoch Powell's infamous "rivers of blood" speech of 1968, discussed in Harris Joshua, Tina Wallace, and Heather Booth, *To Ride the Storm: The 1980 Bristol "Riot" and the State* (London: Heinemann Educational, 1983), 96, and in Fryer, *Staying Power*, 384.

11. For an *entrée* into the vast postwar literature see, in addition to works already cited, Amrit Wilson, *Finding a Voice; Asian Women in Britain* (London: Virago, 1981); Bob Hepple, *Race, Jobs, and the Law* (Harmondsworth: Penguin, 1968); and Paul Foot, *Immigration and Race in British Politics* (Harmondsworth: Penguin, 1965).

12. The most prominent proponent of the latter is the prolific John Rex. See especially Banton, "Mixed Motives and the Processes of Rationalization," 534–47, and John Rex, "Kantianism, Methodological Individualism, and Michael Banton," 549–62, in *Ethnic and Racial Studies* 8 (October 1985).

13. Paul Gilroy, *"There Ain't No Black in the Union Jack": The Cultural Politics of Race and Nation* (Chicago: University of Chicago Press, 1987); also C.C.C.S., *The Empire Strikes Back: Race and Racism in 70s Britain* (London: Hutchinson, 1982). The Institute of Race Relations publishes the journal *Race and Class*, edited by A. Sivanandan.

14. Kenneth Little, *Negroes in Britain: A Study of Racial Relations in English Society*, Introduction by Leonard Bloom (1948; London: Routledge & Kegan Paul, 1972); Banton, *The Coloured Quarter*. Of Banton's substantial *oeuvre*, this latter work remains the most important for historians.

15. Edward Scobie, *Black Britannia: The History of Blacks in Britain* (Chicago: Johnson Publishers, 1972); James Walvin, *Black and White: The Negro in English*

Society, 1555–1945 (London: Allen Lane, 1973); Fernando Henriques, *Children of Conflict: A Study of Interracial Sex and Marriage* (New York: E. P. Dutton, 1975); Cedric Robinson, *Black Marxism: The Making of the Black Radical Tradition* (London: Zed Press, 1983); Fryer, *Staying Power*; Rozina Visram, *Ayahs, Lascars, and Princes: The Story of Indians in Britain, 1700–1947* (London: Pluto, 1986); Ron Ramdin, *The Making of the Black Working Class in Britain* (London: Gower, 1987). Also see Beverly Bryan, Stella Dadzie, and Suzanne Scafe, *The Heart of the Race: Black Women's Lives in Britain* (London: Virago, 1985); Caroline Adams, ed. and comp., *Across Seven Seas and Thirteen Rivers: Life Stories of Pioneering Sylheti Settlers in Britain* (London: Tower Hamlets Arts Project, 1987); Gundara and Duffield, *Essays on the History of Blacks in Britain*.

16. Kenneth Lunn, "Race Relations or Industrial Relations? Race and Labour in Britain, 1880–1950"; Jacqueline Jenkinson, "The Glasgow Race Disturbances of 1919"; and Neil Evans, "Regulating the Reserve Army: Arabs, Blacks and the Local State in Cardiff, 1919–1945," all in Kenneth Lunn, ed., *Race and Labour in Twentieth Century Britain* (London: Frank Cass, 1985).

17. I use the word "men" deliberately. With few exceptions this scholarship has been written from a "gender-neutral" perspective that precludes implicit or explicit discussion of women. But see Sidney Collins, *Coloured Minorities in Britain: Studies in British Race Relations Based on African, West Indian, and Asian Immigrants* (London: Lutterworth, 1957).

18. Colin Holmes, *John Bull's Island: Immigration and British Society, 1871–1971* (London: Macmillan, 1988); Tony Kushner and Kenneth Lunn, eds., *Traditions of Intolerance: Historical Perspectives on Fascism and Race Discourse in Britain* (Manchester: Manchester University Press, 1989); Colin Holmes, ed., *Immigrants and Minorities in British Society* (London: George Allen & Unwin, 1978); Kenneth Lunn, ed., *Hosts, Immigrants, and Minorities: Historical Responses to Newcomers in British Society 1870–1914* (London: Wm. Dawson & Sons, 1980).

19. The inability to explain such anomalies without a structural analysis is most apparent in Lunn, "Race Relations or Industrial Relations?" especially 10–17, ironic because Lunn calls for just such analysis, 1–2, 17, 24–25.

20. P.C. Thomas Cleminson to Chief Immigration Superintendant, Salford, 4 June 1930, HO45/14299/562898/1.

21. On the press as an agent in political process, see Richard Hoggart, "Foreword" to Glasgow University Media Group, *Bad News*, vol. 1 (London: Routledge & Kegan Paul, 1976), ix; Tuen A. van Dijk, *Racism and the Press* (London: Routledge, 1991), ix; Paul Gordon and David Rosenberg, *Daily Racism: The Press and Black People in Britain* (London: Runnymede Trust, 1989), 1; Stephen Koss, *The Rise and Fall of the Political Press in Britain*, vol. 2: *The Twentieth Century* (Chapel Hill: University of North Carolina Press, 1981), 7.

22. Jeffrey Weeks, *Sex, Politics and Society: The Regulation of Sexuality since 1800* (London: Longman, 1981), 38–40; Davidoff, "Class and Gender in Victorian England"; Michael Roper and John Tosh, eds., "Introduction" to *Manful Assertions: Masculinities in Britain since 1800* (London: Routledge, 1991), 1–24; Robert Miles, *Racism and Migrant Labour* (London: Routledge & Kegan Paul, 1982),

esp. 9–21; Ernest Krausz, *Ethnic Minorities in Britain* (London: McGibbon & Kee, 1971), 10; Joanna DeGroot, " 'Sex' and 'Race': The Constructions of Language and Image in the Nineteenth Century," in Susan Mendus and Jane Rendall, eds., *Sexuality and Subordination: Interdisciplinary Studies of Gender in the Nineteenth Century* (London: Routledge, 1989), 89–128.

23. See, for example, Edward Said, *Orientalism* (New York: Random House, 1978); Henry Louis Gates, Jr., ed., *Race, Writing, and Difference* (Chicago: University of Chicago Press, 1985); Ranajit Guha, Gayatri Spivak, and Edward Said, eds., *Selected Subaltern Studies* (Oxford: Oxford University Press, 1989); Brantlinger, *Rule of Darkness*; Dominick LaCapra, ed., *The Bounds of Race: Perspectives on Hegemony and Resistance* (Ithaca: Cornell University Press, 1991); Catherine Hall, *White, Male, and Middle Class: Explorations in Feminism and History* (London: Polity, 1992).

24. Barbara Harrell-Bond, Allen M. Howard, and David E. Skinner, *Community Leadership and the Transformation of Freetown (1801–1976)* (The Hague: Mouton, 1978), 3–17, 304–6; Charles VanOnselen, *New Babylon: Studies in the Social and Economic History of the Witwatersrand, 1886–1914,* vol. 1 (London: Longman, 1982): xvii and passim; Sidney Mintz, "Groups, Group Boundaries, and the Perception of 'Race,' " *Comparative Studies in Society and History* 13 (October 1971): 437–50; Jonathan Okamura, "Situational Ethnicity," *Ethnic and Racial Studies* 4 (October 1981): 452–65; G. Carter Bentley, "Ethnicity and Practice," *Comparative Studies in Society and History* 29 (January 1987): 24–55.

25. Allen Howard, Patrick Manning, and Peter Weiler, "Structures and Consciousness in World History," 6, and Charles Bright and Michael Geyer, "For a Unified History of the World in the Twentieth Century," 77, in *Radical History Review* 39 (September 1987); Eric Wolf, *Europe and the People without History* (Berkeley: University of California Press, 1982), 361–62; Gerald Sider, "When Parrots Learn to Talk, and Why They Can't: Domination, Deception, and Self-Deception in Indian-White Relations," *Comparative Studies in Society and History* 29 (January 1987): 3–23; Eric Hobsbawm and Terence Ranger, eds., *The Invention of Tradition* (Cambridge: Cambridge University Press, 1980); Cynthia Enloe, *Ethnic Soldiers: State Security in Divided Societies* (Athens: University of Georgia Press, 1980), 104.

26. For critiques, see Michel Giraud, "The Distracted Look: Ethnocentrism, Xenophobia, or Racism?" *Dialectical Anthropology* 12, 4 (1987): 413–19; Etienne Balibar and Immanuel Wallerstein, *Race, Nation, Class: Ambiguous Identities* (London: Verso, 1991), 48, 77; Edna Bonacich and John Modell, *The Economic Basis of Ethnic Solidarity: Small Businesses in the Japanese American Community* (Berkeley: University of California Press, 1980), esp. 2–3, 258.

27. Use of cumbersome terms such as "Black and Asian" or anachronisms such as "coloured" in the name of precision or historical accuracy does equal violence to the men's self-identification, which was based in most cases neither on superficial physical resemblance, nor on broad geographical origin—such as "Asian"—but on a complex of kin, religious, and local loyalties. This self-identification was disregarded by the authorities in much the same way as they disregarded the men's

most vigorously asserted claim—to British nationality. Also see comments by Banton, *The Coloured Quarter*, 16; Little, *Negroes in Britain*, 141, 295. As Eric Wolf points out, the terms "Negro" and "Indian" themselves obscured the diversity of African and American peoples. *Europe and the People without History*, 380.

I choose to capitalize the term "Black" to emphasize that like Italian, Jew, and Catholic, Black is a socially constructed category and not a physical description. I refrain from capitalizing "white" because the term describes an equally diverse population whose composition and boundaries have yet to be subjected to systematic scholarly scrutiny. This usage is also endorsed by many practitioners in the field, including Marika Sherwood, *Newsletter of the Association for the Study of African, Caribbean, and Asian Culture and History in Britain* 3 (May 1992), 2, and is found in Audre Lorde, *Sister Outsider: Essays and Speeches* (Trumansburg, N.Y.: Crossing Press, 1984), e.g., 117. Although I agree that racial differences have been shaped at least in part by the Manichean dichotomies ubiquitous in modern Western culture, it is still not sufficient to say that "Black" is merely "non-white" and that "white" is merely "non-Black." On the category "Black," see Paul Spickard, *Mixed Blood: Intermarriage and Ethnic Identity in Twentieth Century America* (Madison: University of Wisconsin Press, 1989), 20–22. On recent efforts to define "white" as a racial or ethnic category, see Ann L. Stoler, "Carnal Knowledge and Imperial Power: Gender, Race, and Morality in Colonial Asia," in Micaela di Leonardo, ed., *Gender at the Crossroads of Knowledge: Feminist Anthropology in the Postmodern Era* (Berkeley: University of California Press, 1991), 52–53 and passim; Gilroy, *"There Ain't No Black in the Union Jack,"* 122–23. Gilroy himself is reading rather creatively from Dick Hebdige, *Subculture: The Meaning of Style* (London: Methuen, 1979), esp. 62–67. For a recent American effort, see David Roediger, *The Wages of Whiteness: Race and the Making of the American Working Class* (London: Verso, 1991).

28. E. N. Cooper to the Home Office, 17 February 1921, HO45/11897/332087/20; Tony Lane, *Grey Dawn Breaking: British Merchant Seafarers in the Late Twentieth Century* (Manchester: Manchester University Press, 1986), 18; David Byrne, "The 1930 'Arab Riot' in South Shields: A Race Riot That Never Was," *Race and Class* 18 (1977): 265. In addition, a diverse population can be found defined as "black" or "coloured" in, among many sources, Cardiff Immigration Officer S. A. Wilkes to the Home Office, April 1921, HO45/11897/332087/24; David Caradog Jones, *The Economic Status of Coloured Families in the Port of Liverpool* (Liverpool: Liverpool Social Science Department, Statistics Division, 1940), 11; Reverend St. John B. Groser et al., "Conditions of Life of the Coloured Population of Stepney," pp. 1–2, MT9/3952; Leo Silberman and Betty Spice, *Colour and Class in Six Liverpool Schools* (Liverpool: University Press of Liverpool, 1950), 7. For an example of Indian seamen referring to themselves, if ruefully, as "black," see "Inspection of Lascars' Food," 1908, L/E/7/604.

29. See, among many others, Christine Bolt, *Victorian Attitudes to Race* (London: Routledge & Kegan Paul, 1971), and Lorimer, *Colour, Class, and the Victorians*, esp. 111–13, 128, the pioneering works on Victorian racial thought. See also Penelope Hetherington, *British Paternalism and Africa 1920–1940* (London:

Frank Cass, 1978), esp. 76–85; Terence Ranger, "The Invention of Tradition in Colonial Africa," in Hobsbawm and Ranger, *The Invention of Tradition*, 211–62.

30. Davidoff, "Class and Gender in Victorian England," esp. 88, 91, 130; Catherine Hall, "The Economy of Intellectual Prestige: Thomas Carlyle, John Stuart Mill, and the Case of Governor Eyre," *Cultural Critique* 12 (Spring 1989): 167–96; Satya P. Mohanty, "Drawing the Color Line: Kipling and the Culture of Colonial Rule," LaCapra, *The Bounds of Race*, 332–38, 341–42, 335–36. On imperial manhood, see John Mackenzie, "The Imperial Pioneer and Hunter and the British Masculine Stereotype in Late Victorian and Edwardian Times," in J. A. Mangan and James Walvin, eds., *Manliness and Morality: Middle-Class Masculinity in Britain and America, 1800–1940* (Manchester: Manchester University Press, 1986), 177, 180–82, 186; J. A. Mangan, "The Grit of Our Forefathers: Invented Traditions, Propaganda, and Imperialism," in Mackenzie, *Imperialism and Popular Culture*, esp. 115, 120, 122. On the Manichean Other, see Abdul JanMohamed, "The Economy of Manichean Allegory: The Function of Racial Difference in Colonialist Literature," 80–89 in Gates, *Race, Writing, and Difference*; DeGroot, " 'Sex' and Race.' " This Manichean construction was not confined to colonized people, but was employed in the eighteenth century in relation to the French. See Linda Colley, *Britons: Forging the Nation 1707–1837* (New Haven: Yale University Press, 1992). On the feminization and defamation of colonized men, see Mrinalina Sinha, "Gender and Imperialism: Colonial Policy and the Ideology of Moral Imperialism in Late Nineteenth Century Bengal," in Michael Kimmel, ed., *Changing Men: New Directions in Research on Men and Masculinity* (Beverly Hills: Sage, 1987), 217–31; John Roselli, "The Self-Image of Effeteness: Physical Education and Nationalism in Nineteenth-Century Bengal," *Past and Present* 86 (February 1980): 121–48, esp. 122–23, 138–39; Uma Chakravarti, "Whatever Happened to the Vedic *Dasi*? Orientalism, Nationalism, and a Script for the Past," in Kumkum Sangari and Sudesh Vaid, eds., *Recasting Women: Essays in Indian Colonial History* (New Brunswick: Rutgers University Press, 1990), esp. 47, 49; Thomas C. Holt, " 'An Empire over the Mind': Emancipation, Race, and Ideology in the British West Indies and the American South," in J. Morgan Kousser and James M. McPherson, eds., *Region, Race, and Reconstruction: Essays in Honor of C. Vann Woodward* (New York: Oxford University Press, 1982), 283–313; Patrick Brantlinger, "Africans and Victorians: The Geneology of the Myth of the Dark Continent," in Gates, *Race, Writing, and Difference*, 185–222, esp. 198, 206.

31. On the fallacy of biological notions of race, see George Stocking, *Victorian Anthropology* (New York: Free Press, 1987), esp. 106–7, 228–29; Nancy Stepan, *The Idea of Race in Science: Great Britain, 1800–1960* (London: Macmillan, 1982); Stephen Rose, " 'It's Only Human Nature': The Sociobiologists' Fairyland," *Race and Class* 20, 3 (1979): 277–87; Stephen Rose and Hilary Rose, "Less Than Human Nature: Biology and the New Right," *Race and Class* 27, 3 (1986): 47–66.

32. Eric Wolf makes a somewhat useful distinction between race, which he sees as imposed by the demands of the global labor market, and ethnicity, which he alleges reflects the authentic experiences of people themselves. *Europe and the People*

without History, 380–81. British imperialists, however, also manipulated definitions of ethnicity.

33. The question of whether British working people supported or shared middle- and upper-class fascination with and support for imperialism, with all its racist implications, remains unresolved, but see Richard Price, *An Imperial War and the British Working Class: Working-Class Attitudes and Reactions to the Boer War, 1899–1902* (London: Routledge & Kegan Paul, 1972); Mackenzie, *Propaganda and Empire*.

34. Evans, "Regulating the Reserve Army"; Stephen Castles and Godula Kosack, *Immigrant Workers and Class Structure in Western Europe* (1973; London: Oxford University Press, 1985); Fryer, *Staying Power*; Ramdin, *The Making of the Black Working Class*.

35. John Bodnar, *The Transplanted: A History of Immigrants in Urban America* (Bloomington: University of Indiana Press, 1985); George Bond, Walton Johnson, and Sheila Walker, "Introduction" to *African Christianity: Patterns of Religious Continuity* (New York: Academic Press, 1979); Frederick Cooper, "Urban Space, Industrial Time, and Wage Labour in Africa," in Frederick Cooper, ed., *Struggle for the City: Migrant Labour, Capital, and the State in Urban Africa* (London: Sage, 1983), 15; Wolf, *Europe and the People without History*; Shula Marks and Peter Richardson, eds., "Introduction" to *International Labour Migration: Historical Perspectives* (Hounslow, U.K.: Maurice Temple Smith, 1984), 1–18.

36. Compare the treatment in Kenneth Lunn, "The Seamen's Union and 'Foreign' Workers on British and Colonial Shipping, 1890–1939," *Bulletin—Society for the Study of Labour History* 53, pt. 3 (Winter 1988): 5–13; Lunn, "Race Relations or Industrial Relations?"; and Anne Dunlop, "Lascars and Labourers: Reactions to the Indian Presence in the West of Scotland During the 1920s and 1930s, *Scottish Labour History Society Journal* 25 (1990): 40–57, with the apologetic treatment in the official history in Arthur Marsh and Victoria Ryan, *The Seamen* (London: Malthouse, 1989).

I. "I Can Get No Justice": Black Men and Colonial Race Relations on the Western Front

1. The phrase is that of Rozina Visram, *Ayahs, Lascars, and Princes: the Story of Indians in Britain, 1700–1947* (London: Pluto, 1986), 113–14; also see Gregory Martin, "The Influence of Racial Attitudes toward India during the First World War," *Journal of Imperial and Commonwealth History* 14 (January 1986): 91ff.

2. The phrase is that of Sir Algernon Rumbold, *Watershed in India 1914–1922* (London: Athlone Press, 1979), 314–17; also see Leo Spitzer, *The Creoles of Sierra Leone: Responses to Colonialism, 1870–1945* (Madison: University of Wisconsin Press, 1974), esp. 3, 49, 154–56; Albert Grundlingh, *Fighting Their Own War: South African Blacks and the First World War* (Johannesburg: Ravan Press, 1987); Jenny Gould, "Women's Military Services in First World War Britain," in Margaret Randolph Higonnet, Jane Jenson, Sonya Michel, and Margaret Collins

Weitz, eds., *Behind the Lines: Gender and the Two World Wars* (New Haven: Yale University Press, 1987), 125.

3. Sir Charles Lucas, ed., *The Empire at War*, 5 vols. (London: Humphrey Milford/Oxford University Press, 1921–24), 2:332–35; 4:14–17, 119–30, 215, 225, 501. The volumes of this survey contain the most complete account of colonial support for Britain's war effort. Also see Philip Mason, *A Matter of Honour: An Account of the Indian Army, Its Officers, and Men* (New York: Holt, Rinehart and Winston, 1974), esp. pp. 405–70; Akinjide Osuntokun, *Nigeria in the First World War* (London: Longman, 1979), esp. 198, 236–39, 245, 313; Michael Summerskill, *China on the Western Front: Britain's Chinese Workforce in the First World War* (London: Michael Summerskill, 1982), esp. 37, 182; Peter B. Clarke, *West Africans at War: 1914–1918, 1939–1945: Colonial Propaganda and Its Cultural Aftermath* (London: Ethnographica, 1986); Grundlingh, *Fighting Their Own War*, esp. 10–11, 20, 39–40, and passim; B. P. Willan, "The South African Native Labour Contingent, 1916–1918," *Journal of African History* 19, 1 (1978): esp. 61–86. On Black men recruited in Britain, see *The Seaman*, 22 October 1915; also "British Arab's Gallantry," *The Seaman*, 21 December 1915; 14 January 1916; 7 December 1917. On French use of Black troops in Europe see Peter Fryer, *Staying Power: The History of Black People in Britain* (London: Pluto, 1984), 316–21; Rob Reinders, "Racialism on the Left: E. D. Morel and the 'Black Horror on the Rhine,'" *International Review of Social History* 13 (1968): 1–28; and Sally Marks, "Black Watch on the Rhine: A Study in Propaganda, Prejudice, and Prurience," *European Studies Review* 13 (1983): 297–334.

4. Mason, *A Matter of Honour*, 411; Visram, *Ayahs, Lascars, and Princes*, 116, 260. British War Cabinet papers CAB/24 GT 6399 and Lucas, *The Empire at War*, passim; Grundlingh, *Fighting Their Own War*, 96; Summerskill, *China on the Western Front*, 163; "Lascars and Seamen: Number Killed and Imprisoned during the War," L/E/7/1154/1229; Dinkar Dattatraya Desai, *Maritime Labour in India* (Bombay: Servants of India Society, 1940), 210; *Syren and Shipping* [a trade journal], 4 June 1919, 880; R. H Thornton, *British Shipping* (Cambridge: Cambridge University Press, 1939), 95.

5. Mason, *A Matter of Honour*, 410–11 and chap. 16, 17, and 18, pp. 405–70 passim; Jeffrey Greenhut, "The Imperial Reserve: The Indian Corps on the Western Front, 1914–1915," *Journal of Imperial and Commonwealth History* 12 (October 1983): 54; Summerskill, *China on the Western Front*, 22, 31–33, 56; Osuntokun, *Nigeria in the First World War*, 238, 244–46; Willan, "The South African Labour Contingent," 63. On treating colonized people as a natural resource, see Mary Louise Pratt, "Scratches on the Face of the Country; or, What Mr. Barrow Saw in the Land of the Bushmen," in Henry Louis Gates, ed., *Race, Writing, and Difference* (Chicago: University of Chicago Press, 1985).

6. J. P. MacLay of the Ministry of Shipping, November 1917, CAB24/GT7541, 3 June 1919; CAB24/GT2660; CAB24/GT2596; also see Daryl Klein, *With the Chinks* (London: John Lane, Bodley Head, 1919), 22, 172, 197.

7. 16 May 1917, CAB24/GT729; CAB24/GT1398. Derby was actually speaking of Chinese laborers in this instance. Most Chinese were not formally

colonized by Britain, but their experience in some ways resembled that of colonized Black people, although there were also significant differences that scholars have yet to adequately explore. Consequently they occupy an ambiguous place in the work at hand; see Ng Kwee Choo, *The Chinese in London* (London: Oxford University Press for the Institute of Race Relations, 1968); J. P. May, "The Chinese in Britain, 1860–1914," in Colin Holmes, ed., *Immigrants and Minorities in British Society* (London: George Allen & Unwin, 1978); Maria Lin Wong, *Chinese Liverpudlians* (Birkenhead: Liver Press, 1992); Maurice Broady, "The Social Adjustment of Chinese Immigrants in Liverpool," *Sociological Review* 3 (July 1955): 65–75.

8. Rumbold, *Watershed in India*, 20–37, 54–58, 94–99; Stephen Cohen, *The Indian Army: Its Contribution to the Development of a Nation* (Berkeley: University of California Press, 1971), 70–72; Robert Huttenback, *Racism and Empire: White Settlers and Colored Immigrants in the British Self-Governing Colonies, 1830–1910* (Ithaca: Cornell University Press, 1976), 21.

9. D. N. Singh, "The Indian Press and the War," *Asiatic Review* 5 (July–November 1914): 402.

10. Sir Roper-Lethbridge, "The War and the Mighty Voice of India," *Asiatic Review* 5 (July–November 1914): 269–79; Huttenback, *Racism and Empire*; Mason, *A Matter of Honour*, 25, 41, 408–11; Rumbold, *Watershed in India*, 7, 12, 13, 54–58, 94–99; Martin, "The Influence of Racial Attitudes"; Greenhut, "The Imperial Reserve," 55; Cohen, *The Indian Army*, 65, 67, 93; also see Lieutenant-Colonel Lord Ampthill, Indian Adviser to the Directorate of Labour, Indian Expeditionary Force, France, to Lt. General Herbert Cox of the India Office, 25 July 1917; 27 October 1917, L/MIL/5/738; Anthony H. M. Kirk-Greene, "'Damnosa Hereditas': Ethnic Ranking and the Martial Races Imperative in Africa," *Ethnic and Racial Studies* 3 (October 1980): 397; Gould, "Women's Military Services in First World War Britain," 114–25.

11. Quoted in Singh, "The Indian Press and the War," 396–402; also see Yusaf Ali, "India and the War"; *Asiatic Review* 5 (July–November 1914): 411, 413; and Roper-Lethbridge, "The War and the Mighty Voice of India." Also see Yusuf Ali, "The British Indian Army in Europe," *Asiatic Review* 5(July–November 1914): 282–89; Cohen, *The Indian Army*, 65, 67; Mason, *A Matter of Honour*, 408–11; Grundlingh, *Fighting Their Own War*, 13–14, 39, 50–51, 71, 133–34, 167–68; see Willan, "The South African Native Labour Contingent," 65–67; David Killingray and James K. Matthews, "Beasts of Burden: British West African Carriers in the First World War," *Canadian Journal of African History* 13 (1979): 15; Osuntokun, *Nigeria in the First World War*, 11, 64, 87–93, 291, 298–300, 307. Spitzer, *The Creoles of Sierra Leone*, 144, 154–56. On the meaning of African-American war service, John Whiteclay Chambers, *To Raise an Army: The Draft Comes to Modern America* (New York: Free Press, 1987), 37, 65, 93, 108, 156.

12. Cohen, *The Indian Army*, 70–72; Willan, "The South African Native Labour Contingent," 65–67; Grundlingh, *Fighting Their Own War*, 14, 39, 167; Rumbold, *Watershed in India*, 20–21, 23, 25, 31–33, 35, 37, 54–58, 94–99; also

Cynthia Enloe, *Ethnic Soldiers: State Security in Divided Societies* (Athens: University of Georgia Press, 1980), 225–27.

13. Killingray and Matthews, "Beasts of Burden," 20–21; James K. Matthews, "World War I and the Rise of African Nationalism: Nigerian Veterans as Catalysts of Change," *Journal of Modern African Studies* 20, 3 (1982): 493–502; Osuntokun, *Nigeria in the First World War*, 75–79; Grundlingh, *Fighting Their Own War*, 167–68. The dissenter is Lewis J. Greenstein, "The Impact of Military Service in World War I on Africans: The Nandi of Kenya," *Journal of Modern African Studies* 16 (September 1978): 495–507.

14. Yusaf Ali, "India and the War," *Asiatic Review* 5 (July–November 1914): 412; also proceedings of a meeting of the East India Association, 14 December 1914, *Asiatic Review* 6 (January–May 1915): 171.

15. Harold Peterson, *With The Indian Army in the Great War, 1916–1919: A Personal Narrative* (Harold Peterson, 1970), 21; Cohen, *The Indian Army*, 35, 42–43, 51, 84–87; Enloe, *Ethnic Soldiers*, 41; Mason, *A Matter of Honour*, 22–23; Greenhut, "The Imperial Reserve," 54, 58, 70. On African "martial races," see Kirk-Greene, " 'Damnosa Hereditas.' " Paternalistic relations were also cultivated between European officers and the ranks in the West African Frontier Force and the Chinese Labour Corps. Lucas, *The Empire at War*, 4:117; Klein, *With the Chinks*, 31, 35, 37, 39, 77, 90ff, 100, 114, 176; Terence Ranger, "The Invention of Tradition in Colonial Africa," in Eric Hobsbawm and Terence Ranger, eds., *The Invention of Tradition* (Cambridge: Cambridge University Press, 1986), 225–26.

16. Cohen, *The Indian Army*, 68–70; Enloe, *Ethnic Soldiers*, 48–49, 134–35; Matthews, "World War I and the Rise of African Nationalism."

17. Censor of Indian Mails, L/MIL/5/825: These excerpts consist of eight bound volumes of typed translated fragments numbered consecutively, interleafed with periodic summary reports. Most reports were signed by E. B. Howell, Chief Censor. The bulk are from December 1914 to November 1915. Subsequent citations will be to page and/or excerpt number. Many letters were written for common rather than personal consumption, in some ways an unusual advantage for our purpose, since personal letters often invite the criticism of unrepresentativeness. On self-censorship by the South African Native Labour Corps and the Chinese Labour Corps, see Grundlingh, *Fighting Their Own War*, 109–10, Summerskill, *China on the Western Front*, 102.

18. On a similar process in another context, see Eugene Genovese's essay "On Paternalism," in *Roll, Jordan, Roll: The World the Slaves Made* (New York: Vintage, 1976), esp. 5–7.

19. Dogra Bali Ran no. 4065, Kitchener Imperial Hospital, Brighton, to Gangaram Kangra, 28 October 1915, 1208/48.

20. Gholam Haider to Khan Sahib, 1307/.

21. Khadim Ali Khan, Pavilion Hospital, Brighton, to Jabar Khan, Indian Convalenscent Home, Boulogne, 1078/8; also see 1077/; 1079/92; 1185/8; 1233/4, also 1147/42; 1083/, 19 October 1915; *Asiatic Review* 5 (July–November 1914):

423–24. The Ottoman Sultan Mehmet V declared war on the Entente in November 1914, posing a potential conflict between religious and secular loyalties for Islamic British subjects. See Syud Hossain, "England, Turkey, and the Indian Mahome-dans," *Asiatic Review* 6 (January–May 1915): 145–55.

22. 1357/; also Bhagwan Singh, Brighton, 1398/46; 1309/.

23. Subadar Sar Buland, Karachi, to Allah Mir Khan, 57th Rifles, France, 1110/53.

24. 40th Pathans, France to Dost Muhammad, India, 1135/18.

25. N.K. Ibrahim Khan, 55th Rifles,/57th to Sepoy Akbar Khan, same regiment, in Hospital no. 12, Marseilles, 1187/15. Also 1442/28, 1438/22.

26. Leonore Davidoff, "Class and Gender in Victorian England: The Diaries of Arthur J. Munby and Hannah Cullwick," *Feminist Studies* 5 (Spring 1979): 87–141; Joanna DeGroot, " 'Sex' and 'Race': The Contruction of Language and Image in the Nineteenth Century," in Susan Mendus and Jane Rendall, eds., *Sexuality and Subordination: Interdisciplinary Studies of Gender in the Nineteenth Century* (London: Routledge, 1989); Kenneth Ballhatchet, *Race, Sex and Class under the Raj: Imperial Attitudes and Policies and Their Critics, 1793–1905* (London: Weidenfeld and Nicolson, 1980); Jane Haggis, "Gendering Colonialism or Co-lonising Gender? Recent Women's Studies Approaches to White Women and the History of British Colonialism," *Women's Studies International Forum* 13, 1/2 (1990): 105–15. Ann L. Stoler, "Making Empire Respectable: Race and Sexual Morality in Twentieth Century Colonial Cultures," *American Ethnologist* 16 (No-vember 1989): 634–60.

27. The phrase is that of American missionary Harold Peterson, *With the Indian Army*, 35; also Grundlingh, *Fighting Their Own War*, 15, 72; Spitzer, *The Creoles of Sierra Leone*, 155; Osuntokun, *Nigeria in the First World War*, 311; Ann Laura Stoler, "Rethinking Colonial Categories: European Communities and the Bound-aries of Rule," *Comparative Studies in Society and History* 13 (1989): 134–61; Ann Laura Stoler, "Carnal Knowledge and Imperial Power: Gender, Race, and Morality in Colonial Asia," in Micaela di Leonardo, ed., *Gender at the Crossroads of Knowl-edge: Feminist Anthropology in the Postmodern Era* (Berkeley: University of California Press, 1991), 51–101. Louis Greenstein offers the minority view that the "mys-tique" never existed, in "The Impact of Military Service," 504.

28. Klein, *With the Chinks*, 125–26, 134, 145, 208.

29. 1157/59.

30. 1214/57; also 1210/51.

31. 1216/59 1 November 1915; also 1387/36; D. Thomson, to Mrs. Thomson in Hull, 1299/; 1167/74. For conflicts, see E. Charles Vivian, *With the Royal Army Medical Corps at the Front* (London: Hodder and Stoughton, 1914); Grundlingh, *Fighting Their Own War*, 100, 122–26.

32. Amirah Inglis, *The White Women's Protection Ordinance: Sexual Anxiety and Politics in Papua* (New York: St. Martin's, 1975); Stoler, "Making Empire Re-spectable"; Stoler, "Carnal Knowledge," 59, 67, and passim.

33. 1204/40. Also see 1202/37; 1142/31; 1361; 1289/47; 1385/33. White men were almost never mentioned.

34. Grundlingh, *Fighting Their Own War*, 38, 47.

35. Mary Booth, *With the British Expeditionary Force in France*, 2d ed. with a Preface by Arthur E. Copping (London: Salvation Army, 1916), 12; Pathan Sowar Sirdar Khan FPO 13, France, to India, 1276/31, 1356; N. D. Sircar, storekeeper, K. I. H. Brighton, in English, 1292/45; 1151/50; Censor's Summary 843–48, 30 October 1915; 1289/47. It is well to recall that British women's "respectability" was open to interpretation on class and race bases. See Judith Walkowitz and Daniel Walkowitz, " 'We Are Not Beasts of the Field': Prostitution and the Poor in Plymouth and Southampton during the Contagious Diseases Act," in Mary Hartmann and Lois Banner, eds., *Cleo's Consciousness Raised: New Perspectives on the History of Women* (New York: Harper Colophon, 1974); John Gillis, "Servants, Sexual Relations and the Risks of Illegitimacy in London, 1801–1900, *Feminist Studies* 5(Spring 1979), 142– 73; Anna Clark, "Rape or Seduction? A Controversy over Sexual Violence in the Nineteenth Century," in London Feminist History Group, eds., *The Sexual Dynamics of History* (London: Pluto, 1983), 13–27.

36. On hospital visits, see Visram, *Ayahs, Lascars, and Princes*, 129, and Martin, "The Influence of Racial Attitudes," 94–99. On similar military strategies in other contexts, see Walkowitz and Walkowitz, " 'We Are Not Beasts of the Field' "; Cynthia Enloe, *Does Khaki Become You? The Militarization of Women's Lives* (Boston: South End Press, 1983); Susan Gubar, " 'This Is My Rifle, This Is My Gun': World War II and the Blitz on Women," in Higonnet et al., *Behind the Lines*, 227–59. On "the economy of self-sacrifice" and its postwar repercussions for white soldiers, see Eric Leed, *No Man's Land: Combat and Identity in World War I* (Cambridge: Cambridge University Press, 1979), 204.

37. Greenhut makes this argument in "The Imperial Reserve," 69.

38. Sikh FPO 13 to Mohant Partab Das, Patiala, 1084/17.

39. 1404/58; 1450/37; also 1436/19. On family tensions, 1078/7; 1188/16; 1374/12; 1432/12 18 December 1915; 1432/12 18 December 1915; 1272/; 1313/ no. 903/908 Indian Mail Censor's Office Boulogne, signed E. B. Howell, Chief Censor, 4 December 1915; also 1380/26, 1443/29. On European troops, see Leed, *No Man's Land*.

40. 1114/61; 1131/7.

41. 1309; 1355; 1338, 1339. Censor's reports, 6 and 27 November, 4 and 11 December 1915; 1341; Hossain, "England, Turkey, and the Indian Mahomedans," esp. 151; Letter to the Editor, *Asiatic Review* 6 (January–May 1915): 326–28; Syud Hossain, "India and the House of Lords," *Asiatic Review* 6 (January–May 1915): 357; Zamar Khan to Rawalpindi, 1148/45. See also 113/58; 2722; Clarke, *West Africans at War*, 18; Osuntokun, *Nigeria in the First World War*, 139–41.

42. Nemesio 1295; 1108/51; 1289/47; 1396/44; 1183/3; Sepoy Kharka of 57th Wilde's Rifles from the Pavilion Hospital at Brighton, 1441/27; also 1154/ 57, /57A; 1205/43; 1270/21; 1154/57. Godbole, 1289/47, 1290–91. For further examples of low morale, 1340; 1417/99; 1318; 1454/41; also Philip Mason, *A Matter of Honour*, 409, 418, 422, 425. The censor mentioned "electrical treatment" applied to "cure" "malingerers," Censor's report 6 November 1915, 860/865. On segregation in hospitals, see Visram, *Ayahs, Lascars, and Princes*, 123–34; also

Martin, "The Influence of Racial Attitudes." On class and gender implications of "malingering," see Elaine Showalter, "Rivers and Sassoon: The Inscription Male Gender Anxieties," in Higonnet et al., *Behind the Lines*, 61–69. For a photograph of Indian convalescents taking "electrical and galvanic treatments at the Kitchener Hospital, Brighton," see Kusoom Vadgama, *India in Britain: The Indian Contribution to the British Way of Life* (London: Robert Royce, 1984), 100.

43. Greenhut, "The Imperial Reserve," 54–56, 60–64, 66–67, 69; Martin, "The Influence of Racial Attitudes," esp. 103. This conclusion also ignored the British Army's similar inability to function in Africa. Osuntokun, *Nigeria in the First World War*, 240.

44. See reports to the War Cabinet, Spring 1917: CAB24/GT778, Spring 1917; CAB24/GT797, 15 May 1917; CAB24/40/GT3244, January 1918; Lucas, *The Empire at War*, 3: 394–96; 4: 118, 130, 215–25, 470–96, 501; Grundlingh, *Fighting Their Own War*, 57–114; Peterson, *With the Indian Army in the Great War* 11; Vadgama, *India in Britain*, 99; Visram, *Ayahs, Lascars, and Princes*, 260.

45. Kasri Nath, Third Indian Labour Corps, Memorandum to Lt.-Col. Lord Ampthill, 10 July 1917, L/MIL/5/738; Yusaf Ali, "India and the War," *Asiatic Review* 5 (July–November 1914): 412; Grundlingh, *Fighting Their Own War*, 15–16, 58–79, 96, 168; Willan, "The South African Native Labour Contingent," 67–68; Klein, *With the Chinks*, 110, 132; Lucas, *The Empire at War*, 336; Summerskill, *China on the Western Front*, 41, 152–58, 168–70; Osuntokun, *Nigeria in the First World War*, 247, 252, 256; Killingray and Matthews, "Beasts of Burden," 11–14.

46. On migration within the empire, see Huttenback, *Racism and Empire*; Hugh Tinker, *Separate and Unequal: India and Indians in the British Commonwealth, 1920–1950* (London: C. Hurst, 1976).

47. Grundlingh, *Fighting Their Own War*, passim; Killingray and Matthews, "Beasts of Burden," 11, 16–18; Osuntokun, *Nigeria in the First World War*, 238, 244–46, 255. The South African Native Labour Contingent was withdrawn in January 1918 because the authorities were unable to contain their sometimes violent resistance to discrimination and segregation in France. Willan, "The South African Native Labour Contingent," 68–79; Grundlingh, *Fighting Their Own War*, 110–14.

48. Lieutenant-Colonel Lord Ampthill, Indian Adviser to the Directorate of Labour in France, repeatedly protested the Army's ill-use of the Indian Labour Companies, charging the authorities with "colour prejudice." See esp. Ampthill to Herbert Cox in the India Office, 27 August 1917, L/MIL/5/738. Cabinet discussions also revealed negligence and inefficiency in the Chinese Labour Corps. CAB24 GT3400, 18 January 1918. Also see CAB24/GT1398; Klein, *With the Chinks*, 12, 18. The question of commissions for Indian officers was a longstanding grievance of colonial origin. Rumbold, *Watershed in India*, 66; Visram, *Ayahs, Lascars, and Princes*, 114; Martin, "The Influence of Racial Attitudes," 101–5.

49. An example was the demand of the postwar National Congress of British West Africa, for "full citizenship . . . or full independence." Osontokun, "Nigeria in the First World War," 91–93; also see Greenstein, "The Impact of Military

Service," 503, 507. Eric Leed suggests European soldiers similarly understood their military service in terms of an "economy of sacrifice," an explicit "exchange" in which they subordinated personal goals to the collective, entitling them to claim "honor," and "prestige," and to make postwar "political and economic demands" on the state and the society. *No Man's Land*, 204, 208. In the colonized situation, it appears these claims were held against the British government and its imperial power; and that they were placed not only on behalf of individual veterans, but of all colonized people.

2. "A Shame on Britain's Part": Problems of Empire in the Postwar Order

1. The chronology of British imperial decline remains contentious, but see John Darwin, "The Fear of Falling: British Politics and Imperial Decline since 1900," *Transactions of the Royal Historical Society* 36 (1986): 27–43; and "Imperialism in Decline? Tendencies in British Imperial Policy between the Wars," *Historical Journal* 23, 3 (1980): 657–79; Aaron Friedberg, *The Weary Titan: Britain and the Experience of Relative Decline, 1895–1905* (Princeton: Princeton University Press, 1990). Also see Rudolf von Albertini, "The Impact of Two World Wars on the Decline of Colonialism," *Journal of Contemporary History* 4 (1969): 17–36.

2. Richard Price, "Labour Process and Labour History," *Social History* 8 (January 1983): 65–70; Richard Price, *Masters, Unions and Men: Work Control in Building and the Rise of Labour 1830–1914* (Cambridge: Cambridge University Press, 1980), 236–41; Patrick Joyce, *Work, Society and Politics: the Culture of the Factory in Later Victorian England* (New Brunswick: Rutgers University Press, 1984), 334–38; George Dangerfield, *The Strange Death of Liberal England, 1910–1914* (1935; New York: Putnam, 1980); Paul Thompson, *The Edwardians: The Remaking of British Society* (Chicago: Academy Chicago, 1985).

3. In the interwar years, heightened labor and nationalist insurgency also prompted a more explicitly "segregationist stance" in many European colonies. Ann Laura Stoler, "Carnal Knowledge and Imperial Power: Gender, Race and Morality in Colonial Asia," in Micaela di Leonardo, ed., *Gender at the Crossroads of Knowledge: Feminist Anthropology in the Postmodern Era* (Berkeley: University of California Press, 1991), 86.

4. "The otherness of the colonized ... was the bedrock of all colonialism. Yet ... to correct difference ... was one of the justifications ... for colonialism." Persis Charles, "The Name of the Father: Women, Paternity, and British Rule in Nineteenth Century Jamaica," *International Labor and Working Class History* 41 (Spring 1992): 19; also Leo Spitzer, *The Creoles of Sierra Leone: Responses to Colonialism, 1870–1945* (Madison: University of Wisconsin Press, 1974), 154–74, 199; Hugh Tinker, *Separate and Unequal: India and Indians in the British Commonwealth, 1920–1950* (London: C. Hurst, 1976), 22–23, 37; Robert A. Huttenback, *Racism and*

Empire: White Settlers and Coloured Immigrants in the British Self-Governing Colonies, 1830–1910 (Ithaca: Cornell University Press, 1976).

5. Keith Middlemas, *Politics in Industrial Society* (London: Andre Deutsch, 1979), 20–22; Arthur Marwick, *The Deluge: British Society and the First World War* (Boston: Little, Brown, 1965), 23, 97–105, 203; James Cronin, "Coping with Labour, 1918–1926," in James Cronin and Jon Schneer, *Social Conflict and the Political Order in Britain* (New Brunswick: Rutgers University Press, 1982), 118; *Labour and Society in Britain* (London: Batsford, 1984), 10–12, 32; Sidney Pollard, *The Development of the British Economy, 1914–1980* (London: Edward Arnold, 1983), 1–50; Susan Pedersen, "Gender, Welfare and Citizenship in Britain during the Great War," *American Historical Review* 95 (October 1990): 983–1006; James E. Cronin, *The Politics of State Expansion: War, State, and Society in Twentieth-Century Britain* (London: Routledge, 1991), esp. 65–77; Ralph Desmarias, "Lloyd George and the Development of the British Government's Strikebreaking Organization," *International Review of Social History* 20 (1975): part 1, 1–15, esp. 8; Paul Gordon, *Policing Immigration: Britain's Internal Controls* (London: Pluto, 1985); Jane Morgan, *Conflict and Order: The Police and Labour Disputes in England and Wales, 1900–1939* (Oxford: Clarendon, 1987).

6. The quote is from Spitzer, *The Creoles of Sierra Leone*, 154–74, 199; Nicholas Mansergh, *The Commonwealth Experience: From British to Multiracial Commonwealth*, vol. 2 (Toronto: University of Toronto Press, 1982); R. J. Moore, "India and the British Empire," in C. C. Eldridge, ed., *British Imperialism in the Nineteenth Century* (London: Macmillan, 1984), 64–85; Tinker, *Separate and Unequal*, 10, 22; Algernon Rumbold, *Watershed in India 1914–1922* (London: Athlone, 1979), 314–17.

7. Marwick, *The Deluge*, 26, 97–105, 203. For political claims based on military service see Rumbold, *Watershed in India*, 300; Stephen Cohen, *The Indian Army: Its Contribution to the Development of a Nation* (Berkeley: University of California Press, 1971), 80. J. M. Barbalet, *Citizenship: Rights, Struggle, and Class Inequality* (Milton Keynes, U.K.: Open University Press, 1988), 37–40; T. H. Marshall, *Class, Citizenship, and Social Development: Essays by T. H. Marshall* with an Introduction by Seymour Martin Lipset (Garden City, N. Y.: Doubleday, 1964), 111–17; on expanded state provision, see James E. Cronin, *The Politics of State Expansion: War, State, and Society in Twentieth-Century Britain* (London: Routledge, 1991); on masculinity and war, see Nancy C. M. Hartsock, "Masculinity, Heroism, and the Making of War," in Adrienne Harris and Ynestra King, eds., *Rocking the Ship of State: Toward a Feminist Peace Politics* (Boulder, Colo: Westview Press, 1989), 133–52; Jenny Gould, "Women's Military Services in First World War Britain," in Margaret Higonnet et al., eds., *Behind the Lines: Gender and the Two World Wars* (New Haven: Yale University Press, 1987), 114–25; Susan Pederson, "Gender, Welfare, and Citizenship in Britain during the Great War," *American Historical Review* 95 (October 1990):983–1006.

8. Special Report 10, "Unrest among the Negroes," 7 October 1919, CAB24 GT8289. On Indian nationalism and race discrimination against Indians abroad, see Huttenback, *Racism and Empire*; Robert Huttenback, "No Strangers within

the Gates: Attitudes and Policies towards the Non-White Residents of the British Empire of Settlement," *Journal of Imperial and Commonwealth History* 1 (May 1973): 271–302; T. G. Fraser, "The Sikh Problem in Canada and Its Political Consequences, 1905–1921," *Journal of Imperial and Commonwealth History* 7 (October 1978): 35–55.

9. Mansergh, *The Commonwealth Experience*, vol. 2; Rumbold, *Watershed in India*, 58–59; Cohen, *The Indian Army*, 76; Tinker, *Separate and Unequal*, 34–39, 44, 46. State efforts did, however, include covert repression: see Kusoom Vadgama, *India in Britain: The Indian Contribution to the British Way of Life* (London: Robert Royce, 1984), 159, for an account of the treatment of Shapurji Saklatvala, a Labour and Communist Member of Parliament.

10. Huttenback, "No Strangers within the Gates," 271–302; Huttenback, *Racism and Empire*, 22; Tinker, *Separate and Unequal*, 22–23, 37; E. Agnes R. Haigh "India after the War," *Asiatic Review* 5 (July–November 1914): 415–22; Memoranda 20, 147, 5 August 1921, Joint Standing Aliens and Nationality Committee, L/E/7/1224/702 (hereafter abbreviated J.S.A.N.C. and cited by individual memorandum numbers). In the nineteenth century, the principle of racial equality, "no distinction in favour of or against race or colour," had been widely espoused by promoters of British imperialism, for example, Joseph Chamberlain, quoted by Shah Mohammed Naimatullah, "Lord Hardinge and Indians in South Africa," *Asiatic Review* 3–4 (January–May 1914): 54–57. "Equal and impartial protection of the law" was promised to "our subjects, of whatever race or creed, freely and impartially," by "Victoria's Proclamation, 1 November 1858:" (in C. H. Philips, H. L. Singh, and B. N. Pandey, eds., *The Evolution of Indian and Pakistan, 1858–1947: Select Document* [London: Oxford University Press, 1962], vol. 4, 10–11), and was widely interpreted to imply racial equality. Also see Percival Spear, *India: A Modern History* (Ann Arbor: University of Michigan Press, 1961), 278; Bernard S. Cohn, "Representing Authority in Victorian India," in Eric Hobsbawm and Terence Ranger, eds., *The Invention of Tradition* (Cambridge: Cambridge University Press 1983), 165–209.

11. David Feldman, "The Importance of Being English: Jewish Immigration and the Decay of Liberal England," in David Feldman and Gareth Stedman Jones, eds., *Metropolis London: Histories and Representations Since 1800* (London: Routledge, 1989), 57–58; Bernard Gainer, *The Alien Invasion: The Origins of the Aliens Act of 1905* (London: Heinemann, 1972), 54–55, 144–45, 208–9 and passim; John Garrard, *The English and Immigration: A Comparative Study of the Jewish Influx, 1880–1910* (London: Oxford University Press for the Institute of Race Relations, 1971). J.S.A.N.C. Memoranda nos. 27, 39, 50; See also *Parliamentary Debates* (*Parl. Deb.*) (Commons) 5th ser., 108(1918): 11 July 1918; and Cabinet Memoranda CAB24/GT4402, 1 May 1916; GT 4931, June 1918; GT4961, GT 5075, GT5409, GT 6869, GT7581, GT7724; CAB24/76 GT6971 12 March 1919; Paul Gordon, *Policing Immigration: Britain's Internal Controls* (London: Pluto, 1985), 9; and Panikos Panayi, *The Enemy in Our Midst: Germans in Britain during the First World War* (New York: Berg, 1991). On Britishness, see Satya P. Mohanty, "Drawing the Color Line: Kipling and the Culture of Colonial Rule," in Dominick

LaCapra, ed., *The Bounds of Race: Perspectives on Hegemony and Resistance* (Ithaca: Cornell University Press, 1991); Catherine Hall, "The Economy of Intellectual Prestige: Thomas Carlyle, John Stuart Mill, and the Case of Governor Eyre," *Cultural Critique* 12 (Spring 1989): 167–96.

12. Cabinet Memorandum 12 March 1919, CAB24/76 GT6971.

13. The quote is from a Cabinet Memorandum, 18 June 1919, proposing an amendment to Article 22B of the Aliens Restriction Order, CAB24/GT7504. The vast bulk of aliens control work was designed to regulate the labor supply, albeit with marginal effectiveness. See J.S.A.N.C. Memoranda nos. 32; 39, 20 May 1919; 40, 23 May 1919; 45, 18 June 1919; 62, 29 July 1919; 67, 92, 8 January 1920; 97; and economic arguments, 50, 17 June 1919; 122, 28 June 1920; 124, 16 July 1920; 138, February 1921.

14. This process can be traced through the Minutes of the Joint Standing Aliens and Nationality Committee, 1919–1926, L/E/7/1224/702; also found in HO45/19966/374304.

15. J.S.A.N.C. Memoranda nos. 165, 18 October 1922; 167, 3 November 1922; 191, 15 October 1925; Cabinet Memorandum 11 August 1919, CAB24/GT7958; Foreign Office to the India Office, 16 March 1921, L/P&S/12/3311.

16. Interdepartmental meeting of representatives of the Home Office, India Office, High Commissioner for India, Board of Trade, and Colonial Office, 2 November 1928; and "Coloured Seamen," note of a conference held at the Home Office on 5 November 1928, L/E/9/953.

17. See, for example, J.S.A.N.C. Memorandum 20, March 1919; India Office Political and Judicial Department discussions in 1939, L/P&J/8/8; John Pedder in Home Office minute, January 1923, HO45/11897/332087/70. See also chapter 6.

18. Central-Register of Aliens, HO45/12258/391001, esp. /1, 7 October, 1919; report by H. R. Scott, W. Haldane Porter, and Sir Leonard Dunning of the Aliens Department staff, 3 November 1920, /15; also /13; /18; /19. On passport control, J.S.A.N.C. Memoranda nos. 58, 28 April 1922; 67; 69, 19 September 1919; 143, 10 June 1921; 156, 24 March 1922. Also see Memoranda nos. 167, 3 November 1922; 168, 18 October 1922; 191, 15 October 1925, HO45/19966/374304; and Cabinet Memorandum 11 August 1919, CAB24/GT7958. On gendered dimensions of nationality policy, see Francesca Klug, "Oh, To Be in England: The British Case Study," in Nira Yuval-Davis and Floya Anthius, eds., *Women-Nation-State* (London: Macmillan, 1984), 17–18.

19. See especially paragraphs 162, p. 42; 176, p. 55; 178 and 179. *Manual on Merchant Shipping and Seamen*, issued by the International Seafarers' Federation, n.d. [ca. 1918–22], Mss175/5/27i. The measure of the difficulty of policing Black seamen can be taken by observing the work it generated for the Aliens Department. Although control of European immigration apparently proceeded routinely, requiring a minimum of involvement from Whitehall in the business of local immigration officers, "coloured" workers and seamen from the colonies took an increasing and at times dominant proportion of the Aliens Department's work between 1920 and 1939.

20. Peter Linebaugh, "Labour History without Labour Process," *Social History* 7 (October 1982): 327; John Mackenzie, *Propaganda and Empire: The Manipulation of British Public Opinion 1880–1960* (Manchester: Manchester University Press, 1984), 187.

21. Derek Aldcroft, *The British Economy, I: Years of Turmoil, 1920–1951* (Atlantic Highlands, N.J.: Humanities Press, 1986), 34–35; and "The Depression in British Shipping, 1901–1911," *Journal of Transport History* 7 (May 1965): 14–23; Sidney Pollard, *The Development of the British Economy, 1914–1980* (London: Edward Arnold, 1983), 75–76; Labour Research Department (L.R.D.), *Shipping*, Studies in Labour and Capital no. 4 (London: Labour Publishing Department, 1923), 14–16; *Syren and Shipping*, 19 June 1919, 1076; Ralph Davis, "Introduction" to Adam Willis Kirkaldy, *British Shipping: Its History, Organization, and Importance* (1914; New York: Augustus M. Kelly, Publishers, 1970), also 168, 207.

22. Francis Hyde, *Shipping Enterprise and Management, 1830–1939: Harrison's of Liverpool* (Liverpool: Liverpool University Press, 1967), 161–77; L.R.D., *Shipping*, 5, 10–12, 21–22, 31–33, 40; S. G. Sturmey, *British Shipping and World Competition* (London: Athlone, 1962), 36–37.

23. L.R.D., *Shipping*, 43–44; R. H. Thornton, *British Shipping* (Cambridge: Cambridge University Press, 1939), 85–86, 96, 101, 109, 119, 127; Sturmey, *British Shipping*, 22–26, 34–56, 60; Davis, "Introduction" to Kirkaldy, *British Shipping*, vi, also 166; Tony Lane, *Grey Dawn Breaking: British Merchant Seafarers in the Late Twentieth Century* (Manchester: Manchester University Press, 1986), 11; E. S. Gregg, "The Decline of Tramp Shipping," *Quarterly Journal of Economics* 1 (1926): 338–46, esp. 340–41; Derek Aldcroft, "Port Congestion and the Shipping Boom of 1919–1920," *Business History* 3 (June 1961): 97–106.

24. Davis, "Introduction," vi; Hyde, *Shipping Enterprise and Management*, 63, 131, 137, 143–49, 156; Sturmey, *British Shipping*, 61–68; P. N. Davies, *The Trade Makers: Elder Dempster in West Africa, 1852–1972* (London: George Allen & Unwin, 1973), 216–17; Lane, *Grey Dawn Breaking*, 7. On the contemporary industry, see Paul Chapman, *Trouble on Board: The Plight of International Seafarers* (Ithaca: ILR Press, 1992).

25. Seven companies owned three quarters of British liner tonnage. L.R.D., *Shipping*, 22, 28–29, 31; Kirkaldy, *British Shipping*, 172–73; Aldcroft, "The Depression in Shipping"; Hyde, *Harrisons*, 149–52; also see Harris Joshua, Tina Wallace, and Heather Booth, *To Ride the Storm: The 1980 Bristol "Riot" and the State* (London: Heinemann Educational, 1983), 29.

26. Minutes of Proceedings of Conference, International Joint Conference between Shipowners and Seamen, 22 and 24 January 1921, Mss175/5/22i; also quoted by George Hardy in *The Struggle of British Seamen* (London: Dorrit, 1927), 11. Some tramp companies were so desperate for a return on their investments that they accepted freights below the cost of the voyages. Sturmey, *British Shipping*, 67–68.

27. L.R.D., *Shipping*, 26; Minutes of the Seventh Meeting of the National Maritime Board, April 1921, 76–89, Mss175/523i.

28. Hardy, quoting from *Lloyd's Register*, *The Struggle of British Seamen*, 18–20, also 21; Thornton, *British Shipping*, 250–51; Max Fletcher, "From Coal to Oil in British Shipping," *Journal of Transport History* 3 (February 1975): 1–19.

29. Weston to Turner, 6 August 1935, enclosure to Appendix IV National Maritime Board to Tramp Shipping Subsidy Committee, IOR L/E/9/955. In the liner ports of Liverpool and London, Black men worked on both standard and special labor contracts called Lascar articles of agreement; meanwhile men migrated from other ports to Bristol and the Tyne to seek work at standard rates. Lane, *Grey Dawn Breaking*, 8; M. J. Daunton, "Jack Ashore: Seamen in Cardiff Before 1914," *Welsh History Review* 9, 2 (1975): 176–203.

30. On union busting, see L.R.D., *Shipping*, 49; John Saville, "Trade Unionism and Free Labour: The Background to the Taff Vale Decision," in Michael Flinn and T. C. Smout, eds., *Studies in Social History* (Oxford: Clarendon, 1974), 249–76; Ron Bean, "Employers' Associations in the Port of Liverpool," *International Review of Social History* 21, 3 (1976): 380–81; Geoffrey Alderman, "The National Free Labour Associations: A Case Study of Organised Strikebreaking in the Late Nineteenth and Early Twentieth Centuries," *International Review of Social History* 21, 3 (1976): 309–36. On working conditions, Kirkaldy, *British Shipping*, 269–70; on "casual" labor, David Caradog Jones, *The Social Survey of Merseyside*, 2 vols. (Liverpool: University of Liverpool Press, 1932), 2:88. W. E. Home, *Merchant Seamen: Their Diseases and Their Welfare Needs* (New York: Dutton, 1922), 6.

31. See Paul Rich, *Race and Empire in British Politics* (Cambridge: Cambridge University Press, 1986), esp. 5.

32. J.S.A.N.C. Memorandum no. 147, 5 August 1921.

3. BLACK SEAMEN IN BRITISH SHIPS: THE USES OF RACE FOR BRITISH SHIPOWNERS

1. For the latter, see Stephen Castles and Godula Kosack, *Immigrant Workers and Class Structure in Western Europe* (New York: Oxford University Press, 1985); Claude Meillassoux, *Maidens, Meal, and Money: Capitalism and the Domestic Community* (Cambridge: Cambridge University Press, 1975).

2. See Arthur J. McIwan, "Employers' Organizations and Strike-breaking in Britain, 1880–1914," *International Review of Social History* 29 (1984): 1–33, esp. 7–9, 31–33; Martin Daunton, "Jack Ashore: Seamen in Cardiff before 1914," *Welsh History Review* 9, 2 (1975): 176–203; John Saville, "Trade Unions and Free Labour: The Background to the Taff Vale Decision," in Michael Flinn and T. C. Smout, eds., *Essays in Social History* (Oxford: Clarendon, 1974), 251–76.

3. Thomas Brassey, *British Seamen* (London: Longmans Green, 1877), 35–37; R. H. Thornton, *British Shipping* (Cambridge: Cambridge University Press, 1939), 221–22. The Navigation Acts stipulated that three quarters of crew members of ships sailing into British ports must be British sailors. Bob Hepple, *Race, Jobs, and the Law* (Harmondsworth: Penguin, 1968), 63.

4. Trade Union delegation to the Board of Trade, March 1914, MT9/ 1087.M835119.

5. Joseph Havelock Wilson, *My Stormy Voyage through Life* (London: Co-operative Press, 1925), 78, 98, 127–28; Wilson to the International Transportworkers' Federation, 15 August 1910, Mss159/3/B/63/2; General Secretary Edmund Cathery to the Registry of Friendly Societies, FS 12/189 (NUS 1493T).

6. Hepple, *Race, Jobs, and the Law*, 63; Tony Lane, *Grey Dawn Breaking: British Merchant Seafarers in the Late Twentieth Century* (Manchester: Manchester University Press, 1986), 17; Brassey, *British Seamen*, 36; F. J. A. Broeze, "The Muscles of Empire-Indian Seamen and the Raj, 1919–1939," *Indian Economic and Social History Review* 18 (January–March 1981): 43–67. On the extensive use of Asian contract labor in the postemancipation British empire, see Hugh Tinker, *A New System of Slavery: The Export of Indian Labour Overseas, 1830–1920* (London: Oxford University Press for the Institute of Race Relations, 1974), 41; Hugh Tinker, *Separate and Unequal: India and the Indians in the British Commonwealth, 1920–1950* (London: Hurst, 1976). Also see Appendix 1.

7. Minute by Hoskin, 5 August 1929, and Board of Trade Minute, 3 October 1927, MT9/2735 M.4184; W. E. Home, *Merchant Seamen: Their Diseases and Their Welfare Needs* (New York: Dutton, 1922), 87; Federation of Nigeria, *Report of the Board of Enquiry into the Trade Dispute between the Elder Dempster Lines Ltd. and the Nigerian Union of Seamen* (Lagos: Federal Government Printer, 1959), esp. 31–34; 79–81; 118–24; P. G. Kanekar, *Seamen in Bombay: Report of an Enquiry into the Conditions of Their Life and Work* (Bombay: Servants of India Society, 1925), Mss159/5/3/587, 17; A. Colaco, ed., *A History of the Seamen's Union, Bombay* (Bombay: Pascoal Vaz, 1955), 87–88, Mss159/5/3/588.

8. Inspection of Lascars' Food," L/E/7/604; The Merchant Shipping Act, 1894, L/E/9/936; "Employment of Lascars on British Ships," MT9/3083 M.11232. In 1939 striking Indian seamen's demands included warm clothing. See chapter 8. Ghee is clarified butter used in Indian cooking.

9. Thornton, *British Shipping*, 221–22; Brassey, *British Seamen*, 19; and see Hepple, *Race, Jobs, and the Law*. 64. Mortality reported in *The Seaman*, 15 May 1914; House of Commons debates 3 and 9 March 1908, *Parl. Deb.*, 4th ser. vol. 185 (1908): 493–508, 1115; and 6, 7, 22 and 23 April 1909, *Parl. Deb.*, 4th ser. vol. 3 (1909): 1131–32, 1253–54, 1786, 1869–70; (20 March 1914): 7; Home, *Merchant Seamen*, 87, 94.

10. India Office Records L/E/7/936; "Inspection of Lascars' Food," 1908, L/ E/7/604; Kanekar, *Seamen in Bombay*, 9–13; Letter from Charles Ainsworth to the *Telegraph* reprinted in *The Seaman*, 29 November 1933, 2; on Trinidadians, see N.U.S. Executive Council Minutes, 7 July 1939, p. 4, Mss175/1/1/9; on West Africans, see chapter 4.

11. For relative proportions of "free" and "lascar" labor, see Table 2. Paul Tofahrn, Secretary of International Transportworkers Federation, delegation to the Ministry of War Transport, 11 May 1942, MT9/3657 M.7724; Lane, *Grey Dawn Breaking*, 17; Hepple, *Race, Jobs, and the Law*, 63, esp. chap. 4; Brassey, *British Seamen*, 36; India Office Records, L/E/7/936; "Elder Dempster, 1925–

1935," MT9/2735; Catherine Betty Abigail Behrens, *Merchant Shipping and the Demands of War* (London: HMSO, 1955), 157; "Engagement of Natives of India under European Articles, and Position of Eurasian Seamen," 20 November 1903, L/E/7/481; Colaco, *History of the Seamen's Union, Bombay*, 58; E. J. Turner of the India Office, 10 October 1936, MT9/2778.

12. Section 29 of Act V. of 1883, quoted in "Inspection of Lascars' Food," L/E/7/604; Hepple, *Race, Jobs, and the Law*, 63.

13. J. G. Dendy, Chief Superintendant, Port of London, to Hoskin of the Board of Trade, 7 August 1923, L/E/7/1152.

14. David Caradog Jones, *The Social Survey of Merseyside*, 2 vols. (Liverpool: Liverpool University Press, 1932), 2:102, 98; and see R. Bean, "Employers' Associations in the Port of Liverpool 1890–1914," *International Review of Social History* 21 (1976): 366–67.

15. Eric Sager, *Seafaring Labour: The Merchant Marine of Atlantic Canada, 1820–1914* (Toronto: McGill-Queen's University Press, 1989), 10–11, 246, 261, 264–65.

16. Brassey, *British Seamen*, 11, 17, 35–36; Sager, *Seafaring Labour*, 248–49, 262–63; James C. Healey, *Foc'sle and Glory Hole: A Study of the Merchant Seaman and His Occupation* (New York: Greenwood Press, 1969), 29–34; Captain Kent, "Sailors: Past and Present," *Syren and Shipping*, 27 June 1917, 805.

17. Thornton, *British Shipping*, 82; Harris Joshua, Tina Wallace, and Heather Booth, *To Ride the Storm: The 1980 Bristol "Riot" and the State* (London: Heinemann 1983), 14–15. Eric Taplin, *Liverpool Seamen and Dockers 1870–1890* (Hull: University of Hull Press, 1974), 14; Tony Lane reports that many of the men called "Somalis" were actually from the Sudan, Aden, Yemen, and Zanzibar. *Grey Dawn Breaking*, 18, 21, 32–33, 153–55, 175, 167–69, 174. David Byrne, "The 1930 'Arab Riot' in South Shields: A Race Riot That Never Was," *Race and Class* 18, 3 (1977): 263; Kanekar, *Seamen in Bombay*, 11; "Types of Indian Seamen," *Syren and Shipping*, 3 January 1945, 117. On similar racial divisions in the U.S. industry, see "Rose Shovell, Glory Hole Sailor," an interview by Joe Doyle in *The Hawsepipe: Newsletter of the Marine Workers' Historical Association* 11 (January–February 1992): 11. Also see reference to racially segregated "checkerboard crews" in "Memorial for Josh Lawrence, 1917–1991," p. 19 of the same issue.

18. Thornton, *British Shipping*, 83, 87; Joshua, Booth, and Wallace, *To Ride the Storm*, 14–15; Andrew Porter, *Victorian Shipping, Business and Imperial Policy: Donald Currie, the Castle Line, and South Africa* (New York: St. Martin's Press, 1986), 246; Taplin, *Liverpool Seamen and Dockers*, 14; Appendix IV, National Maritime Board to the Tramp Shipping Subsidy Committee, July 1935, L/E/9/955; Adam Willis Kirkaldy, *British Shipping: Its History, Organization, and Importance* (1914, New York: Augustus M. Kelly, 1970), 205. Between 1863 and 1914 firemen earned more than certificated or licensed "Able Seamen" (ABs) and much more than unlicensed "Ordinary" seamen. Sager, *Seafaring Labour*, 247–48. Joe Stack, "Shooting Ashes on the Old George Washington," *The Hawsepipe* 8 (February–March 1989): 12. Although the latter is a description of an American ship, the work process was much the same, as was the racial division of labor.

19. Thornton, *British Shipping*, 250.

20. Stack, "Shooting Ashes on the Old George Washington," 12; Thornton, *British Shipping*, 250.

21. Taplin, *Liverpool Dockers and Seamen*, 14; Behrens, *Merchant Shipping*, 163; Weston to Turner, 6 August 1935, L/E/9/955; also see Board of Trade, *Census of Seamen* (1937), 4; Bean, "Employers' Associations," 366–67; Lane, *Grey Dawn Breaking*, 9–10, 32–33; Tony Lane, "Neither Officers nor Gentlemen," *History Workshop Journal* 19 (Spring 1985): 131; Thornton, *British Shipping*, 82–83, 86, 223, 250.

22. Thornton, *British Shipping*, 82–83, 85–87, 119, 213–15, 225–27, 250; Joshua, Wallace, and Booth, *To Ride the Storm*, 14–15; Porter, *Victorian Shipping*, 246; Taplin, *Liverpool Seamen*, 14; National Maritime Board to the Tramp Shipping Subsidy Committee, July 1935, L/E/9/955; Kirkaldy, *British Shipping*, 205; Brassey, *British Seamen*, 6, 10, 60, 164–65, 315, 373, 378; N.U.S. Correspondence Mss175/3/14/1&2.

23. Brassey, *British Seamen*, 8 and passim; Home, *Merchant Seamen*, 87; Kirkaldy, *British Shipping*, 205; Porter, *Victorian Shipping*, 246. Sager, *Seafaring Labour*, 247–48; Peter N. Davies, *The Trade Makers: Elder Dempster in West Africa 1852–1972* (London: George Allen & Unwin, 1973), 154.

24. Caradog Jones, *The Social Survey of Merseyside*, 2:102, 98; Board of Trade Memorandum, July 1935 L/E/9/955; Kenneth Little, *Negroes in Britain: A Study of Racial Relations in English Society*, Introduction by Leonard Bloom (1948; London: Routledge & Kegan Paul, 1972), 95; and see Bean, "Employers' Associations," 366–67.

25. Lane, *Grey Dawn Breaking*, 17–18, 21, 167–74. Thornton, *British Shipping*, 221–22; Byrne, "The 1930 'Arab Riot,'" 263. Board of Trade Memorandum, July 1935, L/E/9/955.

26. Kanekar, *Seamen in Bombay*, 11; "Types of Indian Seamen," *Syren and Shipping*, 3 January 1945, 117.

27. Hermon McKay to Tony Lane, *Grey Dawn Breaking*, 162–63; also 19, 152–55, 167–71, 175; Federation of Nigeria, *Report of an Enquiry*, 16–20, 28 and passim; Hepple, *Race, Jobs, and the Law*, 64; Behrens, *Merchant Shipping*, 156; Lane, "Neither Officers nor Gentlemen," 137; *Maritime Board Year Book* 1923, p. 7; and see 1935, 1936, 1937, 1938, 1939, 1940, 1949; Francis E. Hyde, *Shipping Enterprise and Management; 1830–1939: Harrisons of Liverpool* (Liverpool: Liverpool University Press, 1967), 153; Minute of a meeting at the India Office, 23 February 1944, L/E/9/97g.

28. See *Maritime Board Year Book* 1923–49. The National Maritime Board was a wartime organization which brought shipowners to the bargaining table with the seamen's unions under government sponsorship. After the Armistice the N.M.B. became voluntary. See Leslie Hughes Powell, *The Shipping Federation: A History of the First Sixty Years, 1890–1950* (London: 52 Leadenhall St., 1950), 38–39; Kirkaldy, *British Shipping*, 269–70; and see J. O'Connor Kessack quoted in *The Seaman*, 17 April 1914; *The Seaman*, 29 November 1933, 2, quoting a letter from G. C. Howe, Master Mariner, published by the *Telegraph*, 24 November

1933; see also *The Hawsepipe* 6 (March 1987): 1; and Daunton, "Jack Ashore," 190–91. Segregated quarters were new with steam. Sager, *Seafaring Labour*, 249.

29. *The Seaman*, 1 (April 1911):47–48; Thornton, *British Shipping*, 213–23; Brassey, *British Seamen*, 6, 10, 16, 164–65, 315, 373, 378.

30. Thornton, *British Shipping*, 221. Although Thornton asserts the men were paid standard wages, Black seamen were exempt by statute from N.M.B. rates.

31. Porter, *Victorian Shipping*, 246.

32. Thornton, *British Shipping*, 221–22, 225–26; Letter from Charles Ainsworth to the *Telegraph*.

33. John Springhall, "Building Character in the British Boy: The Attempt to Extend Christian Manliness to Working-Class Adolescents, 1880–1914," in J. A. Mangan and James Walvin, *Manliness and Morality: Middle-Class Masculinity in Britain and America, 1800–1940* (Manchester: Manchester University Press, 1986), 69–70. Also Leonore Davidoff, "Class and Gender in Victorian England: The Diaries of Arthur J. Munby and Hannah Cullwick," *Feminist Studies* 5 (Spring 1979): 90–91, 95–96, 131, and passim; Jeffrey Weeks, *Sex, Politics and Society: The Regulation of Sexuality since 1800* (London: Longman, 1981); John R. Gillis, *Youth and History: Tradition and Change in European Age Relations, 1770–Present* (New York: Academic Press, 1974), 133–42, 171–73; Thornton, *British Shipping*, 225–26; *Syren and Shipping*, 30 July 1919, 424.

34. Anna Davin, "Imperialism and Motherhood," *History Workshop* 5 (Spring 1978): 9–66; Louis Chevalier, *Laboring Classes and Dangerous Classes in Paris during the First Half of the Nineteenth Century*, trans. Frank Jellinek (Princeton: Princeton University Press, 1973), esp. 360–61, 419ff. and passim; Springhall, "Building Character in the British Boy," 54–55, 58; Ann Laura Stoler, "Carnal Knowledge and Imperial Power: Gender, Race and Morality in Colonial Asia," in Micaela di Leonardo, ed., *Gender at the Crossroads of Knowledge: Feminist Anthropology in the Postmodern Era* (Berkeley: University of California Press, 1991), 52, 56, 75. On "splitting," see Davidoff, "Class and Gender," 92, 95.

35. *Syren and Shipping*, 3 April 1918, 15; 9 July 1919, 115; 6 August 1919, 509–10; Michael Howard, "Empire, Race, and War in pre-1914 Britain," in Hugh Lloyd-Jones, Valerie Pearl, and Blair Warden, eds., *History and Imagination: Essays in Honour of H. R. Trevor-Roper* (London: Duckworth, 1981), 342–45; C. I. Hamilton, "Naval Hagiography and the Victorian Hero," *Historical Journal* 23, 2 (1980): 397; Anne Bloomfield, "Drill and Dance as Symbols of Imperialism," in J. A. Mangan, ed., *Making Imperial Mentalities: Socialisation and British Imperialism* (Manchester: Manchester University Press, 1990), 82; also John Mackenzie, *Propaganda and Empire: The Manipulation of British Public Opinion 1880–1960* (Manchester: Manchester University Press, 1984); Porter, *Victorian Shipping*, 30, 62, 272–82.

36. *Syren and Shipping*, 20 June 1917, 735; 10 and 17 April 1918, 83 and 138; 26 June 1918, 712; 16 April 1919, 174; 13 August 1919, 646; 20 August 1919, 691; 9 April 1919, 114; 24 April 1919, 199; and see Hugh Clegg, *A History of British Trade Unions Since 1889*, vol. 2: *1911–1933* (Oxford: Clarendon, 1985), 141, 164.

37. *Syren and Shipping*, 27 March 1918, 851; 24 April 1919, 199; 17 April 1918; 18 June 1919, 1056.

38. "Scheme Proposed by the Hull Fishing Vessel Owners' Association," 1935, MT9/2745; Caradog Jones, *The Social Survey of Merseyside*; Thornton, *British Shipping*, 221–22; *Syren and Shipping*, 20 June 1917, 733; also *The Hawsepipe* 6 (September 1987): 2, 10.

39. For a discussion of these terms in relation to various models of labor market segmentation, see Samuel Cohn, *The Process of Occupational Sex-Typing: The Feminization of Clerical Labor in Great Britain* (Philadelphia: Temple University Press, 1985), esp. 17–19.

40. "Inspection of Lascars' Food," L/E/7/604.

4. A "Blot on Our Hospitality": Recolonizing Black Seamen Ashore in Britain

1. On the first question, see Gary S. Cross, *Immigrant Workers in Industrial France: The Making of a New Laboring Class* (Philadelphia: Temple University Press, 1983), 42–43; 224–25; Stephen Castles and Godula Kosack, *Immigrant Workers and Class Structure in Western Europe* (Oxford: Oxford University Press for the Institute of Race Relations, 1973); Harold Wolpe, "The Theory of Internal Colonialism: The South African Case," in Ivar Oxaal, Tony Barnett, and David Booth, eds., *Beyond the Sociology of Development* (London: Routledge & Kegan Paul, 1975); Claude Meillassoux, *Maidens, Meal, and Money: Capitalism and the Domestic Community* (Cambridge: Cambridge University Press, 1981); John Cell, *The Highest Stage of White Supremacy: The Origins of Segregation in South Africa and the American South* (Cambridge: Cambridge University Press, 1982). On the second, see Martin Daunton, "Down the Pit: Work in the Great Northern and South Wales Coalfields, 1870–1914," *Economic History Review* 34 (November 1981): 578–97; Robert S. Lynd and Helen Merrell Lynd, *Middletown: A Study in Modern American Culture* (1929; New York: Harvester/Harcourt Brace Jovanovich, 1956); Patrick Joyce, *Work, Society, and Politics: The Culture of the Factory in Later Victorian England* (New Brunswick: Rutgers University Press, 1980).

2. For debates regarding the relationship between the state and other "governing institutions," see Keith Middlemas, *Politics in Industrial Society: The Experience of the British System since 1911* (London: André Deutsch, 1979); James Cronin, "Coping with Labour, 1918–1926," in James E. Cronin and Jonathan Schneer, *Social Conflict and the Political Order in Modern Britain* (New Brunswick: Rutgers University Press, 1982), 113–45; Richard Price, "Corporatism," in *Masters, Unions, and Men: Work Control in Building and the Rise of Labour 1830–1914* (Cambridge: Cambridge University Press, 1984), 282–83. On the links between governing elites in the domestic and imperial spheres, see P. J. Cain and A. G. Hopkins, "Gentlemanly Capitalism and British Expansion Overseas, I: The Old

Colonial System, 1688–1850," *Economic History Review* 2d ser. 39, 4 (1986): 501–25; and "II: The New Imperialism, 1850–1945," *Economic History Review* 2d ser. 40, 1 (1987): 1–26; Lance E. Davis and Robert A. Huttenback, *Mammon and the Pursuit of Empire: The Economics of British Imperialism* (Cambridge: Cambridge University Press, 1988).

3. H. A. Jury Report, "Common Lodging Houses," 5 May 1922, India Office file "Lascar Accommodation in U.K.," L/E/7/1152.

4. Lawrence to Kay Menzies, 8 May 1923, L/E/7/1152. Destitute Indian subjects who appealed to the High Commissioner for aid were housed in the Asiatic Home at the Indian taxpayer's expense until a ship could be found for them. They were not free agents: a man who refused a job was denied further aid. If no job was available the High Commissioner paid for his repatriation. As British subjects, Indian seamen could not be forced to leave the United Kingdom under other circumstances. Minute of interdepartmental meeting at the Colonial Office, 4 Sept 1930, L/E/9/954. The principal legislation in force during the interwar period was the Merchant Shipping Act of 1894, which was further amended in 1906. An Indian Merchant Shipping Act was first passed in 1923, but similarly offered little protection to Indian seamen.

5. Cobb to Peel, 11 May 1922, L/E/7/1152.

6. Jury reports, 5 May 1922, 24 May 1922; Kay Menzies to Cobb, 15 June 1922, L/E/7/1152.

7. Kay Menzies to Cobb, 15 June 1922, L/E/7/1152. On the P.& O., see Adam Willis Kirkaldy, *British Shipping: Its History, Organization, and Importance* (New York: Augustus M. Kelly, 1970 [1914]), 72, 103, 170–171; Andrew Porter, *Victorian Shipping, Business, and Imperial Policy: Donald Currie, the Castle Line, and South Africa* (New York: St. Martin's 1986), 59, 62, 85, 219.

8. India Office to W. Duke, 7 July 1922. The delegation consisted of Earl Winterton, M.P., Parliamentary Secretary to the India Office; Viscount Ednam, M.P., M.C.; Lord Cobb; Principal Medical Officer of the L.C.C.; the Reverend George Dempster, Missionary Superintendant of the Port of London and supervisor of the British and Foreign Sailors' Society's Sailors' Palace in Commercial Road; and Captain T. G. Segrave, C.B.E., R.I.M., a shipping surveyor and adviser to the High Commissioner and the India Office. Report by Captain Segrave, 29 November 1922, L/E/7/1152.

9. Report by Captain Segrave, 29 November 1922, L/E/7/1152. In Southeast Asia, a *godown* is a warehouse—from the Malay *godong*. On the P.&O., see Stephanie Jones, *Trade and Shipping: Lord Inchcape, 1852–1932* (Manchester: Manchester University Press, 1989).

10. Ibid.

11. For Gilbert's question and Winterton's reply, see *Parl. Deb.*, Commons, 5th ser., 159(1922):2346–47; also see 9 July 1923, 166(1923):895–96. Mr. Kabeer-ud-din Ahmed raised Gilbert's question in the Indian Legislative Assembly on 23 January 1923, p. 1346. See transcript in L/E/7/1152. Note by Winterton, 8 December 1922, and "Notes of a conference held in Room 26A House of

Commons on 8 December to discuss Lascar accommodation in British home ports." Participants included the P.&O., the Ellerman Line and their affiliates Ellerman City and Hall and Ellerman and Bucknall, the Anchor Line, Bibby and Brocklebank, the Clan Line, Harrison's, Michael Brett for the Shipping Federation, the Rev. Dempster, Captain R. C. Warden and A. S. Hoskin for the Board of Trade, and Winterton, E. J. Turner, Captain Segrave, and Sir Malcolm Seton for the India Office. Also see Peel to Shaw, 1 January 1923; Shaw to Peel, 3 and 9 January 1923, L/E/7/1152.

12. Minute of Conference 22 February 1923, L/E/7/1152.

13. Ibid., p. 3.

14. Ibid., p. 8; Michael Brett was secretary of the Shipping Federation between 1901 and 1933 and general manager from 1933 to 1935. L. H. Powell, *The Shipping Federation: A History of the First Sixty Years, 1890–1950* (London: 52 Leadenhall St., 1950), 132. Reconstitution of racial boundaries to preclude solidarity between marginalized white and Black people was a feature of colonial and postcolonial societies, including the American South and European colonies. See Victoria Bynum, *Unruly Women: The Politics of Social and Sexual Control in the Old South* (Chapel Hill: University of North Carolina Press, 1992); Ann Laura Stoler, "Carnal Knowledge and Imperial Power: Gender, Race, and Morality in Colonial Asia," in Micaela di Leonardo, ed., *Gender at the Crossroads of Knowledge: Feminist Anthropology in the Postmodern Era* (Berkeley: University of California Press, 1991).

15. Minute of Conference 22 February 1923, pp. 7, 10, 14, L/E/7/1152.

16. Ibid., pp. 19–21. On fears of the poor, see Judith Walkowitz and Daniel Walkowitz, "'We Are Not Beasts of the Field': Prostitution and the Poor in Plymouth and Southampton under the Contagious Diseases Act," in Mary Hartmann and Lois Banner, eds., *Cleo's Consciousness Raised: New Perspectives on the History of Women* (New York: Harper Colophon, 1974), 192–225; Louis Chevalier, *Laboring Classes and Dangerous Classes in Paris during the First Half of the Nineteenth Century*, trans. Frank Jellinek (Princeton: Princeton University Press, 1973).

17. For Dempster's comments, see Minute of Conference 22 February 1923, L/E/7/1152. For evidence of enticement by boardinghouse keepers, see Segrave's report of 29 November 1922, L/E/7/1152. In lieu of a passport, a seaman carried a discharge book, containing his work record.

18. Turner to the High Commissioner for India, 23 April 1923; Ellerman & Bucknall to the India Office 10 April 1923, L/E/7/1152.

19. Turner to the High Commissioner, 23 April 1923; Turner to the Government of India, 13 March 1923, p. 5, L/E/7/1152.

20. Turner to the High Commissioner and the Shipping Federation, 6 July 1923; report of resolutions of meeting 22 February 1923. Note of a telephone conversation between Baines and Whatmore 2 March 1922. Much correspondence to shipowners went entirely unacknowledged: see Turner to Dempster 2 March 1923; Dempster to Baines, 19 and 20 March; Baines in India Office Minute, 31 March 1923; E. C. Stephens, Lash's replacement, to Baines. Turner again sent

confirmations to February conference participants on 6 April: Turner to Clan, Harrison, Ellerman & Bucknall, Anchor, P.&O., the High Commissioner, Merchant Marine Department of the Board of Trade, L/E/7/1152.

21. Board of Trade memorandum to "Authorities responsible for the licensing of seamen's lodging houses in London, Liverpool, Glasgow, Cardiff, Penarth, Barry, and Newport"; enclosed in Board of Trade to India Office, 13 and 27 March 1923; Board of Trade Mercantile Marine Department letter to Supervisors of Mercantile Marine Offices signed C. H. Grimshaw, 10 April 1923. Turner to Segrave, 28 July 1923. The India Office intended to placard shipping offices and to translate the posters into various appropriate "Indian dialects." Hoskin to Turner, 23 July, 1923, L/E/7/1152. The Kroo or Kru were a seafaring people of West Africa.

22. Hoskins to Tomkins 16 August 1923. On the Board of Trade's precipitate retreat, see commentary within the India Office: Segrave to W. D. Tomkins, 23 August 1923; Silver, 27 August 1923; Tomkins to Segrave 18 August 1923; C&R minute, Tomkins and Patrick, 10 September 1923; Turner to Tomkins, 20 September; Tomkins to Hoskin, 23 February 1924. Turner to Hipwood, 6 March 1924. Employers in the provinces also rapidly abandoned their agreements. See George Sim to India Office, 23 April 1924; Sim to Turner, 7 May 1924; M. Ahmed to India Office, 9 April 1924; 14 April note by Tomkins; Michael Brett to Tomkins, 7 May 1924, L/E/7/1152. On subsequent efforts, see "The Promotion of Seamen's Welfare in Port, 1929, 1940–44," L/E/9/457.

23. Dendy to Board of Trade, 7 August 1923. Dendy was "Senior Chief Superintendant" and inspector of Mercantile Marine Offices, L/E/7/1152.

24. On corruption, see Martin Daunton "Jack Ashore: Seamen in Cardiff Before 1914," *Welsh History Review* 9, 2 (1975): 184; Kenneth Little, *Negroes in Britain: A Study of Racial Relations in English Society*, Introduction by Leonard Bloom (London: Routledge & Kegan Paul, 1972), 61.

25. Public documents relating to the Elder Dempster Agreements can be found at the Public Record Office (P.R.O.) at Kew, in the Board of Trade Mercantile Marine Department papers, file MT9/2735, labeled, "Elder Dempster 1925–35." Subsequent citations will be to this file or to its subdivisions, such as M.3580; and in documents of the Home Office Aliens Department, HO45, also in the P.R.O.

26. Elder Dempster was a cargo liner firm with scheduled runs to Liverpool, *not* a tramp company. R. H. Thornton, *British Shipping* (Cambridge: Cambridge University Press, 1939), 150. Peter N. Davies, *The Trade Makers: Elder Dempster in West Africa, 1852–1972* (London: George Allen & Unwin, 1973), 24–27, 162; Porter, *Victorian Shipping*, 263–74; *Syren and Shipping*, 2 July 1919, 42; 19 June 1918, 655; 6 June 1917, 651. Mail subsidies were in themselves a form of state support.

27. Davies portrays Elder Dempster's mid-twentieth-century "Africanisation" of their staff as a blow for racial equality. *Trade Makers*, 74, 340–41. The company more likely switched to Africans because they were cheaper. See, for instance, Federation of Nigeria, *Report of the Board of Enquiry into the Trade Dispute between*

the *Elder Dempster Lines Ltd. and the Nigerian Union of Seamen* (Lagos: Federal Government Printer, 1959). On aliens legislation, see Thornton, *British Shipping*, 219; Bernard Gainer, *The Alien Invasion: The Origins of the Aliens Act of 1905* (London: Heinemann, 1972); John Garrard, *The English and Immigration: A Comparative Study of the Jewish Influx, 1880–1910* (London: Oxford University Press for the Institute of Race Relations, 1971); David Feldman, "The Importance of Being English: Jewish Immigration and the Decay of Liberal England," in David Feldman and Gareth Stedman Jones, eds., *Metropolis London: Histories and Representations since 1800* (London: Routledge, 1989).

28. Elder Dempster to Home Office, 20 January 1927, MT9/2735 M.15067; Davies to Home Office, 11 January 1933, report of a visit to Liverpool, p. 4. MT9/2735 M.3580.

29. Cooper to shipowners, 11 June 1925; copy to the Board of Trade, 21 July 1925, MT9/2735. The revealing quote appeared much later, in a letter dated 11 January 1933, Cooper to Board of Trade, MT9/2735 M.3580. On Holt, Henry Tyrer, and other competitors, see Davies, *Trade Makers*, 5, 12, 14, 92ff, 101–4. The Coloured Alien Seamen Order will be more fully analyzed in chapter 6.

30. Cooper to shipowners, 11 June 1925.

31. Holt & Co. to E. N. Cooper, 16 June 1925, MT9/2735.

32. On "imperial manhood," see Leonore Davidoff, "Class and Gender in Victorian England: The Diaries of Arthur J. Munby and Hannah Cullwick," *Feminist Studies* 5 (Spring 1979): 87–141; Satya P. Mohanty, "Drawing the Color Line: Kipling and the Culture of Colonial Rule," in Dominick LaCapra, ed., *The Bounds of Race: Perspectives on Hegemony and Resistance* (Ithaca: Cornell University Press, 1991); John Mackenzie, "The Imperial Pioneer and Hunter and the British Masculine Stereotype in Late Victorian and Edwardian Times," in J. A. Mangan and James Walvin, eds., *Manliness and Morality: Middle-Class Masculinity in Britain and America, 1800–1940* (Manchester: Manchester University Press, 1986), esp. 177, 180–82, 186. On the policing function of the Home Office, see Jane Morgan, *Conflict and Order: The Police and Labour Disputes in England and Wales, 1900–1939* (Oxford: Clarendon, 1987). By September 1925 the Home Office was engaged in preparations to break the impending General Strike. Charles Loch Mowat, *Britain between the Wars, 1918–1940* (London: Methuen, 1956), 294. For a sanguine view of the Immigration Service, see T. W. E. Roche, *The Key in the Lock: A History of Immigration Control in England from 1066 to the Present* (London: John Murray, 1969).

33. Cooper to the Home Office, 17 February 1921, HO45/11897/332087/20.

34. E. N. Cooper to the Home Office, 4 January 1926, HO45/12314/476761/63. On colonial gender and race relations, see Amirah Inglis, *The White Women's Protection Ordinance: Sexual Anxiety and Politics in Papua* (New York: St. Martin's, 1975); Ann Laura Stoler, "Carnal Knowledge and Imperial Power: Gender, Race and Morality in Colonial Asia," in Micaela di Leonardo, ed., *Gender at the Crossroads of Knowledge: Feminist Anthropology in the Postmodern Era* (Berkeley: University of California Press, 1991).

35. Cooper to the Home Office, 17 February 1921, HO45/11897/332087/23;

Cooper to the Home Office, 16 March 1922, HO45/11897/332087/60. The Home Office repeated Cooper's arguments to the Colonial Office, 18 January 1926, HO45/12314/476761/63.

36. G. E. Baker and Hoskins, Board of Trade Minute III, 4 and 6 August 1925, MT9/2735.

37. Colonial Office to Board of Trade, 17 September and 9 November 1927; Board of Trade Minute by Hoskin, 5 August 1927, and Board of Trade Minute, 3 October 1927, MT9/2735 M.4184. The automatic transfer was a feature of Asiatic articles, described in clause 125 of the Merchant Shipping Act, 1894.

38. Minute of Interdepartmental meeting at Mercantile Marine Office, 23 June 1927, MT9/2735. The term "bluff" was used by a Board of Trade legal adviser.

39. Elder Dempster to Board of Trade, 24 December 1927, MT9/2735 M.4184.

40. Board of Trade Minute, 1 September 1927, MT9/2735. It is not at all clear that all the West African seamen in question were actually Kru. British authorities seem to have used the term "Kroo" somewhat indiscriminately. Board of Trade to Elder Dempster, relaying offer from Haldane Porter, 23 June 1927, MT9/2735.

41. G. E. Baker, Minute, 28 January 1927, MT9/2735 M.4184. Home Office papers, September 1927, HO45/13392/493912/30. Board of Trade to Colonial Office, 10 January 1928; Elder Dempster to Board of Trade, 17 April 1927; Board of Trade to Colonial Office, 9 May 1928; Minute cited in "History of the Joint Agreement." The procedure was described in Board of Trade Departmental Paper 491, "General Minutes to Superintendants" issued July-September 1928, p. 230ff, on "Coloured Seamen," MT9/2735 M.3580. Also see Board of Trade Minute, May 1932, MT9/2735.

42. Minute of Interdepartmental meeting, 23 June 1927, MT9/2735; Superintending Inspector, Liverpool, November 1929, MT9/2735 M.3580.

43. Report from Liverpool Immigration Office MT9/2735 M.9553.

44. Cooper to Home Office, 20 May 1932, MT9/2735.

45. Joint meeting of the Board of Trade, Home Office, Colonial Office, 24 March 1933, MT9/2735; Minute of meeting at the Home Office 10 September 1935, MT9/2735 M.15067.

46. Bloomfield, Chief Mercantile Marine Superintendant of the Port of Liverpool, to the Board of Trade, 31 May 1932, MT9/2735.

47. Garro-Jones to W. J. Hicks, 14 May, 16 May and 23 May 1928, *Parl. Deb.* (Commons) 5th ser., 217(1928):673–74, 1041–1042, 1906–1907; 21 June 1928, *Parl. Deb.* 5th ser., 218(1928):1733–34. Zarlia had been exempt from military service due to his "essential" work with the Gas Company. MT9/2735 M.8521.

48. Memorandum of Aliens and Nationality Committee meeting 13 November 1925, HO45/12314/476761/57; Home Office to Colonial Office, 19 December 1925 and 5 January 1926, HO45/12314/476761/62 and /63; E. N. Cooper to the Home Office, 4 January 1926, HO45/12314/476761/63.

49. Superintending Inspector, Liverpool, November 1929, MT9/2735 M.3580; "Proposed Termination of the Elder Dempster Agreements," 19 December 1934; minute of meeting at the Home Office, 10 September 1935, MT9/2735

M.15067. On the company's bankruptcy and reorganization in autumn 1929, see Davies, *Trade Makers*, 254–69.

50. Minute of meeting at the Home Office, 10 September 1935, MT9/2735 M.15067.

51. Hunter and Pollard Report, pp. 46–47, Appendix on Liverpool, p. 15, L/ E/9/457.

52. See Federation of Nigeria, *Report of the Board of Enquiry*, 5–6, 19, 40; also see M. E. Fletcher, *Report on an Investigation into the Colour Problem in Liverpool and Other Ports* (Liverpool: Association for the Welfare of Half-Caste Children, 1930), 18. On "racialization," see Mohanty, "Drawing the Colour Line," in LaCapra, ed., *The Bounds of Race*, 311–43. On "naturalizing," see Joanna DeGroot, " 'Sex' and 'Race': The Construction of Language and Image in the Nineteenth Century," in Susan Mendus and Jane Rendall, eds., *Sexuality and Subordination: Interdisciplinary Studies of Gender in the Nineteenth Century* (London: Routledge, 1989), 89–128.

53. Document 11, 16 March 1938, E. J. Foley of the Board of Trade to Denis H. Bates of Cunard, MT9/2778; Board of Trade papers, 1939, MT9/3083 M.11232. On latitude limits, see Appendix to chapter 3. Also see minutes of the N.U.S. Temporary Management Committee, 27 September 1934, Mss175/1/3/ 1&2, f51.

54. Telegrams, Document 5, 12 October 1936, MT9/2778; for its implementation, see MT9/3083 M.11232.

55. 13 June 1939 and memorandum on Financial Resolution 25 May 1939, MT9/3083 M.9050.

56. Ibid.

57. See Cronin, "Coping with Labour"; Price, "Corporatism"; Cross, *Immigrant Workers in Industrial France*.

5. "We Shall Soon Be Having 'Rule Britannia'
Sung in Pidgin English":
The National Union of Seamen and the Uses of Race

1. Braithewaite to the N.U.S. Temporary Management Committee, July 1929, N.U.S. correspondence, Mss175/3/28.

2. Also see Executive Council Minutes for 23 September 1921, f284, 11 January 1922, f329, Mss175/1/4.

3. The terms "super-exploitation" and "super-profits" refer to the extra profits to be gained from labor paid even less than regular waged workers who are simply exploited in the sense that their wages amount to less than the value their labor adds to the goods they produce. For the best articulation of this process, see Claude Meillassoux, *Maidens, Meal, and Money: Capitalism and the Domestic Community* (Cambridge: Cambridge University Press, 1975).

4. Harris Joshua, Tina Wallace, and Heather Booth, *To Ride the Storm: the 1980 Bristol "Riot" and the State* (London: Heinemann, 1983), 16–19, 25, 28,

36–38; Edward Scobie, *Black Britannia: A History of Blacks in Britain* (Chicago: Johnson Publishing, 1972), 160–67; Kenneth Little, *Negroes in Britain: A Study of Racial Relations in English Society*, rev. and ed. with a new foreword by Leonard Woolf (1948; Routledge & Kegan Paul, 1972), esp. 57–59, 83–84, 98–99; James Walvin, *Black and White: The Negro in English Society 1555–1945* (London: Allen Lane, 1973), 209; Ron Ramdin, *The Making of the Black Working Class in Britain* (London: Gower, 1987), 74–83, 100, 126, 488–92; Kenneth Lunn, "The Seamen's Union and 'Foreign' Workers on British and Colonial Shipping, 1890–1939," *Bulletin: The Society for the Study of Labour History* 53, 3 (1988): 5–13. Also see Paul Gordon and Danny Reilly, "Guestworkers of the Sea: Racism in British Shipping," *Race and Class* 28, 2 (1986): 73–82.

5. See debate among Jonathan Zeitlin, " 'Rank and Filism' in British Labour History: A Critique," Richard Price, " 'What's in a Name?' Workplace History and 'Rank and Filism'," and James E. Cronin, "The 'Rank and File' and the Social History of the Working Class," *International Review of Social History* 34 (1989): 34–102; and between Price, "The Labour Process and Labour History," *Social History* 8 (January 1983): 57–75, and Patrick Joyce, "Labour, Capital, and Compromise: A Response to Richard Price," *Social History* 9 (January 1984): 67–76; Price, "Conflict and Cooperation: A Reply to Patrick Joyce," and Joyce, "Languages of Reciprocity and Conflict: A Further Reply to Richard Price," *Social History* 9 (May 1984): 217–31. Also see Madge Dresser, *Black and White on the Buses: The 1963 Colour Bar Dispute in Bristol* (Bristol, U.K.: Bristol Broadsides [Co-op] Ltd., 1986); Beatrix Campbell, *Wigan Pier Revisited: Poverty and Politics in 80s Britain* (London: Virago, 1984); Michael Savage, *The Dynamics of Working-Class Politics: The Labour Movement in Preston, 1880–1940* (Cambridge: Cambridge University Press, 1987); Kate Purcell, "Militancy and Acquiescence amongst Women Workers," in Sandra Burman, ed., *Fit Work for Women* (London: St. Martin's, 1979), 112–33; Barbara Taylor, "The Men Are as Bad as Their Masters...': Working Women and the Owenite Economic Offensive, 1828–1934," in Taylor, *Eve and the New Jerusalem: Socialsim and Feminism in the Nineteenth Century* (New York: Pantheon, 1983), 83–117; Sonya Rose, "Gender Antagonism and Class Conflict: Exclusionary Strategies of Male Trade Unionists in Nineteenth Century Britain," *Social History* 13 (May 1988): 191–208; Jan Lambertz, "Sexual Harassment in the Nineteenth Century English Cotton Industry," *History Workshop* 19 (Spring 1985): 29–61; Heidi Hartmann, "Capitalism, Patriarchy, and Job Segregation by Sex" in *Signs*, special supplement to volume 1 (1976): 137–69.

6. See Richard Price, *Masters, Unions and Men: Work Control in Building and the Rise of Labour 1830–1914* (Cambridge: Cambridge University Press, 1980), esp. 244–67, 282–83; and James Cronin, "Strikes 1870–1914," 75 and note 6 p. 93, in Chris Wrigley, ed., *A History of British Industrial Relations 1875–1914* (Amherst: University of Massachusetts Press, 1982), 72–98; Frank Broeze, "Militancy and Pragmatism: An International Perspective on Maritime Labour, 1870–1914," *International Review of Social History* 36 (1991): 165–200; Hugh Clegg, *A History of British Trade Unions since 1889*, vol. 2: *1911–1933* (Oxford: Clarendon Press, 1985), 408, 523. With specific reference to the N.U.S, see Basil Mogridge,

"Militancy and Inter-Union Rivalries in British Shipping, 1911–1929," *International Review of Social History* 6 (1961): 375–412, and "Labour Relations and Labour Costs," in S. G. Sturmey, *British Shipping and World Competition* (London: Athlone, 1962); M. J. Daunton, "Jack Ashore: Seamen in Cardiff before 1914," *Welsh History Review* 9, 2 (1975): 176–203; and "Inter-Union Relations on the Cardiff Waterfront: Cardiff 1888–1914," *International Review of Social History* 22, 3 (1977): 350–78; David Byrne, "The 1930 'Arab Riot' in South Shields: A Race Riot That Never Was," *Race and Class* 18 (1977): 261–77.

7. On the earlier period see Joseph Havelock Wilson, *My Stormy Voyage through Life* (London: Cooperative Press, 1925), 122–26; Board of Trade papers, MT9/2737 .M4541; Clegg, *A History of British Trade Unions*, 33–41, 523; Mogridge, "Militancy and Inter-Union Rivalries"; Daunton, "Jack Ashore." On the later period, see Clegg, *A History of British Trade Unions*, 385; Tony Lane, *Grey Dawn Breaking: British Merchant Seafarers in the Late Twentieth Century* (Manchester: Manchester University Press, 1986), 7; Gordon and Reilly, "Guestworkers of the Sea," 78.

8. This apologia is the apparent interpretation in Arthur Marsh and Victoria Ryan, *The Seamen* (Oxford: Malthouse Publishing, 1989).

9. Wilson, *Stormy Voyage*, 185, 199, 186.

10. Ibid., 78, 98, 127–28, 197; Wilson to the International Transport Workers' Federation, August 15, 1910, Mssl59/3/B/63/2; General Secretary Edmund Cathery to Registry of Friendly Societies FS12/189 (NUS 1493T); Minutes of the N.U.S. Executive Council, 16 July 1920, Mss175/1/1/4, f19.

11. Wilson, *Stormy Voyage*, 43–44; Minutes of the Executive Council 23 September 1921, ff284–5, Mss175/1/1/4. David Byrne reports that Wilson reputedly had a soft spot for Lascars. "The 1930 Arab 'Riot,' " 266.

12. For a similar contradictory case, see Dresser, *Black and White on the Buses*, 13–14, 21 and passim. One contrasts such covert and ambivalent manifestations of racism with more overt and unapologetic contemporaneous forms such as Jim Crow or Nazi anti-semitism.

13. *The Seaman* was edited in the interwar period by S. G. LeTouzel, the anonymous "Man at the Wheel," who was also London district secretary for the Catering Section.

14. N.U.S. deputation to the Board of Trade, 19 March 1914 and 1 February 1916, MT9/1087 M.8351 and M.3691. See Havelock Wilson in the House of Commons, 13 March 1908 and 11 March 1909, reproduced in Mss175/3/14/1&2; Minutes of the N.U.S. Executive Council, 1 April 1921, f188, Mss175/1/4.

15. *The Seaman*, 1 April 1911, 47–48, Mss159/5/3/497.

16. See Joshua, Wallace, and Booth, *To Ride the Storm*, 17–19; Daunton, "Inter-Union Relations," esp. 370–72; Daunton, "Jack Ashore."

17. On "Chinese Campaign" expenditures, see FS12/189 (NUS 1493T); on Wilson's parliamentary campaign, see *The Seaman*, 6 February 1914, 4. Wilson had made his parliamentary opponent's employment of aliens an issue in 1906 too. A. W. Purdue, "George Lansbury and the Middlesbrough election of 1906,"

International Review of Social History 18 (1973): 332–52, esp. 347; On a similar situation, see Robert A. Huttenback, "No Strangers within the Gates: Attitudes and Policies towards the Non-White Residents of the British Empire of Settlement," *Journal of Imperial and Commonwealth History* 1 (May 1973): 271–302, esp. 281.

18. *The Seaman*, 15 May 1914, 17 April 1914; 1 May 1914, 4; Report of a meeting of the Newport Trades Council, *The Seaman*, 9 January 1914, 6 (f46).

19. Ibid., 20 March 1919, 4; 1 May 1914, 5. Also see Edward Said, *Orientalism* (New York: Vintage, 1979).

20. Ibid., 1 May 1914, 3.

21. Ibid., 15 May 1914, 6; 17 April 1914, 4.

22. Meetings with Board of Trade President John Burns, 19 March 1914 and 1 February 1916, MT9/1087 M.8351 and M.3691. Also see statement by Havelock Wilson to Board of Trade President John Burns, reprinted in *The Seaman*, 20 March 1914; 17 April 1914. Havelock Wilson's estimate, also possibly inflated, was 9,500. Arthur Greenwood performed the same sleight of hand in 1935 when he counted some 55,000 Lascar seamen as "foreigners" in the campaign for the British Shipping Assistance Act. See typescript of an article by Arthur Greenwood from *John Bull*, 5 January 1935, and related Board of Trade brief, MT9/2737 M.4541.

23. *The Seaman*, 9 January 1914, 6 (f46).

24. Meetings with Board of Trade President John Burns, 19 March 1914 and 1 February 1916, MT9/1087 M.8351 and M.3691; on the "sexualization of western definitions of these non-western societies, and an exoticization of definitions of sexuality in European culture," see Joanna DeGroot, " 'Sex' and 'Race': The Contruction of Language and Image in the Nineteenth Century," in Susan Mendus and Jane Rendall, eds., *Sexuality and Subordination: Interdisciplinary Studies of Gender in the Nineteenth Century* (London: Routledge, 1989), 100.

25. *The Seaman*, 20 March 1914, 4; Triple Alliance Deputation to Lloyd George, 31 January 1917; T.U.C. to the Board of Trade, 14 February 1917; Board of Trade papers MT9/1087 M.1087 and M.5189. Also see article by J. O'Connor Kessack from the *Forward* quoted in *The Seaman*, 17 April 1914, 5.

26. John Burns even disputed Wilson's figures. 19 March 1914 and 1 February 1916, Board of Trade papers, MT9/1087 M.8351 and M.3691; *The Seaman*, 14 November 1915, 4. On the 1911 seamen's strike, see D. E. Baines and R. Bean, "The General Strike in Merseyside," in J. R. Harris, ed., *Liverpool and Merseyside: Essays in the Economic and Social History of the Port and Its Hinterland* (New York: Augustus Kelley, 1969), 239–76, esp. 243.

27. On the N.M.B., see Clegg, *A History of British Trade Unions*, 164, and on the PCs, 328–29; and Byrne, "The 1930 'Arab Riot,' " 266–67. Also L. H. Powell, *The Shipping Federation: A History of the First Sixty Years, 1890–1950* (London: 52 Leadenhall St., 1950), 38–39; Mogridge, "Militancy and Inter-Union Rivalries," 387–88, 391–93. On the incorporation of the broader labor movement in the First World War, see Martin, *T.U.C.*, 132–63.

28. Ninth meeting of the Sailors' and Firemen's Panel of the National Maritime

Board on 7 January 1918. "Chinese Question-Correspondence," Mss175/3/16/1–4; also 10 April 1919 Mss175/3/15/1; N.U.S. Correspondence on the Chinese Question, Mss175/3/16/1–4.

29. 4 March 1920, Mss175/3/15/1. These rates were negotiated in N.M.B. meeting, 4 February 1918, Mss175/3/15/1–14. See *Maritime Board Year Book* for 1923 through 1949, esp. p. 80 of 1949.

30. Secretary's report of International Seafarers' Federation with wage tables for the year ending 30 June 1919 (London: John Kealey and Sons, Ltd.), p. 15; Minutes of the Reconstruction Committee, 9–10 May 1919, Mss175/4/13.

31. "Orientals in British Ships," *The Seaman*, 29 November 1933.

32. Minutes of the N.U.S. Temporary Management Committee, 14 October 1930 and 18 September 1931, 24 August 1932, ff66, 122, 164, Mss175/1/3/1&2; Executive Council Minutes, 7 July 1939 p. 4, Mss 175/1/1/9. Furness Withy was another major shipping firm.

33. *The Seaman*, 22 February 1933, 5; also see an advertisement for the fund in the 15 January 1930 issue of *The Seaman*; Union Annual Report, Mss175/1/5/3; Annual General Meeting 1938, Mss175/1/5/2; Minutes of the Bristol Channel District Committee, 25 March 1944, Mss175/1/4/1&2. A similar "Asian levy" survived until the 1970s and 1980s. Gordon and Reilly, "Guestworkers of the Sea."

34. Byrne, "The 1930 'Arab riot,'" 261–77; Memorandum of a meeting 12 May 1938, document 27, MT9/2778, p. 4; Board of Trade papers, MT9/3083 M.11232 1939.

35. Many matters raised in the Executive Council were referred without discussion "to the Head Office officials to be dealt with." See, for instance, 31 October 1925, Mss175/1/1/6; and see Clegg's comments, *A History of British Trade Unions*, 329, 384. Hardy, *Struggle*, 14–15; *The Seaman*, 26 June 1914, *The Negro Worker* 2 (April 1932): 21.

36. See front page article, *The Seamen*, 9 September 1931; Minutes for 15 February 1930 f27, Mss175/1/3/1; Minutes for 1 November 1933, 27 September 1934, 15 October 1935, Mss175/1/3/2.

37. Mogridge in Sturmey, *British Shipping*, 292, 320, 321. Also see A. R. Griffin and C. P. Griffin, "The Non-Political Trade Union Movement," in John Saville and Asa Briggs, eds., *Essays in Labour History 1918–1939* (Totowa, N.J.: Croom Helm, 1977), 133–62; Clegg, *A History of British Trade Unions*, 328–29, 384–85. Minutes of Proceedings of a Conference with Representative Cooks and Stewards at St. George Hall Westminster, 19 October 1921, Mss175/4/17.

38. See for example the report of the Annual General Meeting of 1938, Mss175/1/5/2; *The Seaman*, 18 February 1929, 7–14; Minutes of the Executive Council for 15 October 1930, p. 11 (f69), Mss175/1/1/7 f69; Joint Meeting of Sailors' & Firemen's Panel and Catering Department Panel, National Maritime Board, 3 July 1925, Mss175/6/NMB/4.

39. For more details see Clegg, *A History of British Trade Unions*, 328–29, 384–85, 401, 408; Mogridge, "Militancy and Inter-Union Rivalries," 391–405; Hardy, *Struggle*, esp. 6; Byrne, "The 1930 'Arab Riot,'" 266–67; Labour Research De-

partment, *Shipping*, 47; and for details of the "non-political Trade Union" campaign, issues of *The Seaman* 1925–26. On the NUS boycott of the General Strike
in Merseyside, see Baines and Bean, "The General Strike in Merseyside," 252; on
the Minority Movement, see Roderick Martin, *Communism and the British Trade
Unions, 1924–1933: A Study of the National Minority Movement* (Oxford: Clarendon
Press, 1969), esp. 48, 70–71, 143.

40. For an early example, see Cathery to Jochade, 23 November 1911, Mss175/
7/ITF/4. See Griffin and Griffin, "The Non-Political Trade Union Movement,"
133, 139–40; Mogridge, "Military and Inter-Union Rivalries"; Clegg, *A History
of British Trade Unions*, 329, 352, 384, 389, 401, 408, 459. On the latter, see
records of the I.S.F., Mss175/5/18–27, especially /18, /19, /20i, /21ii, /23i and
/25ii.

41. Minutes of Proceedings of a Conference held at St. George's Hall, 28 June
1925, re: wages, Mss175/4/19ii, p. 27. On the A.M.W.U., see Clegg, *A History
of British Trade Unions*, 328–29, 385.

42. Minutes of Proceedings of a conference held at St. George's Hall, 28 June
1925, Mss 175/4/19ii; Joint Meeting of Sailors' & Firemen's Panel and Catering
Department Panel, National Maritime Board, 3 July 1925, p. 3, Mss175/6/NMB/
4; Hardy, *Struggle*, 6–9.

43. Executive Council Minutes, 21 July 1925, Mss175/1/1/6; Joint Meeting
of Sailors' and Firemen's Panel and Catering Department Panel, 3 July 1925, p. 5.
Mss175/6/NMB/4; Clegg, *A History of British Trade Unions*, 164, 328–29, 346,
389, 458–59; Powell, *The Shipping Federation*, 32–33. On ship-by-ship arrangements, see Executive Council Minutes, Mss175/1/1/1–10 passim.

44. I.S.F. meeting, Mss175/5/23i; Minutes of Proceedings of Conference, 28
June 1925, Mss175/4/19ii.

45. Executive Council Minutes, 16 July 1923, f214, Mss1/1/5.

46. Minutes 15 February 1930, Mss175/1/3/1&2, f25. On union abuse of the
PC5 and the N.M.B. work ticket for punishment or retaliation, see Mogridge,
"Militancy and Inter-Union Rivalries," 399–400; Clegg, *A History of British Trade
Unions*, 328–29; House of Commons Oral Answers, 11 December 1922, *Parl.
Deb.* (Commons) 5th ser. vol. 159(1923):2335. Philip Cunliffe-Lister to Sidney
Webb 19 July 1928, MT9/3263 M.10115; and Hardy, *Struggle*, 5.

47. Executive Council Minutes, 23 January 1930, p. 10, Mss175/1/1/7. Similar
complaints again appeared in Minutes of the N.U.S. Executive Council, 26 April
1933, p. 2, Mss175/1/1/7, and 7 July 1934, Mss175/1/1/8.

48. 22 October 1931, f104, Mss175/1/1/7.

49. *The Seaman*, 9 September 1931, 1.

50. A.M.W.U. meeting, Antwerp, 30 October 1921, Mss175/3/17/5; Minutes
of Proceedings of a Conference, June 1925, Mss175/4/19ii; also see Clegg, *A
History of British Trade Unions*, 328; Minutes 14 January 1926, p. 100, Mss175/
1/1/6; Hardy, *Those Stormy Years: Memories of the Fight for Freedom on Five Con-
tinents* (London: Lawrence and Wishart, 1956), 175.

51. 10 April 1919, Mss175/3/15/1; N.U.S. Correspondence on the Chinese
Question, Mss175/3/16/1–4; Minutes of the Home Office Aliens Department, 15

and 23 January 1923, HO45/11897/332087/70; N.U.S. Executive Council Minutes 16 April 1935, p. 2 Mss175/1/1/8. Also see Minutes of the Temporary Management Committee, 11–12 November 1930, f75, Mss175/1/3/1.

52. N.U.S. Executive Council Minutes for 23 June 1915, f320, and 25 September 1915, f329, Mss175/1/1/2; also Gainer, *The Alien Invasion*, 23.

53. Minutes of the Executive Council, 11 January 1922, ff327–33, Mss175/1/1/4. It is unclear whether the Mr. O'Connell mentioned here was Harry O'Connell, long-time Black activist and founder in 1935 of the Coloured Colonial Seamen's Union. (See Chapter 7 below, and Peter Fryer, *Staying Power: The History of Black People in Britain* [London: Pluto, 1984], 357).

54. This resolution was moved by district locals in the Bristol Channel: Swansea, Cardiff, Barry, Bristol, and Newport, of whom George Reed was the influential district secretary. Executive Council Minutes, 21 August 1929, Mss175/1/1/7.

55. See Ron Ramdin, *The Making of the Black Working Class in Britain* (London: Gower, 1986) for amplification of this theme.

56. Executive Council Minutes, 28 March 1922, f40, Mss175/1/1/5; 16 July 1920, f34, 11 January 1921, f108, Mss175/1/1/4.

57. Minutes of the Executive Council, 8 July 1930, p.8, f54, 7 July 1933, p. 11 f174, Mss175/1/1/7; Minutes of the Temporary Management Committee, 10 and 23 August 1933, 14 March 1934, Mss175/1/3/2; Minutes of the Executive Council, 11 April 1934, p. 6, Mss175/1/1/8. The Greek Seamen's Union met a similar rebuff. 20 January 1931, f85, and 14 April 1931, f102; Minutes of the Temporary Management Committee, Mss175/1/3/2.

58. Bates of Cunard to the Board of Trade, 5 May 1938, Board of Trade MT9/2778 doc. 15; Executive Council Minutes, 15 July 1938, p. 4, f172, Mss175/1/1/8. For more on the rhetoric of trade union "responsibility" and its application to colonial unions, see Peter Weiler, *British Labour and the Cold War* (Stanford, Stanford University Press, 1988), introduction and chapter 1, "Forming Responsible Trade Unions."

59. *The Seaman*, 12 August 1929, p. 1; A. J. Cook reported in August that the union had stopped its remittances to the Non-Political Trade Union Movement; *The Seaman*, 28 August 1930, 1, 25 September 1929, 28 January 1931; David Byrne reports that the T.U.C. was motivated by fear of a communist takeover of their own Seamen's Section, "The 1930 'Arab Riot,' " 265–66.

60. Like the terms "black" and "coloured," the descriptions "Arab" and "Somali" were somewhat loosely and capriciously applied to men from East Africa and the Arabian peninsula. Most of them were likely Adenese. For the fullest published account of these events, see Byrne, "The 1930 'Arab Riot,' " 264–65.

61. *The Seaman*, 4 February 1929, 3; 18 February 1929, 2–3. *The Seaman* ridiculed Henson and the T.G.W.U. for meeting in Geneva with "Hindu members of the I.T.F., who are there representing seamen" whom "the T&GWU . . . have declared they will drive from the British Mercantile Marine." *The Seaman*, 4 February 1929, 3; 24 June 1929, 1–2; Reed's reply was reprinted in *The Seaman*, 13 May 1929, 5; 27 May 1929, 1, 6.

62. *The Seaman*, 24 June 1929, 1.

63. 16 November 1929, Mss175/1/3/1&2.

64. 11 January 1930, p. 23, Mss175/1/3/1; *The Seaman*, 12 August 1929, 3, 6 November 1929, back page. The delegation included Spence, Reed, and Jarman; M.P.s for Grimsby, Bristol, Birkenhead, Southampton, Commander Kenworthy for Central Hull, and Arthur Henderson, Jr., representing Cardiff South. *The Seaman*, 18 December 1929, 4–5; Reed quoted in *The Seaman*, 18 December 1924, 5 and again 7 May 1930, 2.

65. *The Seaman*, 3 April 1930.

66. Ibid., 18 December 1929, 4–5; 15 January 1930, 2; 15 January 1930, 1–2; 9 April 1930; 26 March 1930, 2; 16 July 1930, 1; 23 April 1930, 5; 3 December 1929, 1; 21 May 1930, 2.

67. Ibid., 23 April 1930; 26 March 1930; 12 March 1930, 4; 23 April 1930, 2; 7 May 1930, 1; 26 March 1930. Conversely, *The Seaman* dismissed Arab seamen's claims of British nationality as a ploy adopted by Italian and French subjects, 12 March 1930, 4; 7 April 1930, 4; 23 April 1930, 5.

68. Ibid., 26 March 1930, 6; 18 December 1929, 4; 23 April 1930, 5; 15 January 1930, 3.

69. Ibid., June 18, 1930, 6; 7 May 1930, 2; 4 June 1930, 2–3; 23 April 1930, 5; 7 May 1930, 2 and 4 July 1930, 3.

70. Names of "Arab and Somali" men were entered on the Joint Supply register and given a numbered card. "They are then presented to the ships' officers requiring seamen of these nationalities in the order of the number shown on their cards." Arabs and Somalis who served on the last voyage of a particular ship got priority. Board of Trade Memorandum 1939, MT9/3263 M.12767. The scheme's principal promoters were District Secretaries Clouston of the Tyne, Reed of the Bristol Channel, Damm of the Continent, and J. H. Tarbitten of the Humber District. *The Seaman*, 2 July 1930, 2, 3; 16 July 1930, 1; HO45/14299/562898/42, /57; Report of a vist to North and South Shields by Mr. Mugliston and Mr. Stovell, HO45/14299/562898/19; and see remarks by the prosecutor in the trial *Rex v. Ali Said*, Mss175/7/LE/103; Minutes of the Temporary Management Committee, 12 September 1930, p. 63; 11 and 12 November 1930, p. 75, Mss175/1/3/1; also see Byrne, "The 1930 'Arab Riot.'"

71. Executive Council Minutes, 9–10 April 1930, Mss175/1/1/7, 33, 36, 46. Measures to exclude new boy ratings were also discussed. Like many white seamen, Black seamen were often unable to afford union dues between voyages, so the question only arose when a man had obtained employment and now had to "buy" the PC5 from the union in the form of past dues.

72. As explained earlier, since men who were between voyages could seldom afford to maintain their union dues, most were forced to pay a £2 flat fee to the union to "buy" the PC5 before signing on a ship. Byrne, "The 1930 'Arab Riot.'" Evidence from the trial of boardinghouse keeper M. Abdul suggests this was precisely the amount charged by the Arab "crimp" or agent, no doubt because it was the going rate. *The Seaman*, 12 August 1929, 3.

73. 19 and 20 May 1932, f156; 1 July 1932, f158; 24 August 1932, f160, Mss175/1/3/1; Thornton, *British Shipping*, 224.

74. Board of Trade Memorandum, 1939, MT9/3263 M.12767; Executive Council Minutes, 20 October 1937, f140; 21 April 1938, pp. 9–10, ff165–66, Mss175/1/1/8 and 7 July 1939, p. 4, Mss175/1/1/9; Bristol Channel District Committee Minutes, 28 April and 23 September 1938, Mss175/1/4/1&2.

75. See Byrne, "The 1930 'Arab Riot,' " and Gordon and Reilly, "Guestworkers of the Sea."

6. Contesting the Boundaries of Race and Nationality:
The Coloured Alien Seamen Order, Policy and Protest

1. Mrs. Mary Fazel to the India Office, 7 September 1925, L/E/9/953 f297.

2. See Aliens and Nationality Committee Memorandum 116 of 18 December 1919 among others, on the status of British-born wives of Germans, L/E/7/1214/ 702; Viceroy to Home Department, Government of India, to India Office L/E/ 9/953.

3. Paul Rich, *Race and Empire in British Politics* (Cambridge: Cambridge University Press, 1986), 122.

4. Kenneth Little, *Negroes in Britain: A Study of Racial Relations in English Society*, Introduction by Leonard Bloom (1948; London: Routledge & Kegan Paul, 1972); and see series of articles appearing in 1935 in *The Keys: Official Organ of the League of Coloured Peoples.*

5. Little wrote that the "police were under a complete misapprehension" about the order, in *Negroes in Britain*, 85–89; also see Peter Fryer, *Staying Power: The History of Black People in Britain* (London: Pluto, 1984), 356; Ron Ramdin, *The Making of the Black Working Class in Britain* (London: Gower, 1987), 75–77, 102, 113, 491–92; James Walvin, *Black and White: The Negro in English Society, 1555–1945* (London: Allen Lane, 1973), 209–10. Only Edward Scobie commented on the order's obviously racist intent, in *Black Britannia: The History of Blacks in Britain* (Chicago: Johnson Publishers, 1972), 161.

6. Rich, *Race and Empire*, 5; Catherine Hall argues that "there was never one colonial discourse in England." "In the Name of Which Father?" *International Labor and Working Class History* 41 (Spring 1992): 24.

7. Paul Rich, "Imperial Decline and the Resurgence of English National Identity, 1918–1979," in Tony Kusher and Kenneth Lunn, eds., *Traditions of Intolerance: Historical Perspectives on Fascism and Race Discourse in Britain* (Manchester: Manchester University Press, 1989), 33–52. For a different view, stressing "persistence of delusions of grandeur," see John Darwin, "The Fear of Falling: British Politics and Imperial Decline since 1900," *Transactions of the Royal Historical Society* 36 (1986): 27–43, esp. 41.

8. Correspondence between A. W. Ruddock and the Home Office, 10 March 1917, HO45/11897/332087; Home Office Aliens Department to South Shields, 18 March 1917, HO45/11897/332087/5; Home Office Minute and Letter to Chief Constable of South Shields, 14 March 1917, HO45/11897/332087/2;

Home Office to Chief Constable of South Shields, 3 April 1917, HO45/11897/332087/7.

9. Stewart to the Secretary of State for India, 28 March 1917, HO45/11897/332087/12; also see Home Office correspondence, 23 July and 2 August 1917, HO45/11897/332087/10.

10. W. Haldane Porter, Chief Inspector of the Home Office Immigration Branch, commented with unconscious irony, "It is difficult to explain even to the educated person the legal difference between a British subject and the British protected person, and quite impossible to make a coloured seaman understand." Interdepartmental meeting, 2 November 1928; Note of a conference at the Home Office, 5 November 1928, L/E/9/953.

11. On the extension of labor contracts, see MT9/2695; Sir John Pedder in Home Office Minute, January 1923, HO45/11897/332087/70; also /29. On the Home Office and workers, see Ralph Desmarias, "Lloyd George and the Development of the British Government's Strikebreaking Organization," *International Review of Social History* 20 (1975), part. I, 1–15, esp. p. 8; Jane Morgan, *Conflict and Order: The Police and Labour Disputes in England and Wales, 1900–1939* (Oxford: Clarendon, 1987).

12. J. W. Oldfield, Newcastle Immigration Officer, to Home Office, 23 January 1920; Home Office Minute 26 June 1920; Correspondence between G. E. Baker of the Board of Trade and the Home Office, June through September 1920; Colonial Office to Home Office conveying Henson's warning, 22 June 1921; Home Office Minute, 18 March 1922; "Deputation to the Board of Trade (Viscount Wolmer) from the Seafarers' Joint Council regarding the Employment of Arabs to the Detriment of British Seafarers," 15 January 1923; Pedder in Home Office Minute, January 1923, HO45/11897/332087/17, /19, /35, /60, /70.

13. See, for example, the case of Ahmed Gabbar, Home Office to the India Office, 20 November 1925, L/E/9/953; Minute of a meeting at the Home Office, January 1928, HO45/13392/493912/42.

14. Home Office Minute, 20 September 1920; Home Office Circular to Immigration Officers 20 October 1920; Home Office Minute, 20 October 1920; and Home Office to Baker of the Board of Trade, 17 November 1920; Home Office to Immigration Officers in Home Office ports, 31 December 1920, HO45/11897/332087/19, /20, /22.

15. Pedder in Home Office Minute, 18 November 1920; Baker to Haldane Porter, Home Office, 4 December 1920; Cooper to Home Office, 17 February 1921; Home Office Minute 20 October 1920; Haldane Porter, Home Office, to Immigration Officers in Home Office ports, 31 December 1920, HO45/11897/332087/19, 20, /22.

16. Cardiff Town Clerk to Home Office, 21 April 1921; Report from His Majesty's Officer in Charge, Cardiff, to Home Office, May 1921; Henry T. A. Bosanquet of the King George Fund for Sailors, 10 June 1921; Grindle of the Colonial Office to the Secretary, Seamen's Union, Cardiff, 22 June 1921. Also see Home Office papers, 13 June 1921; reports from Cardiff, June 1921; Home

Office Minute, April 1921; Home Office draft letter, May 1921, HO45/11897/332087/24, /33, /35, /39.

17. National Maritime Board Sailors' and Firemen's Panel: Report on the Joint Supply System 1924 (13 January 1925), Mss175/6/NMB/3/1; Clipping from *Western Mail*, 15 November 1924, forwarded by Cooper to the Home Office, 19 November 1924, HO45/11897/332087/91. On the pay cut, the strike, and race discrimination, see George Hardy, *The Struggle of British Seamen* (London: Dorrit Press, 1927).

18. Correspondence between George Lansbury and the Home Office, HO45/24820/456725; Board of Trade to Customs and Excise Officers, cc to Henderson, 19 May 1924; Cooper to Home Office, 19 November 1924, enclosing clipping from *Western Mail*, 15 November 1924, HO45/11897/332087/91. Joynson-Hicks was no panderer to labor. His arrival in the Home Office was accompanied by extensive measures to break the anticipated General Strike of 1926. Charles Loch Mowat, *Britain between the Wars: 1918–1939* (London: Methuen, 1956), 193, 294–320, esp. 309, 316. His tenure as Home Secretary also saw intensified aliens restriction along anti-Semitic lines. David Cesarini, "Joynson-Hicks and the Radical Right in England after the First World War," in Kushner and Lunn, *Traditions of Intolerance*, 118–39, esp. 129–30.

19. Cooper to Home Office, 18 October 1924; Home Office Memorandum, 3 November 1924, HO45/11897/332087/91, /94; "Notes of meetings attended by Liverpool Immigration Officers at various ports," Cooper to Carew Robinson, Home Office, 2 April 1925, HO45/12314/476761; Statutory Rules and Orders, 1925, no. 290, 18 March 1925, L/E/9/953; reprinted in Board of Trade Mercantile Marine Department paper no. 461, July-September 1925, p. 120. The Aliens Order of 1920 had required all aliens to register with the police on arrival in the United Kingdom, but seamen had hitherto been exempt for sixty days. The Order of 1925 in effect removed the exemption from alien seamen who were not European, Chinese, or Japanese. The order was initially implemented in Barry Dock, Penarth, Port Talbot, Cardiff, Newport, Swansea, Llanelly, Liverpool, Salford, Newcastle-upon-Tyne, South Shields, Middlesbrough, and Hull. It was broadened in January 1926 to all major British ports.

20. Liverpool Immigration Officer P. R. Fudge to Home Office, 7 September 1925 HO45/14299/562898/97; Home Office instructions to Chief Constables, 23 March 1925, "Registration of Coloured Alien Seamen (Other than Chinese and Japanese)"; J. C. Walton to the Home Office, 4 September 1925; Home Office to India Office, 28 September 1925, L/E/9/953.

21. Numbers registered were reported in a Home Office Memorandum to the India Office, n.d. (October 1925), L/E/9/953; Unemployment figures can be found in National Maritime Board Sailors' and Firemen's Panel: Report on the Joint Supply System 1924 (13 January 1925), Mss175/6/NMB/3/1. See accounts of the enforcement of the Coloured Alien Seamen Order as reported in 1935 by George W. Brown, "Investigation of Coloured Colonial Seamen in Cardiff: April 13th–20th, 1935," *The Keys: Official Organ of the League of Coloured Peoples* 3 (October–

December 1931): 18–22; and by Little, Fryer, and others as in note 5 above. On the British Shipping Assistance Act, 1935, see the relevant India Office file, L/E/9/955.

22. Willet to Haldane Porter, 7 April 1925, also in L/E/9/953; Home Office Minute, 7 May 1925, HO45/12314/476761/14. Pedder in Home Office Minute of meeting with Willett, 8 April 1925, HO45/12314/476761/5, /6.

23. Enclosed in Grindle of Colonial Office to Home Office, 27 April 1925, and see their further letters to the Colonial Office, dated 30 April and 5 May 1925, HO45/12314/476761/17.

24. India Office Minute, 9 June 1925, L/E/9/953.

25. E. J. Turner in India Office Minute, 9 June 1925, L/E/9/953; also see Home Office Memorandum, October 1925, HO45/12314/476761/48.

26. India Office Minute, December 1925, L/E/9/953.

27. By 1939 many Black seamen held passports. See report to the Ministry of Labour by investigators Hunter and Pollard, L/E/9/457.

28. Turner to Home Office, 2 July 1925, L/E/9/953.

29. Interdepartmental meeting at the Colonial Office, 4 September 1930, L/E/9/955. Also see Cooper to Assistant Secretary to the High Commissioner for India, 16 June 1930, HO45/14299/562898/4B.

30. Home Office Minute on Givvons, June 1925; Chief Constable of Manchester to Home Office, 14 April 1925; A. D. Smith, Chief Constable of Glasgow, to Home Office, 17 July and 11 September 1925, enclosing report from Superintending Inspector, Aliens Registration Department of the City of Glasgow Police, HO45/12314/476761/21, /7, /41.

31. Home Office Memorandum to the India Office, n.d., October 1925; Home Office document, Autumn 1925; Home Office Memorandum 3 November 1924, HO45/11897/332087/48, /28, /94; Minute of a meeting at the Home Office, January 1928, HO45/13392/493912/42; Fudge to Home Office 7 September 1925, HO45/14299/562898.

32. C. D. C. Robinson in Home Office Memorandum, October 1927, HO45/13392/ 493912/36. Chief Constable, Cardiff, forwarding a letter from Detective Sergeant Gerald Broben, April 1926; Home Office to Cardiff, 12 May 1926; Home Office to Broben, 18 June 1926, HO45/12314/476761/92, /99, /100, /101; C. E. Baines, India Office, 17 September 1933; India Office Memorandum, 17 September 1933, L/E/9/972; Home Office Minute, 22 November 1927, "Extract from Minutes of Meeting of Aliens Branch Inspectors held at Home Office on 5/10/27; "Coloured Seamen: Difficulties of Administration"; Pedder in Home Office Minute, 6 January 1928, HO45/13392/493912/36; Home Office Memorandum to the India Office, n.d., October 1925, HO45/12314/476761/48; also in L/E/9/953.

33. Notice to Home Office, 19 December 1925, HO45/12314/476761/61.

34. P. S. R. Chowdhury to the Secretary of State for India, 17 February 1926; E. P. Donaldson of the India Office to the Home Office, 2 March 1926, L/E/9/953.

35. Home Office Minute, 1 March 1926, HO45/12314/476761/77; Foreign Office to Home Office, 14 July 1926, L/E/9/953.

36. Newspaper cutting in India Office file L/E/9/953.

37. Note of a conference on 13 December 1926, HO45/13392/493912/11; Report of a meeting to the India Office, 12 December 1925, L/E/9/953; Internal India Office document, n.d. (late October 1925), L/E/9/953; draft of Colonial Office letter to West Indian Governments, 3 December 1925, HO45/12314/476761/58; See, among the copious correspondence from consuls protesting irregular practices, F. Percy-Bush, Consul at Nantes, to Foreign Office, 14 May 1930, L/E/9/954; also W. G. Browning of "E" Division, Glamorgan Constabulary, Barry Dock, 11 October 1928; Board of Trade to Home Office, 11 December 1928, HO45/13392/493912/70, /77; J. P. Gibson of the Colonial Office, 28 July 1930, Cooper to India Office, 16 October 1930, L/E/9/954; "Issue of Travel Documents to Yemenese at Aden, 17 July 1930, enclosed in Assistant Secretary to the Government of India to Secretary, Government of Bombay, HO45/14299/562898/17; Letter from Major H. M. Wightwick, Acting Resident at Aden, 25 July 1931, L/E/9/954.; B. E. Reeve Jones, H.M. Immigration Office, Cardiff, 13 October 1928, HO45/13392/493912/70.

38. Aden resident to India Office; Robinson to India Office, 12 June 1926, L/E/9/953; Home Office to Chief Constable, South Shields, 2 October 1926; Home Office to India Office, 15 October 1926; Harold Swan, Consul at Havre, 16 November 1928; Home Office Minute 4–11 January 1929, HO45/13392/493912/71, /77, /97. Sillery-Vale, Consul at Antwerp, L/E/9/953.

39. J. C. Walton to Colonial Office, 2 July 1925; India Office to Home Office 13 April 1926; Robinson, India Office to Donaldson, Home Office, 19 April 1926, L/E/9/953. On the status of Protected Persons, see correspondence among the Home Office, Colonial Office and Board of Trade in 1920, HO45/13716/417984.

40. J. P. Gibson, Colonial Office, 28 July 1930; Cooper to India Office, 16 October 1930, L/E/9/954; "Issue of Travel Documents to Yemenese at Aden, 17 July 1930, enclosed in Assistant Secretary to the Government of India to Secretary, Government of Bombay, HO45/14299/562898/17; Foreign Office circular T.9496/501/378, 10 October 1931; Note of an Interdepartmental Conference at the Foreign Office 12 March 1931; Foreign Office circular T.3687/501/378 L/E/9/972, also HO45/14299/562898/96, March 1931; and see Board of Trade Mercantile Marine Department Memorandum 446, "General Minute to All Superintendants: 'Coloured Seamen,'" from Baker, 16 December 1932, MT9/2735 M.3580; Foreign Office Circulars T.5918/217/378 and T.12484/217/378, 8 December 1934, and Dominions Office to India Office, 9 November 1934, L/E/9/972; Colonial Secretary to the High Commissioner of the Somali Protectorate, 18 April 1934, L/E/9/972.

41. Aliens and Nationality Committee Memorandum 186, Minute of the 47th meeting at the Home Office, 13 November 1925, L/E/9/953 and HO45/12314/476761/48.

42. Correspondence among Home Office, Passport Office, Colonial Office, A. V. Agius, Trade Commissioner of Malta, and Edward Mifsud of the Office of the Lieutenant Governor of Malta, 10, 11, and 16 May, 14, 19, and 28 June, 23 September 1935, 11 March 1936, L/E/9/972.

43. Correspondence among Home Office, Dominions Office, and Colonial Office, 6 April and 13 May 1936, L/E/9/972. Similarly, Australian restrictions against Chinese were rapidly broadened in the 1890s to all "non-whites." See Robert A. Huttenback, "No Strangers within the Gates: Attitudes and Policies towards the Non-White Residents of the British Empire of Settlement," *Journal of Imperial and Commonwealth History* 1 (May 1973): 271–302, esp. 290.

44. If such men were "made subject to conscription...we should...find it difficult to resist it." M. J. Clauson, India Office Political Department, n.d. (ca. 1942–43), L/E/9/972.

45. Cooper in Home Office Minute, 15 May 1925, HO45/12314/476761/17.

46. Rich, *Race and Empire*, 5.

47. Home Office confidential letter "To the Chief Constable," no. 322, March 1925, "Registration of Coloured Alien Seamen (Other than Chinese and Japanese)," L/E/9/953.

48. *Parl. Deb.* (Commons) 5th ser., vol. 189(1925):1964–1965. See notice of question, 19 December 1925, HO45/12314/476761/61. Also Donaldson, India Office, to Home Office, 2 March 1926, L/E/9/953; Home Office Minutes 11 and 13 March 1926, HO45/12314/476761.

7. "THE HONOUR TO BELONG": BLACK WORKERS AND
   INTERRACIAL SETTLEMENTS IN INTERWAR BRITAIN

1. The 1919 riots have been recounted in several historical surveys although their causes and implications await detailed historical analysis. The most suggestive discussion remains Roy May and Robin Cohen, "The Interaction between Race and Colonialism: A Case Study of the Liverpool Race Riots of 1919," *Race and Class* 14, 2 (1974): 111–26. The present account is based largely on the Home Office file on the riots, HO45/11017/377969. Also see Kenneth Little, *Negroes in Britain: A Study of Racial Relations in English Society*, Introduction by Leonard Bloom (1948; London: Routledge & Kegan Paul, 1972), 79–82; Michael Banton, *The Coloured Quarter: Negro Immigrants in an English City* (London: Jonathan Cape, 1955), 33–34; Edward Scobie, *Black Britannia: A History of Blacks in Britain* (Chicago: Johnson, 1972), 156–58; James Walvin, *Black and White: The Negro in English Society, 1555–1945* (London: Allen Lane, 1973), 206–8; Peter Fryer, *Staying Power: The History of Black People in Britain* (London: Pluto, 1984), 298–316; Jacquelyn Jenkinson, "The Glasgow Race Disturbances of 1919," in Kenneth Lunn, ed., *Race and Labour in Twentieth Century Britain* (London: Frank Cass, 1985), 43–67; Ron Ramdin, *The Making of the Black Working Class in Britain* (London: Gower, 1987), 72–76. In June 1919 alone, there was rioting in Vienna

and Winnipeg and a pogrom in Poland as well as police and teachers' strikes in
Britain. *Daily Herald*, 18 June 1919, 3, 23 June 1919, 2; Charles Loch Mowat,
Britain between the Wars: 1918–1940 (London: Methuen, 1956), 24–25. On the
police strike in Liverpool in June 1919, see D. E. Baines and R. Bean, "The
General Strike in Merseyside," in J. R. Harris, ed., *Liverpool and Merseyside: Essays
in the Economic and Social History of the Port and Its Hinterland* (New York: Augustus
Kelley, 1969), 239–76, esp. 294–95.

2. Statement by a delegation headed by Mr. D. T. Aleifasakure Toummanah
of the Ethiopian Hall, June 1919, and see letter to the editor from a "British
Coloured Soldier," both in the *Liverpool Post*, 11 June 1919, cutting in HO45/
11017/377969, f16.

3. *Daily Herald*, 14, 16, and 17 June, 1919; *Times*, 14 June 1919, 9c; *Observer*,
15 June 1919, 11; Little, *Negroes in Britain*, 81.

4. For repatriation efforts of the early 1920s see HO45/11897/332087/41,
42, 46, 50; on previous efforts see Nigel File and Chris Power, *Black Settlers in
Britain, 1555–1958* (London: Heinemann Educational, 1981), 6–7, 27–41; Michael Banton, "The Changing Position of the Negro in Britain," *Phylon* 14, 1
(1953):74–83.

5. Home Office Minute of a telephone conversation with the Cardiff Chief
Constable, 14 June 1919; also 18 June, HO45/11017/377969/8, f 42, /20, f89;
Office of the Superintending Aliens Officer, Old Harbourmaster's House, Liver-
pool, 11 June 1919; L. Everett, Assistant Head Constable, Liverpool, to the Home
Office, 10 June 1919, HO45/11017/377969/6.

6. Home Office, 17 June 1919, HO45/11017/377969/6.

7. The London Commmittee included Father Hopkins and Edmund Cathery
of the N.S.F.U. "Commissioner of Police: Repatriation of Coloured Men from
the Port of London," September 1919, HO45/11017/377969, f114, f269.

8. Interdepartmental meeting at the Colonial Office, 23 June 1919, HO45/
11017/377969, f141.

9. Draft June 1919 and letter to Chief Constables, 25 June 1919, HO45/
110177/377969, ff111–113, 116–117, f124; J. Richard Lay, Principal Naval Transport Officer, Cardiff, 15 July 1919, HO45/11017/377969, f237; Interdepartmental meeting at the Colonial Office, 23 June 1919, HO45/11017/377969, f141;
Minute of a meeting of the N.S.F.U., B.F.S.S., N.M.B., Board of Trade, and
Chief Constable H. D. Morgan, July 1919, HO45/11017/377969/75, 98.

10. Minute of a meeting, 30 July 1919; "Commissioner of Police, Repatriation
of Coloured Men from the Port of London," HO45/11017/377969 f114; /98,
f251.

11. *Morning Post*, 12 June 1919 and correspondence between the War Office
and the Home Office, HO45/11017/377969; Home Office Minute of a telephone
conversation with the Cardiff Chief Constable, 14 June 1919, HO45/11017/
377969/8, f42.

12. Understanding that reified and static notions of "ethnicity" are highly problematic, I use the term "ethnicity" to describe the personal, nonsecular, frequently
kin-based networks that Black settlers in Britain inhabited and identified with. It

is also necessary to understand race/ethnicity as only one of the variables that also include divisions between men and women, skilled and unskilled, North and South, urban and rural, Home and overseas, that have fissured the British working class.

13. For a discussion of the formation of ethnicity in a process of colonial domination and resistance, see Gerald Sider, "When Parrots Learn to Talk, and Why They Can't: Domination, Deception, and Self-Deception in Indian-White Relations," *Comparative Studies in Society and History* 29 (January 187): 3–23, esp. 17, 21; Persis Charles, "The Name of the Father: Women, Paternity and British Rule in Nineteenth Century Jamaica," *International Labor and Working Class History* 41 (Spring 1992): 4–22.

14. David Caradog Jones, *The Social Survey of Merseyside*, 2 vols. (Liverpool: Liverpool University Press, 1932), 1:74–75; also see *The Seaman*, 26 March 1930, 1, 4; *The Negro Worker* 3 (May 1933): 24–25; Board of Trade Memorandum on the Tramp Shipping Subsidy Committee guidelines, July 1935, L/E/9/955; May and Cohen, "The Interaction between Race and Colonialism." For a case of abandonment, see MT9/2695 M.1821; also Memorandum on the operation of the Aliens Order, October 1925; Report of the Glasgow Immigration Inspector to the Chief Constable of Glasgow, 10 September 1925; Report by Sergeant Broben of the Cardiff Detective Department to the Chief Constable, 23 March 1926, HO45/12314/476761//48, /41, /92.

15. In addition, Black seamen were found in dozens of other British ports. See enumerations under the Coloured Alien Seamen Order, India Office Records, L/E/9/953, L/E/9/954, L/E/9/972.

16. This explanation was advanced by Ministry of Labour investigators Hunter and Pollard in 1939. Report on Seamen in Ports, L/E/9/457. Also see Little, *Negroes in Britain*, 64–65.

17. Hoskin to Turner 23 July 1923, L/E/7/1152; Ministry of Information press release by Miss E. M. Booker, December 1941, L/I/840/462/33g; Caradog Jones, *The Social Survey of Merseyside*, 2:102; Hunter and Pollard Appendix on Southampton, p. 8, L/E/9/457; Rev. St. John Groser et al., "Conditions of Life of the Coloured Population of Stepney," p. 13, Report to the Board of Trade, papers of the Ministry of War Transport, MT9/3952. On migrant enclaves, see John Bodnar, *The Transplanted: A History of Immigrants in Urban America* (Bloomington: University of Indiana Press, 1985); Michael Anderson, *Family Structure in Nineteenth Century Lancashire* (Cambridge: Cambridge University Press, 1971); Virginia Yans-McLaughlin, *Family and Community: Italian Immigrants in Buffalo, 1880–1930* (Ithaca: Cornell University Press, 1978). On the impact of this one employer on the condition of West African households in Liverpool, see M. E. Fletcher, *Report on an Investigation into the Colour Problem in Liverpool and Other Ports* (Liverpool: Association for the Welfare of Half-Caste Children, 1930), 48.

18. *The Seaman* 2 (June 1912): 58.

19. Caradog Jones, *The Social Survey of Merseyside*, 1:82; Constance King and Harold King, *The Two Nations: The Life and Work of Liverpool University Settlement and Its Associated Institutions 1906–1937* (London: Hodder & Stoughton/University of Liverpool, 1938), 17; also see Carlton O. Wilson, "A Hidden History:

The Black Experience in Liverpool, England, 1919–1945," Ph.D. diss., University of North Carolina, 1991.

20. Chief Constable, Cardiff, to the Home Office, 1919, HO45/11017/377969 f71; Cooper to the Home Office, 17 February 1920, HO45/11897/332087/20. Compare Little, *Negroes in Britain*, 68–70.

21. See the annual tallies contained in L/E/9/954, L/E/9/955, and L/E/9/972.

22. Hunter and Pollard Report, pp. 9, 17, L/E/9/457.

23. Caradog Jones noted, "The highest proportion of sons remaining in their father's trade [25 percent] is found among seamen." *The Social Survey of Merseyside*, 2:44; Dinkar Dattatraya Desai, *Maritime Labour in India* (Bombay: Servants of India Society, 1940); A. Colaco, *A History of the Seamen's Union, Bombay* (Bombay: Pascoal Vaz, 1955), 19; R. H. Thornton, *British Shipping* (Cambridge: Cambridge University Press, 1939), 222; P. G. Kanekar, *Seamen in Bombay: Report of an Enquiry into the Conditions of Their Life and Work* (Bombay: Servants of India Society, 1928), 4, 9–11, 17, Mss159/5/3/587; "Types of Indian Seamen," *Syren and Shipping*, 3 January 1945, 117ff; Board of Trade memorandum, MT9/2737 M.4541.

24. Appendix VII, p. 8, L/E/9/457.

25. Cardiff Detective Department, 3 July 1930, and Cardiff Chief Constable to the Home Office regarding "Yusuf Mahomed and other Destitute Somalis in Cardiff," 4 July 1930, HO45/14299/562898/10; Glamorgan Constabulary, Barry Dock, to the Home Office, 14 July 1930, HO45/14299/562898/15.

26. Somali Seamen in Glamorgan," 18 July 1930, HO45/14299/562898/20.

27. Minute of Interdepartmental Meeting at the Colonial Office, 4 September 1930, L/E/9/954.

28. Martin Daunton, "Jack Ashore: Seamen in Cardiff before 1914," *Welsh History Review* 9, 2 (1975): 176–203; transcript of the trial *Rex v. Ali Said*, November 1930, p. 28, Mss175/7/LE/103; William Fishman, *Jewish Radicals: From Czarist Stetl to London Ghetto* (New York: Pantheon, 1974), 30–39; Detective Sergeant Gerald Broben, 8 November 1924, HO45/11897/332087/96; T. Lally, H.M. Immigration Inspector to the Home Office, 11 January 1928, HO45/13392/493912/41; Abbi Farrah, a boardinghouse keeper of Barry Dock was said to be well known in Liverpool and Cardiff as the "local agent of the Somali tribe." *The Seaman*, 23 April 1930.

29. See letter from "loyal West Africans" forwarded to the Board of Trade by the British and Foreign Sailors' Society, 4 October 1921, MT9/2695 M.19615; S. A. Wilkes, Immigration Officer of the Port of Liverpool to the Home Office, April 1921; Chief Constable of Cardiff to the Home Office, 24 September 1923, HO45/11897/332087/24, /78; Home Office Memorandum 17 May 1928, HO45/11392/493912/46; "Yusuf Mahomed and other Destitute Somalis in Cardiff," 4 July 1930, HO45/14299/562898/10; also Daunton, "Jack Ashore": David Byrne, "The 1930 'Arab Riot' in South Shields: A Race Riot That Never Was," *Race and Class* 18 (1977): 261–77; Little, *Negroes in Britain*, 60–63.

30. Home Office Memorandum, 17 May 1928, HO45/13392/493912/46; HO45/14299/562898/36; *The Seaman*, 18 December 1929, 4–6; and 12 March

1930, 4; extract of a report from the Mercantile Marine Officer at Blyth, 5 November 1920 HO45/11897/332087/22; See also the Board of Trade's abortive effort in 1930 to involve shipowners in policing "Lascar deserters"; HO45/14299/562898/8 and /9; Inspector Owen McLenskie to Chief Constable A. D. Smith of Glasgow, under cover to the Home Office 10 September 1925, HO45/12314/476761/41; Interview with Mrs. Nairolla in L/E/7/1152; Also see Anne Dunlop, "Lascars and Labourers: Reactions to the Indian Presence in the West of Scotland during the 1920s and 1930s," *Scottish Labour History Society Journal* 25 (1990): 40–57. John Bodnar has suggested that American trade unions' "failure" vis-à-vis immigrant workers "helped sustain communal solidarity." *The Transplanted*, 92.

31. In Paul Thompson, *The Edwardians: The Remaking of British Society* (Chicago: Academy, 1985), 122–29.

32. See Lisa Norling, "Captain Ahab Had a Wife: Women in the Whaling Industry, 1820–1870," in Lisa Norling and Margaret Creighton, eds., *Iron Men and Wooden Women: Gender and Anglo-American Seafaring, 1700–1919* (Baltimore: Johns Hopkins University Press, 1995). On the National African Sailors' and Firemen's Union, see FS11/266 (1800T); on the 1935 committee, see George W. Brown, "Investigation of Coloured Colonial Seamen in Cardiff, April 15th-20th, 1935," *The Keys* 3 (October–December 1935): 20. *The Keys* was published by the London-based and middle-class League of Coloured Peoples, Britain's major Black advocacy organization in the 1930s and 1940s. On wives in the 1950s, see Sidney Collins, *Coloured Minorities in Britain: Studies in British Race Relations Based on African, West Indian, and Asian Immigrants* (London: Lutterworth, 1957); Rev. St. John Groser et. al., "Conditions of Life of the Coloured Population of Stepney," pp. 23–24, 26, MT9/3952.

33. Home Office to the Board of Trade, 11 January 1933, MT9/2735/M.15067. On entitlement to relief, see Nancie Hare (née Sharpe), "The Prospects for Coloured Children in England," *The Keys* 5 (July–September 1937): 11–12, 25–27; Groser, "The Coloured Population of Stepney," MT9/3952, 6, 9.

34. Nancie Hare, "Cardiff's Coloured Population," *The Keys*, 1 (January–March 1934): 44–45, 61; Hare, "Prospects for Coloured Children"; Thompson, *Edwardians*, 126. On working-class residential patterns, see Anderson, *Family Structure in Nineteenth Century Lancashire*; Michael Young and Peter Wilmott, *Family and Kinship in East London* (1957; London: Penguin, 1977).

35. Liverpool survey, HO45/11017/377969; David Caradog Jones, *The Economic Status of Coloured Families in the Port of Liverpool* (Liverpool: Liverpool Social Science Department, Statistics Division, 1940), 11, 13; Groser, "The Coloured Population of Stepney," 3, 27, MT9/3952.

36. Hare, "Prospects for Coloured Children," 12; Caradog Jones, *The Economic Status of Coloured Families*, 7; Groser, "The Coloured Population of Stepney," 1, 26–27, MT9/3952.

37. "Harriet Vincent passed on marriage from middle class to working class." Thompson, *The Edwardians*, 129. Also see discussion of interracial families, much of it hostile, in Caradog Jones, *The Social Survey of Merseyside*, 1:75, 205; 2:102–

3; King and King, *The Two Nations*, 43, 129–133; Banton, *The Coloured Quarter*, 13.

38. *The Keys* 1 (October–December 1933): 32.

39. Hunter and Pollard Report, Appendix VII, p. 8, L/E/9/457.

40. *The Keys* 5 (July–September 1937): 18.

41. Letter from Syed Fazal Shah, Secretary of the Association, 26 April 1935, India Office file, L/E/9/967; On the foundation of the Home, see Rozina Visram, *Ayahs, Lascars, and Princes: The Story of Indians in Britain, 1700–1947* (London: Pluto, 1986), 34, 49–50.

42. Victor Greene recounts a similar "process of identity-consciousness" when Slavic Catholics in the United States confronted "Irish hegemony" in the church, "For God and Country: The Origins of Slavic Catholic Self-Consciousness in America," *Church History* 35 (1966): 446–60. See also Oscar Handlin, *The Uprooted* (Boston: Little, Brown, 1973), 166–74; and Humbert Nelli, "Italians in Urban America: A Study in Ethnic Adjustment," *International Migration Review* 1 (Summer 1967): 39, 45, on the "reinvention" of Italian ethnicity in the United States; and Sider, "When Parrots Learn to Talk, and Why They Can't," who argues that "ethnic group formation" was "resistance-permeated," 17.

43. Thompson, *The Edwardians*, 126–27; Little, *Negroes in Britain*, 80–81; *Times*, 9 June 1919, 76; *Observer*, 8 June 1919.

44. See *The Seaman*, 9 April 1930, 2; 7 May 1930, 5–6; 21 May 1930, 1; 26 February 1930, 6. Reed under cover of Hoskin to the Home Office, 25 November 1930, HO45/14299/562898/48; N.U.S. Executive Council Minutes for 10 January 1920, f341; 27 March 1920, ff362, 364, Mss175/1/1/3.

45. On objections to "muscling-in" by nonlocal dockers, see Taplin, *Liverpool Seamen and Dockers, 1870–1890* (Hull: University of Hull Press, 1974), 15–16. On the continuing contestation over the use of the term "moral economy," see E. P. Thompson, *Customs and Common* (New York: New Press, 1992).

46. Similar conclusions were reached by Richard Price in *An Imperial War and the British Working Class: Working-Class Attitudes and Reactions to the Boer War, 1899–1902* (London: Routledge & Kegan Paul, 1972).

47. Report of the Glasgow Immigration Inspector to the Chief Constable of Glasgow, 10 September 1925, and "Memorandum on the Operation of the Aliens Order," October 1925, and Detective Sergeant Broben to the Chief Constable, Cardiff, 23 March and 20 May 1926, HO45/12314/476761/41, /48, /92, /99; Cardiff City Police to the Home Office, 24 September 1923 and 12 November 1924, HO45/11897/332087/78, /96; Home Office papers, September 1927, and Carew Robinson in a Home Office Memorandum, October 1927, HO45/13392/493912/30, /36; Liverpool Immigration Inspector Thomas M. Blagg to the Home Office, HO45/14299/562898/48; for a case of abandonment, see MT9/2695 M.1821.

48. See HO45/11897/332087/17, /39; MT9/2695. For discussions by the London Group on African Affairs in 1931, see Rhodes House MssAfr. 1427.

48. For the negotiation of this policy see the Minutes of a Meeting at the Colonial Office, 4 September 1930, L/E/9/972.

50. Cardiff Chief Constable to the Home Office on "Yusuf Mahomed and other Destitute Somalis in Cardiff," 4 July 1930, HO45/14299/562898/10.

51. Report of Cardiff City Police, Sergeant T. Holdsworth, Detective Department, 3 July 1930; Report from Barry by Glamorganshire Chief Constable to the Home Office, 14 July 1930; Report by James Evans, Ministry of Health, "Somali Seamen in Glamorgan," 18 July 1930; correspondence between South Wales police and the Home Office, October through December 1930; Arthur Henderson, M.P. for Cardiff, to the Home Office, 21 November 1930, HO45/14299/562898/10, /15, /20, /32, /48, /54; Minutes of the N.U.S. Bristol Channel District Committee, 28 July 1938, Mss175/1/1/4/1 and 2. Indoor relief, in the form of admission to a workhouse or other institution, was opposed to outdoor relief, which took the form of cash payments enabling people to subsist outside of an institution.

52. Report of a visit to North and South Shields by Mr. Mugliston and Mr. Stovell; Home Office Minute 13 August 1930; and T. Holdsworth, Sergeant, Cardiff City Police, 26 July 1930; Liverpool Immigration Inspector Thomas M. Blagg to the Home Office; Scott of the Home Office to Wilkie of South Shields, 7 October 1930; Home Office correspondence, minutes, and newspaper cuttings, September and October 1930; Home Office Memorandum 3 November 1930, HO45/14299/562898/19, /32, /36, /37, /42, /43, /48, /51, /54; "Behind the Invasion by 'Destitute Arabs,'" *The Seaman*, 22 October 1930, 4–5. On peddling, see Dunlop, "Lascars and Labourers.

53. On good relations with police, see letter from distressed West African seamen in London, MT9/2695 M.19615; Glamorgan Constabulary "E" Division, Barry Dock Police Office, 14 July 1930, HO45/14299/562898/15.

54. Minutes of the Temporary Management Committee, 13 August 1930, ff50, 55–56, Mss175/ 1/3/1 and /2; Minutes of the Executive Council, 15 October 1930, 9–11, 67–69, Mss175/1/1/j7.

55. Home Office to William Wilkie, Borough Police, South Shields, 8 September 1930; Wilkie reporting the rota successful, 15 September 1930; Chief Constable South Shields to the Home Office, 18 August 1930, HO45/14299/562898/19, /22.

56. *The Seaman*, 15 January 1930; Home Office Minute, 20 November 1930, HO45/14299/562898/57; transcript of the trial *Rex v. Ali Said*, Mss175/7/LE/104, 9, 16, 18, 102, 110, 129–30; and 105, 9–10, 80, 103–4; Ali Said also had local convictions dating from 1911. Also see David Byrne, "The 1930 'Arab Riot.'"

57. Home Office Minute, HO45/14299/562898/51; on repatriation, see also HO45/14299/562898/84, /93.

58. Bloomfield to Board of Trade, 31 May 1932; Board of Trade Memorandum to Mercantile Marine Officers no. 446; Board of Trade Minute no. 11, 1933; Liverpool Immigration Officer P. R. Fudge, 8 March 1932; Davies to Home Office, report of a visit to Liverpool, 11 January 1933, 4, MT9/2735. On "the

management of sexuality" as a means of controlling men by controlling their access to women, see Ann Laura Stoler, "Carnal Knowledge and Imperial Power: Gender, Race and Morality in Colonial Asia," in Micaela di Leonardo, ed., *Gender at the Crossroads of Knowledge: Feminist Anthropology in the Postmodern Era* (Berkeley: University of California Press, 1991), 58, 62, 64, 84; Cynthia Enloe, *Does Khaki Become You? The Militarization of Women's Lives* (Boston: South End Press, 1983); Luise White, "A Colonial State and an African Petty-Bourgeoisie: Prostitution, Property, and Class Struggle in Nairobi, 1936–1940," in Frederick Cooper, ed., *Struggle for the City: Migrant Labor, Capital, and the State in Urban Africa* (London: Sage, 1983), 167–94.

59. *Reynolds Newspaper*, 22 June 1919, HO45/11017/377969.

60. E. N. Cooper to the Home Office, 4 January 1926, HO45/12314/476761/63.

61. Register of Friendly Societies, FS11/266 (1800/T).

62. Havelock Wilson himself left the sea early in his career to become a restaurateur to overcome these threats to continuity and stability. *My Stormy Voyage through Life* (London: Cooperative Press, 1925), 96.

63. *The Negro Worker* 1 (October–November 1931): 36; 2 (August 1932): 20; 6 (March 1936): 12. The term "Minority" in this case denoted the unofficial character of the organization relative to a hostile union leadership, not its racial composition which, reflecting the working class as a whole, was predominantly white. A fuller discussion of the communist party's Minority Movement project can be found in Roderick Martin, *Communism and the British Trade Unions, 1924–1933: A Study of the National Minority Movement* (Oxford: Clarendon Press, 1969), esp. 48, 70–71, 143. On Hardy, see Clegg, *A History of British Trade Unions*, 385. The British Shipping Assistance Act subsidized tramp ships, but stipulated that crews must be British. See L/E/9/955; George W. Brown, "Investigation of Coloured Colonial Seamen in Cardiff, April 15th-20th, 1935," *The Keys* 3 (October–December 1935): 18–22; Ramdin, *Making of the Black Working Class*, 78–86, 122–27. On the "colour-bar" means test, which awarded unemployed white men 15 shillings per week but Black men only 10, see *The Keys* 5 (January–March 1937): 44–45, 61; and 6 (July–September 1938): 5. On exclusion of seamen, see HO45/14299/562898/52; *The Negro Worker* 5 (September 1935): 22.

64. On the Cardiff organizations, see *The Negro Worker* 3 (April–May 1933): 24–25; and 4 (June–July 1934): 19; 5 (September 1935): 10–11; *The Keys* 2 (October–December 1934): 20–21, and 6 (July–September 1938): 5; on Shields, see Hunter and Pollard report on North Shields, pp. 3, 5, L/E/9/457; *The Negro Worker* 5 (July–August 1935): 35–37. On Saklatvala, see Visram, *Ayahs, Lascars, and Princes*, 144–58; Ramdin, *Making of the Black Working Class*, 154–60; Fryer, *Staying Power*, 351–53.

65. *The Keys* 2 (October–December 1934): 20–21; *The Negro Worker* 5 (September 1935): 22; 5 (November 1935): 8–9; 7 (February 1937): 4. On Braithewaite/Jones, and on other Black organizations, see Fryer, *Staying Power*, 313–16, 321–34, esp. 345.

66. See accounts of official harassment in *The Negro Worker* 5 (November 1935): 25; 6 (March 1936): 16. For a similar argument, see Ramdin, *Making of the Black Working Class*, 80–81 and passim.

8. "Getting Out of Hand": Black Service and Black Activism in the "People's War"

1. Consistent with the wartime climate of reconciliation and rapprochement, the British government enacted limited but much publicized reforms in public and workplace welfare. Angus Calder, *The People's War: Britain, 1939–1945* (London: Pantheon, 1969); James E. Cronin, *Labour and Society in Britain, 1918–1979* (London: Batsford, 1984), 115–16, 121–23. Tony Lane also takes a dim view of employers and the state, seeking to debunk the notion of "the people's war," and arguing that the rhetoric of class conciliation failed to mask the reality of continuing and deepening social divisions, particularly aboard British merchant ships. He perhaps slights the degree of conflict *between* employers and the state, as well as within the state itself, for example, between the India Office and the Board of Trade. *The Merchant Seamen's War* (Manchester: Manchester University Press, 1990). Feminist historians have concluded much the same. See, especially, offerings by Margaret and Patrice Higgonnet and by Michelle Perrot in *Behind the Lines: Gender and the Two World Wars* (New Haven: Yale University Press, 1987). Also see C. B. A. Behrens, *Merchant Shipping and the Demands of War* (London: H.M.S.O./Longmans, 1955).

2. Ministry of Information memorandum by Miss E. M. Booker, December 1941; V. R. Bhatt for the Principal Information Officer, Government of India Bureau of Public Information, to J. F. Gennings, 2 July 1943, L/I/1/840/462/33g.

3. Minute 8, "Lascar Strike 1939," MT9/3150 M.12623; S. Alley Memorandum, "Indian Seamen in the Merchant Navy," 11 December 1941, MT9/3657 M.14184.

4. Document 26A, 5 September 1939, letter from Shipping Master, Calcutta, MT9/3150.

5. The basic wage at the beginning of the war was about 35s (£1 15/) per month. By the end of the war wages had risen 300 percent, to £5 17/, still less than half of N.M.B. standard wages. War risk bonuses were also disproportionate. Minute 8; Minute 1; also Minute 7, MT9/3150 M.12623; Minute, 16 November 1939; decipher of 2 December 1939 telegram, MT9/3150. For white men's pay scales, see Lane, *The Merchant Seamen's War*, 164.

6. 1 September 1939, MT9/3150 M.12623; Minute, 28 September 1939, of a meeting of Norman, Justice, Noon; also Board of Trade Minute 8, MT9/3150.

7. Minute of a conference with owners, 11 September 1939, p. 2; Minute 7, Document 21; 26 September and 6 October meetings at the Shipping Federation, MT9/3150.

8. Minute, 28 September 1939; F. H. Norman, 14 and 29 September 1939; Lall in Minute 10, MT9/3150.

9. This threat was hollow: men on European articles cost much more, and there were not enough to replace the thousands of Asian seamen in the British service. Minute 8, Document 15, 11 September 1939, MT9/3150.

10. Harold Cayzer to the Board of Trade, 15 September 1939, MT9/3150.

11. Minutes of 26 September and 6 October meetings at the Shipping Federation: news cutting from *Daily Worker*, 23 October 1939, MT9/3150.

12. Minute 7, Document 21; Minute, 11 September 1939, p. 2, MT9/3150.

13. Minute 9, 8 September 1939; Minute 10; Lumby to the Board of Trade, 14 October 1939, MT9/3150; Lumby to the Board of Trade, 4 December 1939, Document 62A, MT9/3150 M.12623.

14. Correspondence between Oliver Stanley and Noon, 10 September 1939; Notes of thanks to Noon and Lall, 11 September 1939; F. H. Norman minute, 1 December 1939, MT9/3150; Minute 9, Document 9, 11 September 1939, MT9/3150 M.12623; "Indian Seamen's Trade Unions," Group no. 141 (Seamen), file 24, L/E/9/97g.

15. 13 December 1939, MT9/3150.

16. Minute, 16 November 1939; decipher of 2 December 1939 telegram; Meeting at the India Office, 13 December 1939, MT9/3150; *Daily Herald* cutting, 1 December 1939, MT9/3150 M.12623.

17. 27 December 1939, MT9/3150 M.16782; Sir Horace Williamson, Board of Trade Document 74A; Minute, 31 January 1940, MT9/3150.

18. Todd to the Board of Trade, September 1939; Minute, 31 January 1940, MT9/3150.

19. 27 and 29 December 1939; Norman to Greaney, 29 December 1939; Government of India to India Office, 6 February 1940, MT9/3150 M.16782; Lumby of the India Office to the Government of India, 13 January 1940; Government of India correspondence, 30 October 1940, MT9/3150.

20. India Office Information Department, Whitehall, December 1941, L/I/1/840 462/33G.

21. Broadcast by Sir M. Azizul Huque, High Commissioner for India, 23 February 1943, L/I/1/978.

22. For more details, see Booker press release, December 1941, L/I/1/840 462/33g; on the broader effort, see Cronin, *Labour and Society in Britain*, 115–16, 121–23; and for an example of the use of such reforms in wartime propaganda, see *The Hook: A Broadsheet for Dockers in the Northwest Ports*, published in 1941 by the Regional Port Director J. Gibson Jarvie. Also see the *Report of the Committee on Seamen's Welfare in Ports* (London: H.M.S.O., 1945), 5–6.

23. *Report of the Committee on Seamen's Welfare*, 7, 12, 38–39. For the British state's handling of I.L.O. recommendations, see "Indian Seamen's Welfare," L/E/9/457.

24. Clipping from the *East London Advertiser*, 20 December 1941, in L/I/1/840. Alley made much the same argument in a memorandum to the Shipping

Federation, "Indian Seamen in the Merchant Navy," MT9/3657 M.14184. On the role of the Shipping Federation and Suhrawardy in the formation of Indian unions, see L/E/9/97g. On N.M.B. wage rises, see Lane, *The Merchant Seamen's War*, 164.

25. "Indian Seamen's Trade Unions," L/E/9/97g. These demands had also been passed as a resolution at the Seamen's Section of a recent India Conference at Central Hall, Bath St., Glasgow.

26. Norman of the Ministry of Shipping to Lumby of the India Office, 11 March 1940; Norman to Lumby, 24 April 1940, L/E/9/97g. As in 1939, the India Office instructed the Admiralty not to prosecute a striking crew so as not to "prejudice" these talks. Cipher telegram, 19 December 1941, MT9/3657 M.14184.

27. Minute 2, 6 January 1942; Minute 5, 12 January 1942; Paul Tofahrn, Secretary of the I.T.F., to the M.W.T., 12 February 1942; I.T.F. Management Committee to the M.W.T., 11 March 1942; M.W.T. to the India Office, 30 March 1942, Document 19, MT9/3657 M.14184; Minute of meeting, 11 May 1942, MT9/3657. Also see Minute 5, document 64 of MT9/3657 M.12623/39.

28. Minute of conference at the Board of Trade, 21 May 1942; M.W.T. to Government of India, 8 July 1942, MT9/3657. In August Bevin and Lord Leathers considered but rejected attributing resistance to wage increases to "native ship-owners" in India. Document 21, 10 August 1942, MT9/3657 M.7724.

29. Surat Alley to Secretary of State for India, 17 October 1942, MT9/3657; Memorandum of a meeting, 27 August 1941; Resolution on the pending griev-ances of the Indian Seamen and their immediate requirements . . . per meeting 31 August 1943 with Lt. Cmdr. Aftab Ali, R.I.N.R., M.L.A., President of the Union, in the Chair; extract from Reuters, 12 September 1943; M. F. Bukht to India Office, 13 September 1943, L/E/9/97g; on American support, see Surat Alley to Joseph Curran of the National Maritime Union of America, 13 December 1942, L/E/9/457. During the war years the British Council House in Barnett Street, Liverpool, operated a "Colour Bar" in the "American Room." St. Clair Drake, "The Colour Problem in Britain: A Study in Social Definitions," *Sociological Review* 3 (December 1955): 197–217.

30. M. F. Bukht to India Office, 13 September 1943, L/E/9/97g.

31. Ibid.

32. *Lloyd's List*, 14 September 1943, *Daily Express*, Scottish ed., 13 Sept 1943, clippings in L/E/9/97g.

33. Telegram, Government of India, Commerce Department, to High Com-missioner for India, 5 December 1943; Rumbold to Silver, 9 December 1943, L/E/9/97g.

34. A transcript of the meeting of 7 January 1944 appears in Minutes of discussions in the India Office, February 1944, L/E/9/97g.

35. Alley to the India Office, 14 January 1944, Oldenbroek to the India Office, 24 January 1944; Munster to Rumbold, note of 23 February interview; Minutes of discussions in the India Office, February 1944, L/E/9/97g.

36. Rumbold to the Secretary, Goverment of India Commerce Department, 7 March 1944; S. R. Zaman to the India Office, 23 May 1944; Munster to Rumbold,

note of 23 February interview; also Minutes of discussions in the India Office, February 1944, L/E/9/97g.

37. The effects of colonial racial ideology are more fully explored in Lane, *The Merchant Seamen's War*, 167, 173–83.

38. Report of Reed's visit, Reuters, 1717, 23 December 1945, clipping in L/E/9/97g. India Office distaste for their role in labor conflicts was perhaps reflected in the note expressing evident relief at the proposed formation of an Indian Maritime Board—Reed's Mission—when the "two parties might be brought face to face round the same table" and the Government of India might cease its "go-between" role. Rumbold to Adams, 29 December 1945, L/E/9/97g. For a fuller discussion of relationships between organized labor in Britain and in the empire, see Partha Sarathi Gupta, *Imperialism and the British Labour Movement, 1914–1964* (New York: Holmes & Meier, 1975); Peter Weiler, *British Labour and the Cold War* (Stanford, Stanford University Press, 1988); and Marjorie Nicholson, *The TUC Overseas: The Roots of Policy* (London: Allen & Unwin, 1986).

39. See, for example, Marika Sherwood, *Many Struggles: West Indian Workers and Service Personnel in Britain (1939–1945)* (London: Karia Press, 1985).

40. 14 May 1946, Federation of Chambers of Commerce, British Empire Publication, p. 3; clippings, *Times*, 28 December 1940; *Times Educational Supplement*, 7 December 1940; Newham of the India Office; telegram India Office to the Government of Bombay and Government of India, 14 June 1941; note, A. J. Fells; clipping from *Newsindia*; note of a meeting at the India Office, 2 April 1941, "European War: Indian Workmen Training in Britain," L/I/1/978.

41. Consistent with the view of British racial conflict as a post-1945 phenomenon, Christopher Thorne, "Britain and the Black G.I.s: Racial Issues and Anglo-American Relations in 1942," *New Community* 3 (Summer 1974): 262–71; Graham Smith, "Jim Crow on the Home Front (1942–1945)," *New Community* 8 (Winter 1980): 317–28; Graham Smith, *When Jim Crow Met John Bull: Black American Soldiers in World War II Britain* (New York: St. Martin's, 1987), debate the impact of the racially segregated U.S. Army on British race relations.

42. Arnold R. Watson, *West Indian Workers in Britain* (London: Hodder & Stoughton, 1942), 3–4, 8, 11–14, 23–24, and passim; also Anthony Richmond, *Colour Prejudice in Britain: A Study of West Indian Workers in Liverpool, 1941–1951* (London: Routledge & Kegan Paul, 1955).

43. The India Office Information Department's handling of several instances of "colour bar" and defamation in the late 1940s contrasted with their cautious attitude in the 1930s and during the war, prefiguring postwar governments' demeanor toward Black migrants in the 1950s. See L/I/1/48; L/I/1/143; and for a discussion of state race politics, see Paul Foot, *Immigration and Race in British Politics* (Harmondsworth: Penguin, 1965).

CONCLUSION

1. "Africa Speaks in Manchester," *Picture Post*, 10 November 1945. On wartime race relations and the impact of the Jim Crow U.S. Army, see Graham Smith,

When Jim Crow Met John Bull: Black American Soldiers in World War II in Britain (New York: St. Martin's, 1987); Graham Smith, "Jim Crow on the Home Front, 1942–1945," *New Community* 8 (Winter 1980): 317–28; Christopher Thorne, "Britain and the Black G.I.s: Racial Issues and Anglo-American Relations in 1942," *New Community* 3 (Summer 1974): 262–71; also see Marika Sherwood, *Many Struggles: West Indian Workers and Service Personnel in Britain (1939–45)* (London: Karia Press, 1985).

2. The literature on postwar migration is vast. In addition to works cited in previous chapters, a sensitive early work incorporating testimony from Black migrants themselves is Daniel Lawrence, *Black Migrants, White Natives: A Study of Race Relations in Nottingham* (Cambridge: Cambridge University Press, 1974); more recent works include Stella Dadzie et al., *Heart of the Race: Black Women in Britain* (London: Virago, 1985); Centre for Contemporary Cultural Studies (C.C.C.S.), *The Empire Strikes Back: Race and Racism in 70s Britain* (London: Hutchinson, 1982); Paul Gilroy, *"There Ain't No Black in the Union Jack": The Cultural Politics of Race and Nation* (Chicago: University of Chicago Press, 1987); Jenny Bourne with A. Sivanandan, "Cheerleaders and Ombudsmen: The Sociology of Race Relations in Britain," *Race and Class* 21 (Spring 1980): 312. On the structural context of restriction, see Paul Foot, *Immigration and Race in British Politics* (Baltimore: Penguin, 1965); A. Sivanandan, *A Different Hunger: Writings on Black Resistance* (London: Pluto, 1983), 131–40; Madge Dresser, *Black and White on the Buses: The 1963 Colour Bar Dispute in Bristol* (Bristol: Bristol Broadsides, 1986); Peter Fryer, *Staying Power: The History of Black People in Britain* (London: Pluto, 1984), 372–73; Edward Pilkington, *Beyond the Mother Country: West Indians and the Notting Hill White Riots* (London: I. B. Tauris, 1988); Kathleen Paul, "The Politics of Citizenship in Post-War Britain," *Contemporary Record* 6 (Winter 1992): 452–73; James Wickenden, *West Indian Migration to Britain* (London: Oxford University Press for the Institute of Race Relations, 1968).

3. On the implications of guest worker institutions in Western Europe, see Stephen Castles and Godula Kosack, *Immigrant Workers and Class Structure in Western Europe* (1973; Oxford: Oxford University Press, 1985); Gary S. Cross, *Immigrant Workers in Industrial France: The Making of a New Laboring Class* (Philadelphia: Temple University Press, 1983); also Paul Gordon and Danny Reilly, "Guestworkers of the Sea: Racism in British Shipping," *Race and Class* 28, 2 (1986): 73–82.

4. Paul Rich, *Race and Empire in British Politics* (Cambridge: Cambridge University Press, 1986), 126.

5. On the construction of "reverse discourses," see Susan Kingsley Kent, *Sex and Suffrage in Britain, 1860–1914* (Princeton: Princeton University Press, 1987), 16; Gyan Prakash, "Can the Subaltern Ride? A Reply to O'Hanlon and Washbrook," *Comparative Studies in Society and History* 34 (January 1992): 168–94.

6. An optimistic sign was the election of London activists Bernie Grant and Diane Abbott to Parliament in June 1987. Ron Ramdin stresses the critical con-

tribution Britain's "Black working class" made to global liberation struggles, in *The Making of the Black Working Class in Britain* (London: Gower, 1987).

7. This book has also aimed to meet D. C. M. Platt's challenge to provide evidence of "the day-to day operations of business" when discussing "economic imperialism." "Economic Imperialism and the Businessman," Roger Owen and Bob Sutcliffe, *Studies in the Theory of Imperialism* (Burnt Mill, Harlow, Essex: Longman, 1972), 310; also see essays in C. C. Eldridge, ed., *British Imperialism in the Nineteenth Century* (London: Macmillan, 1984).

8. For these debates, see Charles Maier, *Recasting Bourgeois Europe: Stabilization in France, Germany and Italy in the Decade after World War I* (Princeton: Princeton University Press, 1975); Keith Middlemas, *Politics in Industrial Society: The Experience of the British System since 1911* (London: Andre Deutsch, 1979) esp. 20–22; James Cronin, *Labour and Society in Britain, 1918–1979* (London: Batsford, 1984), 15; Richard Price, *Masters, Unions and Men: Work Control and the Rise of Labour, 1830–1914* (Cambridge: Cambridge University Press, 1980); Beatrix Campbell, *Wigan Pier Revisited: Poverty and Politics in 80s Britain* (London: Virago, 1984); James Cronin, "Politics, Class Structure and the Enduring Weakness of British Social Democracy," *Journal of Social History* 16 (Spring 1983): 123–42; Michael Savage, *The Dynamics of Working-Class Politics: The Labour Movement in Preston, 1880–1940* (Cambridge: Cambridge University Press, 1987); Jonathan Zietlin, "From Labour History to the History of Industrial Relations," *Economic History Review* 40, 2 (1987): 159–84.

9. Cronin, "Coping with Labour"; Middlemas, *Politics in Industrial Society*, 20–22; Rich, *Race and Empire*.

10. Ramdin, *The Making of the Black Working Class*, 507–8. On labor and working-class "conservatism," see Lunn, "Race Relations or Industrial Relations? Race and Labour in Britain, 1880–1950," in Kenneth Lunn, ed., *Race and Labour in Twentieth Century Britain* (London: Frank Cass, 1985); Zeitlin, "From Labour History to the History of Industrial Relations"; Henry Pelling, *A History of British Trade Unionism* (London; Macmillan, 1963).

11. Errol Lawrence, "Just Plain Common Sense: The 'Roots' of Racism," in C.C.C.S., *The Empire Strikes Back*; Catherine Hall, "In the Name of Which Father?" *International Labor and Working Class History* 41 (Spring 1992): 23–27.

12. "Super-exploitation" and "super-profits" refer to the extra wealth to be extracted from workers who are paid even less than ordinary workers. Claude Meillassoux argues that migrant workers are often paid less than the cost of their reproduction; in this way the host economy effectively drains resources from the migrants' country of origin. *Maidens, Meal, and Money: Capitalism and the Domestic Community* (Cambridge: Cambridge University Press, 1975).

13. See Geoff Eley, "Defining Social Imperialism: Use and Abuse of an Idea," *Social History* 3 (October 1976): 265–90; Lance E. Davis and Robert Huttenback, *Mammon and the Pursuit of Empire: The Economics of British Imperialism* (Cambridge: Cambridge University Press, 1988); P. J. Cain and A. G. Hopkins, "Gentlemanly Capitalism and British Expansion Overseas, II: The New Imperialism, 1850–

1945," *Economic History Review* 2d ser., 40, 1 (1987): 1–26; Miles Kahler and respondents, "Europe and Its 'Privileged' Partners in Africa and the Middle East," *Journal of Common Market Studies* 21 (September–December 1982): 199–226; John Darwin, "British Decolonization since 1945: A Pattern or a Puzzle?" *Journal of Imperial and Commonwealth History* 12 (1984): 187–209; Wolfgang H. Mommsen, "The End of Empire and the Continuity of Imperialism," in Wolfgang H. Mommsen and Jürgen Osterhammel, eds., *Imperialism and After: Continuities and Discontinuities* (London: Allen & Unwin, 1986), 333–58; P. J. Cain and A. G. Hopkins, *British Imperialism: Crisis and Deconstruction, 1914–1990* (London: Longman, 1993).

14. For a discussion of who benefited from imperialism, see Davis and Huttenback, *Mammon and the Pursuit of Empire*; Cain and Hopkins, "Gentlemanly Capitalism." The cultural dimensions of this "recolonization" process in post-1945 Britain have frequently been articulated, but its material and structural dimensions have remained largely unexplored. See, in addition to Gilroy, *There Ain't No Black in the Union Jack*, and C.C.C.S., *The Empire Strikes Back*; John Rex, *Race, Colonialism and the City* (London: Routledge & Kegan Paul, 1973), 79, 85–88, 107; Michael Banton, *White and Coloured: The Behaviour of British People toward Coloured Immigrants* (New Brunswick: Rutgers University Press, 1960), esp. 59, 69. For structural analyses of post-1945 migrant labor, see Castles and Kosack, *Immigrant Workers and Class Structure in Western Europe*; Ceri Peach, *West Indian Migration to Britain: A Social Geography* (London: Oxford University Press for the Institute of Race Relations, 1968). For a discussion of the persistence of imperial links beyond formal decolonization, see Kahler and respondents, "Europe and Its 'Privileged' Partners."

15. On British imperialism since the First World War, see John Darwin, "The Fear of Falling: British Politics and Imperial Decline Since 1900," *Transactions of the Royal Historical Society* 36 (1986): 27–45; John Darwin, "Imperialism in Decline? Tendencies in British Imperial Policy between the Wars," *Historical Journal* 23, 3 (1980): 657–79; John Mackenzie, *Propaganda and Empire: The Manipulation of British Public Opinion, 1880–1960* (Manchester: Manchester University Press, 1984); Huttenback and Davis, *Mammon and the Pursuit of Empire*; Cain and Hopkins, "Gentlemanly Capitalism."

16. John Bodnar, *The Transplanted: A History of Immigrants in Urban America* (Bloomington: University of Indiana Press, 1985); Eric Wolf, *Europe and the People without History* (Berkeley: University of California Press, 1982); Shula Marks and Peter Richardson, eds., Introduction to *International Labour Migration: Historical Perspectives* (Hounslow, U.K.: Maurice Temple Smith, 1984), 1–18.

17. Harold Wolpe, "The Theory of Internal Colonialism: The South African Case," in Ivor Oxaal, Tony Barnett, and David Booth, eds., *Beyond the Sociology of Development* (London: Routledge & Kegan Paul, 1975); Meillassoux, *Maidens, Meal, and Money*; Kahler, "Europe's Privileged Partners"; Ruth Taplin, "Women in World Market Factories: East and West," *Ethnic and Racial Studies* 9 (April 1986): 168–95; Helen Safa, "Runaway Shops and Female Employment: The Search for Cheap Labor," *Signs* 7 (Winter 1981): 418–33; María Patricia Fer-

nández-Kelly, *For We Are Sold, I and My People: Women and Industry in Mexico's Frontier* (Albany: SUNY Press, 1983); Castles and Kosack, *Immigrant Workers and Class Structure in Western Europe*: Alec Wilkinson, *Big Sugar: Seasons in the Cane Fields in Florida* (New York: Knopf, 1989); and on contemporary labor relations in merchant shipping, reflecting the outcome of interwar trends, see Paul K. Chapman, *Trouble on Board: The Plight of International Seafarers* (Ithaca, N.Y.: ILR Press, 1992).

Appendix I

1. Bob Hepple, *Race, Jobs, and the Law in Britain* (Harmondsworth: Penguin 1970), 63–64.

2. R. H. Thornton, *British Shipping* (Cambridge: Cambridge University Press, 1939), 221–22; Tony Lane, *Grey Dawn Breaking: Merchant Seafarers in the Late Twentieth Century* (Manchester: Manchester University Press, 1985), 8.

3. Hepple, *Race, Jobs, and the Law*, 63.

4. "Engagement of Natives of India under European Articles and Position of Eurasians," Despatch no. 117 of 29 March 1901, L/E/7/481.

5. A. Colaco, ed., *A History of the Seamen's Union, Bombay* (Bombay: Pascoal Vaz, 1955), 58, Mss159/5/3/588.

6. "Engagement of Natives of India," L/E/7/481.

7. India Office papers, L/E/9/936 and L/E/7/604.

Index